Humana Festival '93
The Complete Plays

Humana Inc. is one of the nation's largest managed health care companies with more than 1.6 million members in its health care plans.

The Humana Foundation was established in 1981 to support the educational, social, medical and cultural development of communities in ways that reflect Humana's commitment to social responsibility and an improved quality of life.

Smith and Kraus *Books For Actors*

THE MONOLOGUE SERIES
> The Best Men's Stage Monologues of 1992
> The Best Women's Stage Monologues of 1992
> The Best Men's Stage Monologues of 1991
> The Best Women's Stage Monologues of 1991
> The Best Men's Stage Monologues of 1990
> The Best Women's Stage Monologues of 1990
> One Hundred Men's Stage Monologues from the 1980's
> One Hundred Women's Stage Monologues from the 1980's
> Street Talk: Character Monologues for Actors
> Uptown: Character Monologues for Actors
> Monologues from Contemporary Literature: Volume I
> Monologues from Classic Plays
> Kiss and Tell: The Art of the Restoration Monologue

FESTIVAL MONOLOGUE SERIES
> The Great Monologues from the Humana Festival
> The Great Monologues from the EST Marathon
> The Great Monologues from the Women's Project
> The Great Monologues from the Mark Taper Forum

YOUNG ACTORS SERIES
> Great Scenes and Monologues for Children
> New Plays from A.C.T.'s Young Conservatory
> Great Scenes for Young Actors from the Stage
> Great Monologues for Young Actors

SCENE STUDY SERIES
> The Best Stage Scenes of 1992
> The Best Stage Scenes for Women from the 1980's
> The Best Stage Scenes for Men from the 1980's

PLAYS FOR ACTORS SERIES
> Seventeen Short Plays by Romulus Linney
> Eric Overmyer: Collected Plays
> Lanford Wilson: 21 Short Plays
> William Mastrosimone: Collected Plays
> Terrence McNally: Collected Plays

GREAT TRANSLATION FOR ACTORS SERIES
> The Wood Demon by Anton Chekhov

OTHER BOOKS IN OUR COLLECTION
> The Actor's Chekhov
> Women Playwrights: The Best Plays of 1992

If you require pre-publication information about upcoming Smith and Kraus monologues collections, scene collections, play anthologies, advanced acting books, and books for young actors, you may receive our semi-annual catalogue, free of charge, by sending your name and address to **Smith and Kraus Catalogue, P.O. Box 10, Newbury, VT 05051. (800) 862 5423 FAX (802) 866 5346**

Humana Festival '93
The Complete Plays

edited by Marisa Smith

Plays for Actors Series

SK
A Smith and Kraus Book

A Smith and Kraus Book
Published by Smith and Kraus, Inc.

COVER AND TEXT DESIGN BY JULIA HILL
Manufactured in the United States of America

First Edition: August 1993
10 9 8 7 6 5 4 3 2 1

Publisher's Cataloging in Publication
(Prepared by Quality Books, Inc.)

Humana Festival '93 : the complete plays / edited by Marisa Smith.
      p. cm. -- (Plays for actors)
      Complete plays from 1993 Humana Festival, Actors Theatre of Louisville,
      February 25-April 4, 1993.
      ISBN 1-880399-37-7

      1. American drama -- 20th century. I. Smith, Marisa. II. Title: Humana festival,
      nineteen ninety-three. III. Series.

      PS634.H85 1993   812'.54
                             QBI93-1121

Contents

Introduction

The Humana Festival, now in its 18th year, has to date produced 170 new works. The writers who have begun or burnished their careers in this venue read like the Who's Who of American playwriting, and the plays themselves are performed every day of every week of every year somewhere in the world.

Last year's 1993 Humana Festival (each one having its own flavor) was particularly rich in social concerns and cultural diversity. These were blunt plays, not in the sense that they lacked ambiguity, but in the clarity of their deepest concerns. These plays spoke their minds. They confronted abortion and its constellation of issues, suicide when life lacks emotional meaning, the uncharted expanse through which African-American experience now travels, and, among other things, the fact that most of us have forgotten how to work with our hands.

The plays take place in Minnesota, Missouri, Rhode Island, Georgia, Venice, Paris, everywhere in fact other than the great American urban centers where the evening news spends so much of its time. Out of these variable landscapes, they speak of family but without many of the realistic trappings, or even traditional relationships that have been the heart of the American theatre. They mine for intimacy in unlikely places.

To me these works seem transitional in several positive and important ways. Transitional in female/male relationship. Transitional between naturalism and a new, less bounded style. Transitional in terms of our bonds to family, group and nation. We may look back on these plays and see them as part of a fulcrum, part of a key moment of American change.

What else are they? Warm rather than cool. Funny when they ought to be. Filled with a sense of loss merging with a new purpose. Great parts. Actors will like these plays.

You will too.

Jon Jory, Production Director
Actors Theatre of Louisville

Humana Festival '93
The Complete Plays

STANTON'S GARAGE

by Joan Ackermann

Playwright's Biography

Joan Ackermann is a writer, actress, composer and producer. She made her ATL acting and playwriting debut in the 1989 Humana Festival of New American Plays with ZARA SPOOK AND OTHER LURES. In 1981, she co-founded Mixed Company Theatre which she continues to co-direct in Great Barrington, Massachusetts. Her plays that premiered there include ZARA SPOOK AND OTHER LURES, DON'T RIDE THE CLUTCH (both of which were performed at the Edinburgh Theatre Festival Fringe), BED AND BREAKFAST, THE LIGHT OF HIS EYE and YONDER PEASANT. Her most recent works include RESCUING GREENLAND, which premiered at Mixed Company in 1991 and was funded by PBS, and a ten-minute play, QUIET TORRENTIAL SOUND. As a feature writer, Ms. Ackermann's articles have appeared in *Sports Illustrated* (to which she was a special contributor for six years), *Time, The Atlantic, Esquire* and many others. At age 13, she won an award for acting at the New England Boston Globe Theatre Festival and subsequently performed at Harvard, Theatre Workshop of Boston, the Berkshire Public Theatre and in many productions at her own theatre, Mixed Company.

A Note from the Playwright

Mechanics - physical and metaphysical - drew me into this play, along with the fragile hearts and good will of its characters. While I was writing it, I happened to discover my broken tape deck worked again. From my point of view, there was no logical explanation for this. None. Really, none. Something in its inner nature just kicked in, stirred to action, set reels into motion. Several of the characters, often through inadvertent moments of grace and compassion between unlikely pairs, experience the same phenomenon inside them. Something clicks, something gives, something jammed breaks free. They are closer to becoming whole. They move on.

Characters

RON, forty.
HARLON, seventeen.
SILVIO, late fifties.
DENNY, thirty-five.
LEE, forty.
FRANNIE, sixteen.

MARY, sixty.
AUDREY, late fifties.

Directed by Steven Albrezzi

Cast of Characters (in order of appearance)

Ron	Peter Zapp
Harlon	Rob Kramer
Silvio	Bob Burrus
Denny V	Craig Heidenreich
Lee	Priscilla Shanks
Frannie	Jessica Jory
Mary	Adale O'Brien
Audrey	Susan Barnes

Scenic Designer	Paul Owen
Costume Designer	Laura Patterson
Lighting Designer	Karl E. Haas
Sound Designer	Darron L. West
Props Master	Ron Riall
Stage Manager	Julie A. Richardson
Ass. Stage Manager	Amy Hutchison
Production Dramaturg	Julie Crutcher
Casting arranged by Marnie Waxman	

Setting

Time is late summer. Saturday morning. Setting is a small service station in upstate Missouri. Perspective is from the back of the station. Part of the back of the two bay garage is in view stage right, windows in the garage door allow some viewing into garage, and a smaller door stage left of window allows for access in and out of the back of the garage. Downstage of garage are old barrels, engine parts with geranium pots on them, tires, a couple of outside chairs, makeshift table, a small overgrown garden plot—a playing space. Attached to the garage is a large waiting room with counter and cash register, armchair, vinyl couch, a few vending machines, a table with coffee pot, cups, sugar, and a few items for sale—oil, dry gas, anti-freeze, etc. All kinds of possibilities for local color and character. On the upstage wall of waiting room a door leads out front to gas pumps. Backward letters on the large windows read Stanton's Garage; these large windows are quite opaque, although flower boxes may read through them. There is a door between garage and waiting room.

STANTON'S GARAGE

ACT ONE

SCENE 1

At opening Ron is alone on stage sitting in a chair. He gets up and goes over to gum ball machine. Puts in a penny, nothing comes out. He hits it. Puts in another penny. Still doesn't work. He hits it again.

RON: Shit. (*Harlon enters from outside; heads toward cash register.*) This doesn't work. This doesn't work.

HARLON: Huh?

RON: This gum ball machine. It's broken.

HARLON: Yeah. It's broken. (*Pause.*)

RON: I know it's broken. (*Pause.*)

HARLON: (*Counting change.*) You want a gumball? (*Ron stares at him. Harlon takes change, exits. Phone rings. Ron puts two quarters in a candy machine. Nothing comes out.*)

RON: What the fuck. (*He jiggles change return, hits machine, kicks it. Sits down. Harlon enters. He calls into garage.*)

HARLON: Hey, Denny! Denny! You hear about Lonnie Bissell? Jerked himself off with the milker? D'you hear? Spoiled twenty thousand gallons of milk. Drew blood. (*Moves towards phone. To Ron.*) You imagine? (*Picks up phone.*) Stanton's. (*During Harlon's phone call Ron exits into garage.*) Yes, m'am we do. Where you located? Huh? You check your fuel gauge? Just asking. Turn over at all? Is there a little clicking noise when you turn the key? Well, we'll bring it on in, take a look. I don't know if it's serious, m'am, where are you? Can you see an Adopt a Highway sign? I can hold. (*Covering receiver, yelling.*) Hey, Denny! I'm thinking of piercing my ear, what do you think? Think I should? (*Into phone.*) Beg pardon? I know just where you are, m'am, less than two miles away. What kind of car? Huh. Don't see too many of them around here. Oh yeah, we can service it, no problem. (*Ron enters from garage with hammer. Sits.*) Afraid you haven't got much choice. We're the only garage for thirty miles. Be right there. (*Hangs up.*) Looking forward to it. Silvio, I got a tow, you gotta cover for me. Yo! Silvio! (*Harlon goes into garage where Silvio is partially visible through garage door window working on car. Denny is working on another car. From within garage;*) So Denny, think I should pierce my ear? Huh? What do you think? Pierce my ear? (*While Harlon is in garage, Ron hits glass of candy machine with hammer, breaks it, takes out candy bar, cutting himself slightly. Sits. Eats. Harlon and Silvio enter from garage.*)

HARLON: What's eatin' Denny?

SILVIO: I don't know.

HARLON: Why's he acting like that? Huh? Sil?

SILVIO: I don't know.

HARLON: Why's he acting like that? Never seen him act like that.

SILVIO: Doesn't feel right.

HARLON: Doesn't feel right? He doesn't feel right?

SILVIO: Get out of my way.

HARLON: How's he feel wrong? Sil?

SILVIO: Brain tumor, I don't know.

HARLON: Brain tumor? Brain tumor? You shittin' me?

SILVIO: Something.

HARLON: He has a brain tumor?

SILVIO: Thinks he does.

HARLON: Why's he think that? Why's he think he has a brain tumor?

SILVIO: Blow your nose.

HARLON: He's gonna play tonight? Can he play? Silvio? Big game. Play-offs.

SILVIO: Here. (*Hands him a handkerchief.*)

HARLON: (*Blows his nose.*) I'm thinking of piercing my ear, Silvio. What do you think? Think I should?

SILVIO: No.

HARLON: (*Trying to hand him back handkerchief; Silvio won't take it.*) You don't think I should pierce my ear? Little diamond? Little diamond stud?

SILVIO: (*Handing him keys to tow truck.*) Go.

HARLON: I'm going. (*Grabs cap. Exits. Silvio goes behind counter. Reads Penny-Saver. Denny exits garage through back doorway; lights and smokes a cigarette, leaning up against the wall. Silvio sees Ron eating candy; sees broken machine. Goes over and carefully takes out a candy bar for himself.*)

RON: So how much longer?

SILVIO: Ten minutes.

RON: What was it?

SILVIO: Thermostat.

RON: (*Gets up, walks around, sits.*) How far is it to St. Joseph?

SILVIO: St. Joes? Couple hours.

RON: (*Nods.*) How *far* is it?

SILVIO: Couple hours. (*Denny throws cigarette on ground, steps on it. Starts to go, loses his balance and falls over. Stays down for a bit till he gains his equilibrium, stands up, exits.*)

RON: Pretty day, huh? They forecast rain. (*Pause.*) I don't know why it couldn't have rained. I was really looking forward to it raining. (*Silvio doesn't respond. Ron takes gun out of his blazer pocket and aims it at Silvio.*) Give me all your money. (*Cocks gun; Silvio freezes.*) Just kidding. I'm kidding, honest to God, I'm kidding, really, I don't want your money. I don't. Look, here, take my money. (*Reaches into pocket, pulls out handful of cash.*) Go ahead, take some. Take some more, here. Here. (*Leaves it on the counter. Sits, gun in hand.*) Talk to me, Silvio. Talk to me. Tell me something. Come on, tell me something. Anything. I'll be fascinated, I promise. Tell me about. . . second grade. You were in second grade, weren't you? Silvio?

SILVIO: Huh?

RON: Second grade, did you like it? Was it a good experience?

SILVIO: Uh. . .

RON: That's nice. That's interesting. Who was your second grade teacher?

SILVIO: I don't remember.

RON: You don't remember? You don't remember!

SILVIO: Mrs. Foley.

RON: Mrs. Foley. My second grade teacher was Mrs. Brooks. I didn't like Mrs. Brooks. Did you like Mrs. Foley?

SILVIO: Yeah.

RON: Well, there you go. That's the difference. That's the difference right there between you and me, Silvio. Mrs. Foley. Mrs. Brooks. Right there. So. Tell me more. Come on.

SILVIO: (*Struggling to come up with something.*) Third grade?

RON: What about third grade?

SILVIO: I didn't like it.

RON: No?

SILVIO: No.

RON: Why not?

SILVIO: Uh . . .

RON: What happened in third grade? Silvio? What happened in third grade?

SILVIO: My sister died.

RON: Your sister died. (*Explodes.*) Shit! I'm sorry. Was she younger or older? (*Pause.*) Was she younger or older, Silvio?

SILVIO: (*At a loss.*) Not really.

RON: Not really what?

SILVIO: I don't have a sister.

RON: You don't have a sister cause she died, or you never had one?
SILVIO: I never had one.
RON: Oh. That's good. That's a relief. I appreciate your honesty, Silvio. I'm glad you didn't have a sister who died. That's the best news I've heard all month. Now I'll tell you something. Okay? We're having a conversation. All you have to do is look at me and keep your eyes open. Don't look at the gun, Silvio, look up here. Here. (*Points at face with gun.*) You say it'll be ten minutes? Ten minutes till my car is ready?
SILVIO: Denny's working on it.
RON: Denny with the brain tumor?
SILVIO: He's working on it.
RON: Is he good?
SILVIO: He's a genius.
RON: Mm. You know why I'm going to St. Joseph? Silvio? You know why I'm going? I thought you might want to know. I'm going to a wedding. Yeah. (*Shoots gun.*) Jesus fuck, this thing is loaded! Woo! That was quite a noise, wasn't it? Christ. So. I'm going to a wedding. You know who's getting married? My wife. My wife is getting married. (*Scratches head with gun.*) My wife is getting married in St. Joseph. Big wedding, two hundred guests. And you want to hear the irony? The irony is I'm not invited. Can you imagine? My wife is getting married and I'm not even invited. Do you like wine, Silvio? I'll send you some wine. I import wine. I'll send you some. You like red or white? I'll send you red, a nice Cote du Rhone, I'll send you a case of Cote du Rhone. (*Gas pump bell sounds; Silvio starts to go.*)
RON: No, no, no. You stay here. Relax. I'll take care of it. It's the least I can do. (*Ron exits out front door carrying gun by his side. Silvio calls into garage.*)
SILVIO: Denny. Denny—Denny, where the hell are you? Denny? (*Silvio comes out of garage, nervously tries to get a look out front. Goes to the phone, crouches on floor with it, starts to dial. Ron enters. Silvio gets up, hangs up phone.*)
RON: Hey, Silvio, you won't believe this. That's my brother-in-law out there. David. He wants directions to St. Joseph. You got any maps? (*Fires gun again.*) Jesus Christ! This thing is loud. Here, take it. Take it. (*Hands him the gun.*) I don't like it. Take it. It's too loud. (*Sits.*) Go out there, Silvio, go out there and tell David how to get to St. Joseph. Tell my brother-in-law how to get to my wife's wedding. (*Silvio goes out, carrying gun by side.*)
RON: Fuck. (*Silvio enters.*)
SILVIO: He left.

RON: He left? David left? Is my car ready? Is ten minutes up. Silvio? (*Silvio puts gun in pocket, exits into garage. Ron sits, head in hands. Harlon enters, followed by Lee and Frannie.*)

HARLON: Have a seat, ladies. Make yourselves comfortable.

LEE: So you think it's the ignition?

HARLON: Could be. Have some coffee. On the house. Free.

LEE: If it is the ignition, how long will it take to fix?

HARLON: That depends.

LEE: On what?

HARLON: What it is.

LEE: If it's not the ignition, what else could it be?

HARLON: Could be your alternator.

LEE: Alternator.

HARLON: Could be a lot of things. First off we got to charge up your battery. That's gonna take an hour.

LEE: It was running fine. It was running perfectly fine, all the way down from Chicago. Why would it suddenly die?

HARLON: I don't know, m'am. Have a seat, we'll check it out.

LEE: Soon? I'm sorry. I don't mean to be. . . it's just. . . people are waiting for us, expecting us.

HARLON: Just as soon as Denny gets through with this gentleman's car, he'll be right on it. How many holes you have in your ear?

RON: (*Looking up.*) My ear?

LEE: Is Denny good?

FRANNIE: Two in this one; three in this.

HARLON: 't's awesome.

LEE: Is Denny good?

HARLON: He's a genius.

LEE: Is he a good mechanic?

HARLON: Yeah. He's a living legend in his time. Now you have a seat, have a cup of coffee, have a magazine, relax, enjoy your flight. Jesus H. Christ, what happened to the candy machine. (*He looks at Ron.*)

RON: It's broken.

SILVIO: (*In garage.*) Harlon, get in here! (*Harlon exits into garage. Silvio and he converse quietly. Frannie goes to coffee pot.*)

FRANNIE: You want some coffee? Lee?

LEE: No. Yes. Please. Be careful.

FRANNIE: Sugar?

LEE: No.

FRANNIE: How many?

LEE: Two.

FRANNIE: Here. (*To Ron.*) You want some coffee?

RON: Did you say something?

FRANNIE: Would you like some coffee?

RON: Would I like some coffee? (*Pause.*) Are you having coffee?

FRANNIE: Yeah.

RON: I'll join you.

FRANNIE: Sugar?

RON: Okay.

FRANNIE: How many?

RON: As many as you like.

FRANNIE: Cream?

RON: Uh-huh. (*Yes.*)

FRANNIE: It's not real cream.

RON: Not real cream?

FRANNIE: It's powdered. It's a whitener. Kind of like Borax. You want some?

RON: Yes, please.

FRANNIE: Here.

RON: Thank you very much.

FRANNIE: You're very welcome.

RON: Do you live here?

FRANNIE: No. (*Silvio enters. Hands car keys to Ron.*)

SILVIO: Ready to go.

RON: I have to go?

SILVIO: You don't have to go. Your car's ready.

RON: Silvio, I'm just now having a cup of coffee with these ladies here. They've invited me to join them. Invited me. I'll be a few minutes. (*Silvio goes behind counter. Picks up Penny Saver. They all drink coffee. Pause.*)

FRANNIE: Strong.

RON: Did you say something?

FRANNIE: Coffee's strong. Don't you think?

RON: I can't taste it.

LEE: Your hand is cut. (*He looks at cut on hand from glass in candy machine. Looks at Lee. Pause.*)

RON: (*Staring at Lee.*) Well, I guess I'm going. (*Pause.*) I'm going to leave now. (*Stands.*) I'm leaving. You take American Express, Silvio? (*Hands him card. As Silvio runs payment through machine, Ron tears off one of many little air fresheners—meant to be hung from rear-view mirror—wrapped in cellophane on a display card on counter.*)

RON: Why doesn't he fix your gumball machine?

SILVIO: Who?

RON: Denny. The genius. (*Pause.*)

SILVIO: He's vegetarian.

RON: Mm. What is this?

SILVIO: Air freshener. (*Ron unwraps the air freshener, smells it.*)

RON: How many are there?

SILVIO: Fifty. Minus two. That'd be forty-eight.

RON: I'll take them all.

SILVIO: You want them all?

RON: (*Nods. Looks around at products for sale.*) And I'd like a case of antifreeze.

SILVIO: A case?

RON: Please. Thank you. (*Silvio exits into garage. Ron continues smelling the air freshener, looks at Lee who is aware he's watching her. Silvio enters with case of anti-freeze. Puts it on counter.*)

RON: (*Puts air fresheners on them.*) Could you gift wrap these for me?

SILVIO: Huh?

RON: Do you have any wrapping paper? It's a wedding present.

SILVIO: No. (*Pause.*) Sorry. (*Ron nods. Silvio totals bill, hands Ron a receipt.*)

RON: Thank you. Ladies. Thank you for the invitation. (*To Lee.*) Your concern.

FRANNIE: Bye.

RON: Silvio. (*Shakes his hand.*) Thanks for sharing. I'm so glad about your sister.

SCENE 2

> *It is two hours later; the clock says 11:30. Lee is on the phone. Frannie is sitting cross-legged, inspired by the garage, writing in a notebook.*

LEE: No, the MRI was negative. I was calling primarily to find out if the results were in on the anticardiolipins. Really? That's interesting. Well, that explains it. No. No. What we should do is taper off the prednazone and refer him to a rheumatologist. Don't you think? Definitely. I agree. (*Harlon bops by from outside.*) Could you hold on a sec, Peter. (*To Harlon.*) Excuse me, excuse me. Would you ask him again to come out here? Please. Thank you.

HARLON: Sure thing. (*Harlon goes into garage to get Silvio.*)

LEE: Sorry, Peter. So, any more calls? I thought she might. Yup, yup, I'm seeing her on Tuesday, she's just testing the system. She is, very sweet. (*Silvio comes out.*)

LEE: Well, thanks, Peter. (*Silvio sees she's on the phone; starts to go back.*) Wait! (*He stops.*) I'll check in with you later. Bye. (*She hangs up and goes over to him.*) Could you just explain this to me again. Please, I'd really appreciate it. What exactly is a fuel injector?

SILVIO: Injects your fuel.

LEE: Injects fuel. To the engine.

SILVIO: Intake manifold.

LEE: And what, specifically, are you doing to the fuel injector?

SILVIO: Injectors, m'am. You got four. Checking for fuel.

LEE: You're checking for fuel. You've ruled out the ignition?

SILVIO: Got spark. Got to be a fuel problem.

LEE: How long will it take?

SILVIO: They're hard to get at. Injectors.

LEE: Why is that?

SILVIO: 's a lot in the way — air cleaner, fuel rail, hoses, wires, might have to tear off the plenum.

LEE: The plenum?

SILVIO: Might.

LEE: Are you Denny?

SILVIO: I'm not Denny.

LEE: Where is Denny? (*Pause.*)

SILVIO: Break.

LEE: Should we wait for him, before you proceed?

SILVIO: (*Changing the subject.*) Used to be you could look down the carburetor, pump it, see if gas squirts out.

LEE: Why don't you do that now?

SILVIO: Do what?

LEE: Look down the carburetor.

SILVIO: Is no carburetor.

LEE: What do you mean there is no carburetor?

SILVIO: Not in a Volvo.

LEE: My car has no carburetor?

SILVIO: Not in a Volvo.

LEE: If it is the injectors, if one of the injectors is not squirting fuel, then what happens?

SILVIO: Replace it.

LEE: How much would that cost?

SILVIO: Run you 'round a hundred dollars. I can look it up.

LEE: That's all right. Just fix it. Please. It's very important that we leave here by two. At the latest. Two. Do you know how far it is to St. Joseph from here?

SILVIO: You going to St. Joes?

LEE: Yes.

SILVIO: You going to St. Joes?

LEE: St. Joseph. Yes.

SILVIO: Couple hours.

LEE: Thank you. I appreciate your best efforts. (*Silvio exits.*) We should call your father. (*She goes to the phone.*) Shouldn't we? Call your father? Frannie?

FRANNIE: Huh?

LEE: Don't you think we should call your father, let him know?

FRANNIE: Okay.

LEE: (*Lee ponders.*) We shouldn't wait? (*No response.*) We'll wait. We may not have to call him at all. (*She sits. Harlon enters. Puts cash in cash register.*)

SILVIO: (*Calling from garage.*) Harlon!

HARLON: You ladies comfortable? Anything I can get you?

FRANNIE: No thanks.

HARLON: I could turn the fan on. Give you a little breeze. (*Goes to old fan. Tries to turn it on.*) Huh. Something's not. . . (*Fiddling with it; it won't turn on.*) Can't tell if the switch. . . On. (*Puts his hand up to feel breeze.*)Off. On. Off. See if it's plugged in. Plugged in. Plug doesn't look too good.

LEE: Better unplug it. It could start a fire.

SILVIO: Harlon! Get in here!

HARLON: Well, looks like it only works in the off position. (*Harlon exits into garage.*)

LEE: What did he say about the opposition?

FRANNIE: Not the opposition. The off position. The fan only works in the off position.

LEE: (*Ponders.*) Is that funny? (*Pause.*) Do you know what a carburetor does, Frannie?

FRANNIE: No.

LEE: I don't either but I thought I had one. I might have thought it was broken, and it doesn't even exist. What are you writing?

FRANNIE: A poem.

LEE: Everything will be fine. Everything's under control. Your father doesn't even have to know. (*Pause.*) It's hot in here, isn't it?

FRANNIE: It's not too bad. I like it.

LEE: No carburetor. A pygmy in a rain forest understands his world. He sees every moving part.

FRANNIE: My poem has a carburetor in it. In the fourth line.

LEE: How can you have a carburetor in your poem if you don't know what it does?

FRANNIE: I know what it does in my poem.

LEE: It might do more if you knew what it was.

FRANNIE: Maybe not. (*Pause.*) It might do less.

LEE: What?

FRANNIE: Nothing.

LEE: Your father told me to get the car serviced before he left. He must have told me four times. (*Pause.*) Your mother, when I picked you up, your mother asked me if I'd had the car serviced. She seemed to enjoy asking. (*Pause.*) That's a pretty dress. Are you looking forward to the wedding?

FRANNIE: Not particularly.

LEE: No?

FRANNIE: I don't like weddings.

LEE: Why not?

FRANNIE: They're always so sad.

LEE: Frannie, weddings aren't sad. They're joyful, they're life-affirming.

FRANNIE: I don't think they're especially life-affirming. I think funerals are more life-affirming than weddings.

LEE: How can you say that?

FRANNIE: Weddings make you think of divorce. Funerals make you think of life.

LEE: Maybe you haven't been to any good weddings.

FRANNIE: Maybe I've been to too many.

LEE: (*Pause.*) Could you make sure he unplugged that fan? It makes me nervous, the thought of a fire in a garage. What do you think that genius is doing, the living legend in his own time? Christ. What a place to break down. (*Frannie goes over to the outlet and takes out the plug, looks at it, plugs it back in.*) He'll never forget me.

SCENE 3

The clock is now set at 1:45. Lee is by the pay phone on the wall. Frannie is still writing in her journal.

LEE: We should call him. He would want us to call, don't you think? (*She goes to phone; stops.*) I don't want to upset him, unnecessarily. (*Goes over to the garage doorway.*) Excuse me, how's it going in there? Hello! It's been over two hours. Hello!

HARLON: (*Entering from garage.*) 'scuse me. (*He goes to phone. Dials.*)

LEE: (*To Harlon.*) Is Denny back? Is he?

HARLON: Uh. . .no.

LEE: Do you know where he is?

HARLON: Denny? Not exactly.

LEE: Look, Harlon, that is your name isn't it? Harlon, you told me Denny is an excellent mechanic, you assured me he would be working on my car. I've been here four hours and there's been very little to assure me that progress is being made. I'd like to speak to the owner of this garage.

HARLON: You're not alone, m'am. There's a few people in line ahead of you, some with badges.

LEE: Where is he?

HARLON: She. Is in Mexico. (*Points to a postcard on the wall.*) She's right here, by this monument, right where this little arrow's pointing.

LEE: What is she doing in Mexico?

HARLON: Well, put it this way—she can't ever run for President. Come on, Mary Louise. Answer the phone. (*Silvio becomes visible in doorway.*)

SILVIO: M'am.

LEE: Yes?

SILVIO: Figure two are bad.

LEE: Two are bad.

SILVIO: Only a couple 're squirting.

LEE: Well, that's good. Isn't it? That would explain why it won't start?

SILVIO: Mm.

LEE: So, they need to be replaced.

HARLON: (*Into phone.*) Good afternoon. Wake up call.

SILVIO: Might want to replace all four while you're at it.

HARLON: Harlon.

LEE: You think I should?

HARLON: Can you drag your butt over here?

SILVIO: Chances are, two are bad, two are goin'.

HARLON: Now.

LEE: You're telling me I should replace all four.

SILVIO: Not telling you, m'am.

HARLON: Half an hour. Hour. I gotta pick up some parts.

LEE: But you think I should.

HARLON: Good question. He left. Disappeared.

SILVIO: Don't mention his brain. Harlon. Harlon! Don't mention his brain.

HARLON: We don't know.

LEE: If it was your car, would you replace all four injectors?

SILVIO: I wouldn't own a Volvo, m'am.

LEE: Why not? (*He grimaces.*) If you did own one, would you replace them all?

HARLON: We don't know. His car's still out back.

SILVIO: Might.

LEE: How long will that take?

HARLON: Mary, I'm thinking of piercing my ear, what do you think? Think I should?

SILVIO: Couple hours.

LEE: Two hours?

HARLON: He knows about the game.

LEE: That means we'll be out of here by three-thirty. Is that right? (*Silvio studies clock.*)

HARLON: He knows about the game. You think he doesn't know about the game? Whole county knows about the game.

LEE: Do you have the injectors here in stock?

SILVIO: No, m'am.

LEE: How far away is your supplier?

HARLON: You coming?

SILVIO: Ten minutes.

LEE: Each way? (*Gas pump bell outside rings again.*)

SILVIO: With Harlon driving.

HARLON: That's no problem. Bring her with you.

SILVIO: You wanna do 'em all?

HARLON: Bring her along.

LEE: All right.

HARLON: It'll perk him up.

LEE: At your recommendation.

HARLON: He's having too much fun today, anyway, ain't you, Silvie. Adios. (*Hangs up.*) She's coming right over. Bringing Audrey with her.

SILVIO: No!

HARLON: They were just headed out for a picnic. Guess they'll have it here.

SILVIO: No!

HARLON: Hee, hee, hee. (*Silvio exits out front door to pump gas.*) Hey! Should I get a case of tranny fluid while I'm there? Silvio? (*Goes for cap.*)

FRANNIE: You want some company?

LEE: Frannie.

HARLON: Company? You wanna come?

FRANNIE: Yeah.

LEE: I don't think that's a good idea.

FRANNIE: Why not?

LEE: I don't think it is.

HARLON: It's okay by me.

FRANNIE: I'll get us some food. Aren't you hungry?

LEE: No.

FRANNIE: We can stop and get some food, can't we?

HARLON: What kind of food?

FRANNIE: Food.

HARLON: I know where there's food. Sure. Food. Yeah.

FRANNIE: Let's go. We'll pick up some ice, I'll pierce your ear.

HARLON AND LEE: (*Together.*) What?

FRANNIE: I'll pierce your ear when we get back.

HARLON: You will?

LEE: No, she won't.

HARLON: You know how?

LEE: Frannie. Your father wouldn't like this.

FRANNIE: We'll be right back. You probably shouldn't drink any more of that coffee. (*They head out front door as Lee looks through purse for wallet.*)

HARLON: You ever done it before?

FRANNIE: What?

HARLON: Pierced an ear.

FRANNIE: No.

LEE: Frannie, let me give you some money. Frannie. Tell him to drive carefully. (*Door closes.*) Drive carefully! Shit. (*Goes to pay phone on wall.*) Hello, I'd like to leave a message for Henry Britten. Henry Britten, he's the best man. No, don't go get him; don't get him! If you could just kindly give him this message. Tell him Lee called. Lee. Yes, I am playing the piano. I brought sheet music, I'm all set. If you could just tell him. . . (*Denny enters garage through back door, quietly enters waiting room, goes to counter, picks up his keys. Keeps his balance by holding on to walls, counter, etc. Lee hears him, turns around, sees him, too engrossed to think it might be Denny. They stare briefly at each other. He exits into garage, out garage door, off stage.*) . . . we've had a little car trouble, nothing major; we're a little behind schedule, I'm afraid we've missed the luncheon, but we'll be there in plenty of time for cocktails, well before the ceremony. No, please don't get him, I don't want to bother him. Thank you so much. Isn't it, a lovely day for a wedding. Bye, bye. (*She sits. Silvio enters, Silvio enters, picks up two cans of oil and takes them outside. Comes back, rings up gas sale at cash register. Exits into garage, avoiding her view.*)

MARY: (*Mary enters like a bat out of hell fellowed by Audrey who enters cautiously, looking around for Silvio. Fires off her words in one long sentence.*) Damn, it's hot. Whew! Smells like Kuwait in here, hot and oily. Now Audrey, you have a seat, hon, not on the vinyl it'll stick to your thighs, forget about your hair, just forget he's in the next room. Put him out of your mind. You want a saltine? No? Would you care for a saltine? M'am?

LEE: No, thank you.

MARY: Days like this, I just suck 'em. Don't know why, but I do. Suck 'em till it gets dark. Must have been a cow in a past life, stuck on my salt lick. You been here long?

LEE: Yes, I have.

MARY: Mm. (*Goes to doorway.*) What are you doing in there, Silvie, working or fucking the dog? So, where'd he go, huh? Not like him to just wander off. What's wrong with it? They don't like the heat, I know that. Volvos.

LEE: It won't start.

MARY: Won't start? You check the fuses, Silvie? Check the fuses? (*Chuckles.*) Checking them now. Wouldn't be the first time. You okay, Audrey? (*To Lee.*) Having a rough time. Phone calls. Being here ain't helping none but she don't wanna be left alone, do you, Audrey? Well shoot, what happened to the candy machine? I tell you this place is going to hell in a handbasket, glass everywhere, people disappearing, court orders, warrants for arrest, counter's a mess. Now here's someone's wallet. Hundred dollar bills and condoms. (*She studies his license.*) Ron Patrick Maguire is off right now having unsafe sex. He can't pay for. Bills, bills, bills, got more bookwork than a PhD, be here all afternoon. What're you looking for, hon?

AUDREY: The key.

MARY: What key?

AUDREY: (*Whispers.*) The key.

MARY: Don't worry, he's not listening. Here it is. (*Key is attached to a big key ring.*) You'd best take the Penny Saver with you. No telling when that room was stocked last. Not since Bonnie high tailed it for Mexico. (*Audrey exits with key to ladies room.*)

MARY: Damn if my feet haven't grown; these shoes never used to hurt. (*To Lee.*) There's history.

LEE: I beg your pardon?

MARY: History. Between them two, you'll pick up on it. They're what you might call "estranged." Your skin's real nice. You drink a lot of buttermilk? You in a hurry?

LEE: Yes.

MARY: Where're you headed?

LEE: I'm going to a wedding.

MARY: Not yours, I hope.

LEE: Not mine.

MARY: That's good. That's good it's not your wedding.

LEE: It's extremely important that I get there.

MARY: Why's that? (*Takes jar of mayonnaise and several hard boiled eggs out of her bag.*)

LEE: My fiancee is the best man and I'm playing the wedding march.

MARY: Huh. I'm gonna whip up some egg salad, you care for some?

LEE: No, thank you.

MARY: Sure? Hostage in a gas station, bound to be hungry. I'm on a high cholesterol diet myself. Lipid center, that's me, two sticks of butter a day. My niece Claudette? She eats macrobiotic is skinny, pale, got zits, stringy hair and a bad attitude. You ever get squirrely phone calls? Damn, can't get my rings off; look like the Michelin man. First summer I got my answering machine, came home, poured myself a wine cooler, kicked off my shoes and turned to playback. First message: "Mary Louise, I love you." That was the extent. "Mary Louise, I love you." Total stranger, in my dining room. Well. You jump-start a battery, that's about how hard my heart kicked in, pounding, full throttle. Scared? I was living alone, still do. Jackson, my third and last - I don't say final husband - died the year before, prostate cancer, I went round to every room and nailed my windows shut. Lookee here, this one's got a double yolk; twice the cholesterol for the price of one. For weeks, I slept in fear—cold, bone-chilling, can't wear your curlers to bed cause they make too much noise on the pillow fear—knife in hand, lying in wait for the laughing slasher, Ol' Hannibal the Cannibal. Every day I'd get home from work, ease towards that little red flashing light tells you how many messages. Silvie! You working or waxing your porpoise? Don't want him feeling left out. Never heard from him again. Never did. Every so often, in daylight, I'd rewind the tape, study that voice just in case I ran up against it. Now here's some human nature for you. After a couple months I began to listen to the message in a whole new light. I started to hear it like maybe that person did truly love me, not in a perverse want to stalk you in your house kill you with a blunt weapon dress up in your skin kind of way, but sincere. Heartfelt. There was passion in his voice, I don't know what your name is if I did I'd say it now. I couldn't help but start to wonder what the man behind the voice looked like, his forearms, his hands. Yeah. I have regretted to this day taping over that message. Haven't heard a man tell me he loved me since. Could be hearing it three times a day. Sure you don't want any egg-salad?

LEE: I'm going for a walk.

MARY: A walk? You can't walk to anywheres from here. Just a long stretch of highway out there.

LEE: I need some air.

MARY: Okay, honey. Where's your wedding at?

LEE: St. Joseph.

MARY: St. Joe's, last stop of the Pony Express. Too bad. I'd drive you there myself, I could use the breeze, but there's a big game this evening. Semifinals. You're welcome to come, got an extra lawn chair in my Bronco. (*Lee exits out front door. Mary takes the bowl of egg salad along with a bag, exits into garage, out back garage door. Puts bowl and thermos down on a makeshift table. Silvio comes and stands in the garage doorway.*)

MARY: Silvie, you look like you were rode hard and put away wet. Is that a gun in your pocket or are you happy to see me? (*Silvio takes the gun out of his pocket and puts it on the table. Sits. Mary hands him a slice of bread with egg salad on it.*)

MARY: Now what're you doing with that? You need a gun up Josie's trailer park? I thought she kept it quiet up there. Iced tea? (*Looking out towards audience.*) Always did like this view. She's a doctor, that woman. It's on her license plates. (*Silvio reacts strongly.*) What? You need a doctor? You need Click and Clack. You should've called Car-Talk this morning. (*Calling towards ladies room.*) Audrey? Audrey? She's gonna spend the afternoon in there, hiding out from you. Been complaining about phone calls all week. My suspicion is every time the phone rings and it's not you she gets that much more afraid you're never gonna call. That's what scares her. Now I know it's hot; my lipstick is melting. Where is Denny? Where's our shining MVP? (*Lights fade.*)

SCENE 4

The clock says 4:10. Audrey and Lee are both sitting still. Mary is going through the drawers below the counter, trying to organize a mess of bills, papers, eating saltines. Silvio and Harlon are in the garage. Frannie is outside pumping gas. Mary picks up phone, dials.

MARY: Addie, it's Mary, hon, how are you? You haven't seen Denny today, have you, 's he been by? No. Well, just got a notion he might have stopped in, pick up his mail. Oh yes, I heard. Spoiled 20,000 gallons, blood got in the milk. I know, I know. Well, that age. Young Harlon here'd poke the crack of dawn if he could catch it. So, just thought I'd check. You take care, Addie. (*Hangs up.*) Sourpuss. That woman was weaned on a pickle. (*Frannie enters. She is wearing a man's large shirt from the garage over her dress.*)

FRANNIE: (*Handing her a twenty.*) Twelve dollars. Pump two.

MARY: (*Giving her change from the register.*) You're good at this. You want a job? Your daughter's a sweetheart. She favors you. (*Lee and Frannie respond together.*)

LEE: She's not my daughter.

FRANNIE: I'm not her daughter.

MARY: Oh.

FRANNIE: He wants a free glass.

MARY: Free glass? That was last month. Bonnie had a promo going.

FRANNIE: He says the sign is still up; he should get one.

MARY: Who is it? (*Looks out window.*) Should have known. Trudy Minskoff, ugly enough to make a train take a dirt road. Here, give him this. (*Hands Frannie a used styrofoam cup from the coffee table. Frannie exits.*) If my dog was that ugly I'd shave his ass and make him walk backwards. (*She dials phone while looking at old photos.*) So, is she your step-daughter?

LEE: Not yet.

MARY: Not yet. Sounds promising. Oh my Lord, will you look at that, Bonnie in her prom dress. Audrey come take a look. Bonnie in her prom dress with her daddy, out front by the old pumps. Look how skinny Steve is. He never did have a butt. (*Into phone.*) Huh? Who's this? Jim who? What? Jim! I clear forgot I called you. How'd you know it was me? (*To Audrey.*) Look at this one here. Then again . . . (*Tries to take it back but Audrey has taken it and sits down with it. Frannie enters and goes back into garage.*) You haven't seen Denny, have you? Mm. He wandered off, been gone all afternoon. Nope. I tried him. Nope. (*Audrey takes the photo and sits back down. Stares at it.*) Called him. Called her. Well, if you could ask around, he's got me worried. If you track him down, tell him to give a call here. Hey, Jim. (*Lowering her voice.*) You don't know Volvos, do you? Silvie here's got one won't start. '88 240. You know, that was my very first thought, I was thinking might be the brain. Yes, I do. I remember Vic and them lookin' at that car three days couldn't figure out what it needed. Put in a new brain, started right up. Well, thanks for calling,

Jim. How's your arm? Keep it rested, hear? See you at the game. (*Hangs up.*) For the love of God, there's a turtle on the floor.

LEE: Would you do me a favor, please?

MARY: A turtle. On the floor.

LEE: Don't pick him up.

MARY: Now what in your tiny little head brought you here. Nature is just one mystery after another. (*Leans over.*)

LEE: Don't pick him up.

MARY: I'll pick him up. (*Picks him up.*) Are you a pet or are you wild? You're awful cute. Like an RV, little Winnebago, wherever you park, you're home. Care for a saltine?

LEE: Mary! There is a sign, Authorized Personnel Only, on that door and so far I have heeded it.

MARY: You want me to go in for you, don't you? Check your car. (*To turtle.*) Come on, Captain RV, I'm gonna introduce you to Uncle Silvio. (*Mary exits into garage with turtle. Lee notices Audrey is sniffling, studying the photo. Mary comes back with box with turtle in it, moves toward counter.*) Well now, Harlon can't decide which ear to do. She says right ear, he says left. She says left ear means he's gay, men will think he's willin'. I say if you're already walking the planet with a permanent hard-on, giving every man, woman and species you meet a welcome howdy-do, what difference does it make?

LEE: Is my car ready?

MARY: You can call me Mary. I still don't know your name. (*Pause.*) Here's the low down. Silvie's doing a compression check right now. (*Harlon enters from garage. Goes out front door.*)

LEE: A compression check?

MARY: Won't take him thirty minutes.

LEE: What about the injectors?

MARY: Injectors are all in; beautifully installed. All they need is a new pick-up for the distributor, kick them in right. Harlon's gone to pick it up.

LEE: He's getting a new part?

MARY: Just a little one. Little bitty.

LEE: What . . . what is a compression check?

MARY: That's when you put a pressure gauge in each spark plug hole. Read how much pressure each cylinder has, pounds per square inch? Volvo has four. Cylinders. I think, am I right, Audrey? (*Audrey holds up four fingers.*) Four. Yeah, you want to have a hundred and sixty-five pounds of pressure in each. It's a kind of old-fashioned back to basics procedure, but then again that's Silvie.

LEE: Does my car start?

MARY: Audrey, what are you doing looking at that old picture of you and Silvie. You're just gonna get all worked up.

LEE: Does my car start?

MARY: Does it start?

LEE: Does it start?

MARY: Well, no, not exactly. Now, I don't want to alarm you unnecessarily, but I am gonna bring you up to speed here. There's a chance your car might need a new brain.

LEE: A new brain?

MARY: Computer. Seen it before, with a Volvo.

LEE: Is there a car rental agency nearby?

MARY: You mean like Hertz, or Avis?

LEE: Yes.

MARY: Budget. National.

LEE: Yes!

MARY: I know Budget lets you charge it to your Sears card.

LEE: Is there one nearby?

MARY: Uh . . . not nearby. No.

LEE: How close is the nearest car rental agency?

MARY: That'd be back in Hannibal, wouldn't you say Audrey? Audrey, put that picture away, Silvie doesn't even look remotely like that any more. Used to be a courtesy car at the airport back in Monroe city before the town took it over. Yeah, Hannibal's a good hour east on 36 and I know for a fact they close at five. (*Looking up at clock.*) Afternoon really flew, didn't it?

LEE: Is there anyone around here who would rent me a car?

MARY: Mm. Ol' Wilson used to have a second car. A Taurus I think it was, Ford Taurus, yeah. Then again, I think he passed it along to his daughter, the one became a DJ for KMVM? (*To turtle.*) You comfy in there? Oop, we need a pooper scooper; size of a thumbnail. Let me think. There's not many folks would rent their car to a stranger.

LEE: Is there anyone who I could hire to drive me to St. Joseph?

MARY: Mm. Any other day you'd have your pick of the litter but, like I told you, big game today, starts at six, can't think of anyone off hand who isn't going. Burly, maybe. Maybe Burly, you think, Audrey?

LEE: What about Silvio?

MARY: Silvio's scorekeeper. (*Dialing phone.*) Audrey couldn't make the return trip back alone. Can't handle being alone now, been staying with me. I'll try Burly. He's not what you'd call overly hygienic, Burly, doesn't exactly go overboard with the soap, does he Audrey, but he does enjoy a Sunday drive. Just keep your windows down. It's ringing. Still ringing. He's not the type to have an answering machine, Burly, wouldn't want to be beholden to a message. Doesn't like to talk. Never did. Ow, my feet, these damn shoes. Burly's the one drove Denny out to MIT his one semester at the college, didn't he, Audrey? Massachusetts Institute of Technology up in Cambridge, Massachusetts. They gave a full scholarship. He hitch-hiked back. Still ringing. This little turtle resembles a question mark. You asking me a little turtle question? Little philosophical turtle question? Like what am I doing here in the cardboard box smells of tranny fluid?

LEE: Hang up.

MARY: Burly went out with my cousin Angel in high school. Used to mow the town cemeteries, all three of them, didn't he, Audrey? He and Angel used to do the horizontal cha-cha down behind the monuments, in amongst the flags and flowers. Yup, right in the marble orchard.

LEE: Hang up!.

MARY: That's what Jackson, my third and last I don't say final husband, used to call the cemetery. The marble orchard. Course he's planted there right now, on the installment plan. Four years later, I'm still paying monthly for it. Nothing's free in life, not even death.

LEE: (*Over the top.*) Hang up the goddamned phone!! (*She goes and hangs it up.*) Silvio!! And for God's sakes, stop eating those saltines! (*She throws them away.*) Silvio! Don't you wonder why your hands and feet are swollen? Has it occurred to you there might be some simple explanation that would explain why you can't get your rings off, why your feet don't fit into your shoes? You have too much sodium in your diet. Silvio!! (*She takes the broken bell off the counter and throws it. Silvio enters. Audrey rushes out of the room.*) Now look. Listen. We have been here for over seven hours. Seven. I told you when we got here we needed to leave by two. I told you it was very important. . (*Voice breaks.*) I told you . . . You didn't tell me that wasn't possible. You didn't say you couldn't do it. It's now four-twenty. I want my car working in thirty minutes. If not my car, another car. I want a car. . . any car, that's running, that will start and go. . . . out in front of the garage. . . in half an hour. A car that I can get into and drive away in. Have I made myself clear? Do you understand me? And I don't want to hear one detail. One alternator. One plenum. Nothing! (*Screaming.*) What are you staring at?!

MARY: Something's leaking in your blouse.

LEE: My blouse? (*Phone rings.*)

MARY: (*Picking up phone.*) Stanton's Garage. Who? There's no Lee here.

LEE: That's me. I'm Lee. (*Frannie enters from garage and stays by the door.*)

MARY: What? Okay. (*Pause.*) Who is this? Sure, I'll tell her.

LEE: (*Grabbing phone.*) Hello? Hello? Hello? (*Hangs up.*) Who was it?

MARY: I don't know. A man.

LEE: What man?

MARY: I don't know.

LEE: What did he say?

MARY: He said for me to tell you. . .

LEE: What?

MARY: Well, he said, tell her to relax. . .

LEE: Relax?

MARY: . . everything will be okay and. . .

LEE: And what? What?

MARY: He said to tell you he loved you.

LEE: Is this some kind of joke? Who was it?

MARY: I don't know. I truly don't. You want a paper towel?

LEE: What did he say again? Tell me everything. Exactly.

MARY: He said, is Lee there. I said, there's no Lee here, not knowing that was your name. He must have heard you in the background, he said, tell her to relax, everything will be okay, and, . . tell her I love her.

LEE: He said my name. He knew my name?

MARY: Your fiancee?

LEE: How could it be? He doesn't have the number here.

FRANNIE: Hey!

LEE: What?

FRANNIE: The fan. The fan is working.

LEE: I thought you unplugged it. Frannie? (*Lights fade.*)

SCENE 5

> *The clock says 6:10. Audrey and Lee are sitting across from each other. All the others have gone to the game.*

AUDREY: Care for a wipe-n-dry? That's my feeling, there's no comparison between grass fed deer and corn fed beef. (*Pause.*) You'll hear them howl all night. Didn't used to could. I remember first time I heard a coyote I was lying next to Silvie, he asked me, "Audrey, is that your stomach or mine?" Being from such a distance, see. Used to laugh. (*Laughs. Pause.*) You don't care for conversation?

LEE: You didn't want to go to the game with the others?

AUDREY: More useful here. (*Pause.*) I help Silvie with the numbers, hand them up to him. He's scorekeeper. Today's our anniversary.

(*Sniffles.*) Thirty-six years.

LEE: I'm sorry.

AUDREY: You married?

LEE: No.

AUDREY: Ever been married?

LEE: Yes.

AUDREY: Divorced. I've never been divorced. Don't know that I'd be much good at it.

LEE: I'm not divorced, I'm widowed.

AUDREY: Widowed. Mmm. Your husband passed away? Then, too, that's something else again. Was it an accident?

LEE: Was what an accident?

AUDREY: Your husband's death?

LEE: No, illness.

AUDREY: Is that right? Illness. Mm. That's a shame. You being a doctor and all.

LEE: What are you saying?

AUDREY: You must have been. . . well. . .

LEE: What?

AUDREY: ...that much more involved. (*Pause.*) You ever been estranged?

LEE: Estranged. Yes.

AUDREY: Now could you tell me, is that a medical condition?

LEE: No.

AUDREY: Not medical?

LEE: No.

AUDREY: Mm. I wondered. Thought there might be some prescription. First time for me. According to Mary been in it three months now. Three months Silvie's been up the trailer park, in his sister's pop-up camper. Sometimes I think, if she hadn't of had that pop-up camper, he'd still be home. How'd you get out of it?

LEE: I don't remember.

AUDREY: Mm. Still don't know how it happened. Still a mystery. Wake up one morning...before you even open your eyes you know some-things different. Like someone snuck in during the night and re-arranged all your furniture. It's a sick feeling. Just the way he sat there that morning, on the edge of the bed. I could see it in his back.

LEE: Excuse me, I need to make a phone call.

AUDREY: I knew you were thinking. Would you like for me to step out-side?

LEE: No. Thanks for offering. (*Lee goes to phone. Dials in her credit card number.*)

LEE: Hello, is Henry Britten nearby. Yes, I would, please. Thank you.

(*Pause.*)

AUDREY: I'm not listening.

LEE: Hi, sweetheart. I did call. I called twice, you didn't get my messages? I didn't want to bother you, Henry. Can you speak up, sweetheart, I can't hear you very well. I know you would have come, I didn't want you spending half the day in the car, it would have been a four hour drive for you. Somewhere on route 36, between Monroe City and Macon. We did stay in Hannibal, we got up early, we left at 8:30 this morning we've spent ten hours in this garage. It wouldn't start. It wouldn't start! We stopped, Frannie wanted to look at some deer in a cornfield and it wouldn't start up again. Deer in a cornfield! She doesn't see deer in Chicago, pardon? The fuel injectors, two injectors weren't working properly they replaced them. Not yet, they're putting in a little part, a pick up in the alternator.

AUDREY: Distributor.

LEE: Distributor that's what...Yes, you did. You did. You told me to get it serviced. Not that much time, Henry, I've been on call the last three nights in a row. You're right. Please tell them I'm so sorry. Isn't that a band in the background? Can't they play the wedding march? I know he wanted Frannie to be there. Uh, she's at a game, a softball game. There's a big game tonight, playoffs. She's perfectly safe. With friends, new friends, I'll have her call you as soon as she gets back. When the game is over, it should be before dark I would...think. Henry .... sweetheart...don't be angry, please don't be angry. We'll spend the night in a motel and we'll come in the morning, we'll be there for the weekend, everyone will get to see Frannie. No, we're not coming tonight. We can't make it. Henry? Henry? He hung up. (*She hangs up phone. She stares at phone, Audrey moves to another seat. Lee turns slowly, somewhat stunned, trying to collect herself. The pay phone rings. They both look at phone.*)

AUDREY: Don't answer it. (*It continues to ring. Lee picks it up, doesn't say anything. She is crying. She looks through her bag for change. Deposits a few coins. Hangs up phone. Pauses. Goes into garage, gets into car, closes door. After a moment, Audrey goes to doorway.*)

AUDREY: Mind if I join you? I'll ride in the back. (*She exits into garage. Car door shuts. Lights fade.*)

ACT TWO

SCENE 1

Lights up. The clock says 9:35 p.m. Sounds of crickets, locusts, an occasional coyote. Denny, wearing his baseball uniform, which is dirty, is leaning up against the counter, helping Audrey who is desperately looking for the key to the ladies room.

DENNY: Here it is. (*Audrey exits out front door. Silvio enters from garage.*)

DENNY: Did you talk to her?

SILVIO: Yeah.

DENNY: Well? Is she coming out? (*Silvio nods.*) What's she doing?

SILVIO: Sittin'.

DENNY: She's sitting? In her car?

SILVIO: She's comin'. (*Silvio picks up some styrofoam cups from the coffee table, goes to bottom of drawer of counter for whiskey bottle. Pours whiskey into a couple of cups, drinks one down, hands one to Denny.*)

SILVIO: Think she'd like a drink?

DENNY: I don't know.

SILVIO: (*Pondering.*) Think she might?

DENNY: Your call. (*Silvio takes a cup into garage. While he is gone Denny lies down, flat on his back. Off stage we hear Silvio ask her if she'd like a drink. "M'am, would you like a drink? M'am?" No response. He enters without the cup.*)

SILVIO: Left it on the hood. You okay?

DENNY: It's better when I lie down. (*Silvio goes to pour himself another drink.*)

DENNY: I blew the game.

SILVIO: 't's all right.

DENNY: We'd be in the finals.

SILVIO: She'll take a look.

DENNY: She can't see much without an x-ray, Silvie. Be like trying to study an engine through the hood. All she'll see are my old zit marks.

SILVIO: She's from Chicago. Doctor from Chicago.

DENNY: Al Capone's from Chicago.

SILVIO: You won't have to go to the clinic, mess with Chet. (*Pause.*)

DENNY: I'm scared shitless, Silvie.

SILVIO: Probably some simple thing. (*Pause.*)

DENNY: Last time I had this view, Bonnie was on top of me. Hitch hiked all the way from Massachusetts, dead of winter. You know how they say you see your life flash before you, right before you die? It's all up there. (*Pause. Silvio goes to doorway, looks in.*)

DENNY: She's not coming, Silvie.

SILVIO: Just wait. (*Silvie goes to whiskey, pours some more into Denny's cup.*)

DENNY: I've had a good life. I can't complain. I have enjoyed my life on this planet. I love mother earth. I love my fields, my alfalfa, my soybeans—Silvie, I want you take Red. Will you?

SILVIO: Jesus, Denny.

DENNY: You'll take good care of her, I know you will. She likes you. You're a good man, Silvie. Not too many like you around. You're one of a dying breed. (*Audrey enters, avoids looking at Silvio, takes her sweater from a chair, exits.*)

DENNY: Ol' Forbes. You see his expression? Running home from third, all gleeful, wondering what the hell I was doing on the ground. Humped up like a cut worm on a log.

SILVIO: Nice hit. (*Pause.*)

DENNY: No regrets. You have to live in the moment, Silvie. Live in the moment. Life is short. All those cliches you hear, they're true. I'm going home. Silvie, that turtle needs some water.

SILVIO: If you'd maybe take a look at her car, Den. Might put her in a mind to reciprocate.

DENNY: What is it?

SILVIO: Volvo.

DENNY: What's wrong?

SILVIO: Won't start.

DENNY: Check the wires?

SILVIO: Think it's the brain.

DENNY: The brain?

SILVIO: Only thing left. Should I test the sensors? Den? Take me for goddamned ever, should I? Test every one of them Swedish sensors?

DENNY: I'm leaving. (*He gets up and heads for the door.*)

SILVIO: Don't go. Den.

DENNY: Thanks, Silvie. I appreciate it.

SILVIO: Can you drive? Should you be drivin'?

DENNY: Don't forget the turtle. (*Denny exits out front door. Silvio goes to coffee table; pours water into lid and puts it in turtle's box. Sees Audrey's bag. Holds it. Exits out front door. Moments later, door* *opens. It's Mary, carrying blankets, comforter, bag with food, tiny portable TV.*)

MARY: Audrey, you wanna give me a hand with this. Audrey? Jesus Christ, she hiding out again. Silvie, I'm back! Just barely, some fool nearly rammed me, swerved into my lane right before I pulled in. Another coat of paint and he would have had me. Silvie, you there? (*Looks into garage.*) Hm. I don't know whether to make up the couch or the back seat of the car. (*Gets blankets, starts to make up the couch.*) What a day, a day to remember to forget. I was gonna bring the microwave but it doesn't work; turn it on, just sits there, most likely cooking the house, sending deadly nuclear rays back through all the wiring, mutation rays be coming out of every outlet. Silvie, you think that was a double or a triple that Denny hit? Breaks my heart, I can't think about it. That boy just folded like a one egg pudding. I tell you, there're some planets up there doing some kind of wild do-si-do, wreaking havoc down here is what. I never. I just never. And I don't want to, ever again. (*Silvie enters from outside.*) Well, it's not the Motel Six, more like Motel Two and a Half, but it's got its charm. What are you doing out there? Silvie, you look even worse. Guess that new pick-up didn't pick you up much. (*Into garage.*) M'am, now don't you worry about Frannie. She said to tell you she'd be late, not to worry. Harlon's a good boy, he'll watch out for her. (*To Silvio.*) Think she can hear me through the window? Poor thing, I feel bad for her. (*Into garage.*) When she comes back, you give a call, we'll come pick you up, plenty of room at my house. Don't hesitate now. I've left you some oranges in a bag here, oranges, TV guide, and bagel chips, cholesterol free. You want to wave or something, let me know you hear me? (*To Silvio.*) She looks like she's on the road in there, doesn't she? Travelling. Like she's moving, going 55, sitting there in the passenger seat. Looks like she racked up some miles. (*Into garage.*) Don't forget, you got the turtle here to keep you company. If you hear noises at night it's the bats up in the attic - don't be scared. And don't let them coyotes bother you. There's a gun on the counter; you won't need it but you can feel more secure knowing it's there. So. 'night. Me and Audrey are goin'.

SILVIO: I'm taking Audrey home.

MARY: What?

SILVIO: I'm taking Audrey home.

MARY: What do you mean home.

SILVIO: Home.

MARY: Pop-up camper home? 105 Bull Hill Road home?

SILVIO: 105 Bull Hill Road.

MARY: Whatever has possessed you?

SILVIO: Would you get her?

MARY: She's in the ladies room.

SILVIO: She won't come out for me. (*Mary leaves. Silvio sits. Stands. Tries to groom himself—tucks in shirt, spits in hands to pat down hair, combs hair. Takes container of creme type heavy duty hand cleaner and cleans hands. Audrey enters. They look at each other, awkwardly. He hands her her purse.*)

SILVIO: Ready? (*They start to go.*)

AUDREY: Why? I want to know why.

SILVIO: (*Pause. Takes his time.*) I woke up start of May, smelled spring. Window was open. I looked at you and you looked old. And I felt old. So I left.

AUDREY: That's why? (*Takes it in.*) Why are you coming back?

SILVIO: I still feel old. I am old. (*He starts to leave again.*)

AUDREY: That's not good enough.

SILVIO: Huh?

AUDREY: That's not good enough.

SILVIO: For what?

AUDREY: For me to take you back. (*He runs outside. Returns and hands her two numbers from the scoreboard from the softball game.*) (A 6 in her left hand, a 3 in her right) Six runs in the first; three in the second. Sixty-three? (*He switches them.*) Thirty-six? Thirty-six years. (*Smiles.*) You remembered. (*He pats her affectionately on the back of her head. They exit. Mary enters to get her bag and turn out the lights. She stares into the garage at Lee.*)

MARY: Sure you don't wanna come along with me? I just lost my roommate. Alone again. (*Looks down at turtle.*) Tomorrow night, you're coming home with me. (*Mary turns off lights and exits.*)

SCENE 2

> *It is 12:40. Moonlight lights Lee, sitting on the couch. The phone rings. She gets up and goes to it. Almost picks it up. Doesn't. It keeps ringing. Stops ringing. She tests both doors, the one to the outside and the one to the garage to make sure they're locked, the one to the outside and the one to the garage. Sits back on the couch. Lights fade.*

SCENE 3

It is 2:00. In the black there is a knock on the front door. Another knock. More knocks. Louder.

LEE: Frannie. (*Pause.*) Frannie? Is that you?
RON: No.
LEE: Who is it? Who is it?
RON: It's me. A friend.
LEE: Go away.
RON:. I need to see you.
LEE: Go away. I'm calling the police right now.
RON: Just let me in for a minute.
LEE: I have a gun. I'll shoot.
RON: Please don't do that. I have a present for you.
LEE: (*Terrified.*) I'm warning you. I'll shoot. (*There is a crash in the dark as Lee gropes for the gun.*)
RON: Are you okay?
LEE: Leave.
RON: I won't stay long. It's very important.
LEE: Leave! Now! I'll count till three. One. . .
RON: Two. . .
LEE: I'm not kidding.
RON: I know. I have only the highest respect for you.
LEE: Two. (*Pause.*) Three. (*Pause. Lee shoots the gun in the dark. There is the sound of broken glass.*)
RON: No!! Shit—(*Lee turns on lamp on coffee table. Runs to the door.*)
LEE: Oh my God. Did I hit you?
RON: Shit!
LEE: I didn't mean to hit you. Are you hurt? Are you hurt?
RON: I'm very hurt.
LEE: Oh God. (*Unlocks and opens the door.*) I'm sorry. I didn't think it would go through the door. I didn't. . . (*Ron stands there, holding the neck of the broken bottle of wine she shot.*)
RON: What an aim.
LEE: You!
RON: One thousand dollars. This wine is worth one thousand dollars.
LEE: Why didn't you tell me it was you?
RON: A Chateau Petrus.
LEE: You scared me to death.
RON: 1966.

LEE: Jesus, you scared me. Your face. Come in. Did the glass hit your face? (*He comes in. She grabs a towel to blot his face.*)

RON: This is for you.

LEE: My heart. My heart is pounding. Put it. . .(*She takes broken bottle top and throws it away.*) Your eye.

RON: And this. (*Takes cake wrapped in napkin out of his pocket.*)

LEE: You have a black eye.

RON: Wedding cake.

LEE: It's all swollen.

RON: Put it under your pillow. The tooth fairy will come.

LEE: This isn't from the glass.

RON: It's from your fiancee. Who is an asshole. I came to warn you.

LEE: My fiancee? You were at Jay's wedding? Sit down.

RON: All right. Thank you.

LEE: Did someone hit you? How did you do this to your face?

RON: It wasn't easy. It took me all day. First my car overheated. Then they didn't like my wedding present. I thought it was appropriate. Antifreeze. Don't you think that's appropriate, for a wedding? What could be more useful for a long term commitment?

LEE: You're drunk.

RON: And you have incredible legs. I'm sorry, I won't make that kind of remark again.

LEE: What have you got hanging from your ear?

RON: (*Alarmed; knocking it off.*) Is it alive?

LEE: It's an air freshener.

RON: An air freshener? (*He inhales.*) It smells like Chateau Petrus. Breathe deep. (*Inhales again.*) Figure about thirty dollars a breath.

LEE: It's all over your pants.

RON: Should I take them off?

LEE: No. Why didn't you offer to take us with you, this morning?

RON: I didn't know you were going to my wife's wedding.

LEE: Your wife.

RON: I didn't know till I got there and your fiancee was badmouthing you.

LEE: What?

RON: Ow. Excuse me. I think my face is biting me.

LEE: What did he say?

RON: Is there a small wild animal with little pointed teeth, swinging from my cheekbone?

LEE: What did he say?

RON: He said he could never count on you.

LEE: He didn't.

RON: He did.

LEE: He didn't.

RON: He did. In front of everyone—the bartender, me . . .

LEE: He said he can't count on me?

RON: . . . Sheila from Ottawa I met in the beverage tent after I drove into it.

LEE: He said that? I can't believe it.

RON: I can't either. I went up to him and I said, isn't it amazing how the good Lord can build an entire person around an asshole this small? (*Makes a hole with thumb and index finger.*)

LEE: Do you know how much people count on me? How much?

RON: Very, very much.

LEE: Count on me with their lives? He . . . that's . . . I took two days off from work to drive his daughter to his best friend's wedding . I organized his plane ticket.

RON: Where is she? I have some cake for her, too. (*Takes it out of other pocket.*)

LEE: . . . I have no idea: she's had me worried sick. Out in Missouri somewhere. I had his suit drycleaned, picked it up, dropped off his dogs at the kennel, drove him to the airport. I bought and mailed the wedding present he doesn't even know what it is.

RON: Look. He wears his keys on his belt; it's the first sign of an asshole. That's what I came to tell you. Sometimes women don't know, don't see when men are assholes. They have these blind spots.

LEE: I just. . .

RON: It's very frustrating to watch. . . .

LEE: He couldn't have said anything worse.

RON: . . . especially if you're an asshole.

LEE: Okay. Okay. That's it. That's it. Fine. I'm through. Through. It's over. I'm going back to Chicago, first thing, as soon as they fix my car. I can relax. They fix it when they fix it, it doesn't matter any more. Where's that bottle of wine?

RON: You shot it.

LEE: Shit!

RON: That's what I say.

LEE: What an asshole! Excuse me. Is that an asshole? Is he an asshole?

RON: Yes.

LEE: Am I wrong? Help me. Is he?

RON: He is. Bona fide.

LEE: I am engaged to this person. I'm supposed to marry this person in two months? Why? Can you tell me why? I was sitting in that car trying to figure out if I really deserved to feel as bad as I was feeling and

I started to wonder why, someone like me, a woman who has been through med school, who has spent years - in my residency, in my practice, in the hospital - years combatting, successfully, the enormous, colossal egos of male doctors, why would I put myself in a relationship with a man who does nothing but put me down? Does it make sense to you? (*He tries to think of an answer.*) You know, (*Takes a deep breath.*), this year . . . this year . . . has been so strange, I can't tell you. I have lost my nerve, lost it. I've had these . . . fears, these unspecific, low-grade, chronic fears I don't know what they're rooted in. I used to be so tough, you can't imagine, on top of everything. I can't explain it.

RON: (*Getting up and moving to her other side.*) Excuse me . . .

LEE: When I drive? In the rain?

RON: . . . could I just sit on this side? So I can see you with this eye. This is my seeing eye. Without the dog.

LEE: I am terrified of slipping off the road, I take a turn and I see myself just sliding right off the road, like the arm of a turntable, after the record is over, off the road. Other times I'm afraid the tires are going to detach. I can't get on a plane, can't fly any more. Is it natural, do you suppose, just a natural part of aging, becoming more fearful?

RON: I wouldn't know. I'm still quite young.

LEE: At work, I've lost my confidence. Two weeks ago, in the middle of surgery, I walked out. Not just out of the operating room, out of the hospital. I was standing out on the sidewalk with a face mask on, gloves, gown. Out on the sidewalk. (*Pause.*) And do you think he's been the least bit sympathetic? Whenever I try to talk to him about my fears, he looks at me like I'm attacking him, like he's responsible and I'm attacking him. It makes him angry. That's the only emotion he offers me—anger. I think he can't bear thinking I might be more afraid than he is, it terrifies him. . .

RON: It is scary.

LEE: He hung up on me. Whenever I'm in trouble it's always my fault. But it's over. I'm through. He can find someone else to let him down. I'm through with it all. Both of them. Those two, they may as well be married. She's never been on a date, never been kissed.

RON: No?

LEE: Never had a boyfriend, she's been too busy being a housewife since she was nine when her mother threw a chair through the sliding glass door and left. They'll both be delighted I'm leaving. It's over. (*Sighs.*) What a relief. Hooray.

RON: Have some cake.

LEE: Okay. We'll celebrate.

RON: Hurrah.

LEE: Hurrah. You celebrate, too. Doesn't it feel great?

RON: Yes. No.

LEE: No?

RON: It feels awful. See my black eye? That's how it feels, everywhere.

LEE: Suzanne is your ex-wife?

RON: Such an unattractive sound—ex, especially for someone soft you've held naked against your body at night for a decade. Like ax.

LEE: How long have you been divorced?

RON: Five years.

LEE: That's a long time. That's how long ago my husband died.

RON: See, the problem was I never made it to court. For my divorce. I never went. I didn't want to go, I didn't have to go, my lawyer told me, but. . . it was a mistake. You have to go to events like that. You have to be there. You have to be at your. . . birth. To get the full effect. You have to go to funerals, watch the body being lowered into the ground, being covered with dirt, shovelful by shovelful. Then you know. . . you know where the body is. In the ground. There's no doubt. You have to go to your own divorce, sit in the courtroom, hold your coat in your lap, look at the judge, look at your lawyer, look at her lawyer. Make the appropriate expressions. Hear the flies. Then you have something. Then you have pieces, concrete pieces. I can't see it. I don't have her face getting divorced. I never saw our marriage officially pronounced dead. It's been a problem. Do you hear something?

LEE: It's the bats.

RON: Bats?

LEE: In the attic.

RON: I thought it was my face. Something's flapping in my face, but today I saw. I watched, from the roof of the house. (*Pause.*) See, if we had had some anti-freeze, if someone had been kind enough, thoughtful enough to give us anti-freeze, we might have made it. Suzanne. (*He starts to cry.*)

LEE: I'm sorry. If it makes you feel any better, she married a real prick.

RON: Thank you. I knew I could count on you. When you told me this morning my hand was cut, I knew you'd be there for me.

LEE: You really watched from the roof?

RON: Yes I did.

LEE: Did anyone know you were up there?

RON: The bartender. The dog.

LEE: That obnoxious terrier, he won't shut up.

RON: He was with me.

LEE: On the roof?

RON: It was the only way to keep him quiet.

LEE: Was there music for the wedding march?

RON: I don't know.

LEE: I don't care. I'm through.

RON: Can I go to sleep right now?

LEE: Where?

RON: I'm sorry, but I'm going to sleep very immediately.

LEE: You can sleep in my car.

RON: I can't sleep with you? Just kidding. Not really.

LEE: We can put back the seats.

RON: 'kay. (*He stands.*) Maybe I'll fix your car, in my sleep. I wish I could fix your car. I wish I could fix anything. I wish I could fix that gumball machine. I'm going to fix it right now. I am. I am. First, I'm going to approach it, and rub it with this towel. (*Does so.*) In small, tiny, concentric circles. It's hard being a guy who can't fix anything.

LEE: Why don't you try a screwdriver?

RON: No. If I could use a screwdriver, I'd still be married. Now I'm to press my cheek against it, just for a few seconds, rub my tongue around. Now I'm going to sing to it, sweetly, with my forehead. A favorite gumball tune (*Puts forehead on it.*) Who can fix the gumball... sprinkle it with glue. . . la da da da da and make the gum come out... the handyman can. . .the handyman can da da da da da da da and he's a terrific guy. (*Puts in penny. Turns handle. Nothing.*) See. This is what always happens. This is. . . now I'm going to. . . smash it with a hammer.

LEE: No.

RON: (*Heading toward garage.*) Excuse me, I'm going to get a hammer. I know where they keep them.

LEE: Don't.

RON: I tried. I was nice. Reasonable. I'm going to break it. I'm going to pulverize it.

LEE: Here, take this blanket. And pillow.

RON: Thank you. Now your legs are standing up. But you know what?

LEE: What?

RON: I saw her wedding. I have her face getting married, looking up at me on the roof. Her expression, a double exposure. I have it. (*Ron follows her into the garage, she opens car door, puts back seat, gets him settled in the back of the car. She comes back in and lies down. After a few moments, the car horn beeps briefly.*)

LEE: Ron? Ron, did you call me this afternoon? Did you call here?

SCENE 4

It is 4:00 a.m. The slightest bit of morning light should become visible during this scene. Frannie and Harlon enter with flashlight from stage right, carrying a sleeping bag and blanket; Harlon, dressed in his softball uniform, carries a small paper bag.

HARLON: (*Puts down a sleeping bag.*) This here's your mattress. And. . bed covers,

FRANNIE: Voilà.

HARLON: You mind if I stay a minute or two?

FRANNIE: What do you mean, I'm going to do your ear, aren't I?

HARLON: I just didn't know if you'd mind me being in your bedroom. And all.

FRANNIE: It smells like manure.

HARLON: Mm. For Bonnie's tomatoes. She likes everything organic.

FRANNIE: Bonnie in Mexico?

HARLON: It's her garage. Inherited it from her daddy. Yeah, I've never been in a girl's bedroom before.

FRANNIE: Did she break the law?

HARLON: Broke a few laws. Broke a few hearts. There's a warrant out for her arrest.

FRANNIE: What did she do? Tell me.

HARLON: Six counts of fraud, for starters. Bait and switch. Regulation stuff. With the state, with her meters. Some woman sued her. Yeah, I've been in cars, movies, never a girls' bedroom.

FRANNIE: Why did the woman sue her?

HARLON: Bonnie sold her a set of tires she didn't need. Are you going with anyone?

FRANNIE: She sold her a set of tires she didn't need?

HARLON: Yeah, some New York bitch. Givin' Denny a hard time. Course Denny's too nice a guy to say anything.

FRANNIE: Were you honest with us?

HARLON: Huh?

FRANNIE: With Lee and me.

HARLON: Yeah.

FRANNIE: You honestly couldn't fix our car?

HARLON: Uh. . .we don't see too many Volvos.

FRANNIE: Well, I'm glad. I didn't want to go to that wedding.

HARLON: Good. I knew that. Silvie had it fixed within an hour, I pulled a few wires. Just kidding. Do you have a boyfriend?

FRANNIE: No. Look.

HARLON: What?

FRANNIE: The moon.

HARLON: You don't have a boyfriend?

FRANNIE: Look at it, isn't it lovely? Do you know how to tell if the moon is waxing or waning?

HARLON: No.

FRANNIE: If the crescent is this way (*She describes the right half of the circumference of a circle.*) it's waxing, filling out this way. If the crescent is this way (*The left half of the circumference of a circle.*) it's waning. I can always tell what the moon is doing by how I feel. My favorite time to write is just before a full moon, I can stay up two nights in a row writing. Sometimes I can write on a waning moon, but my writing has a very different quality. Very spare.

HARLON: I never met anyone like you.

FRANNIE: Where's the ice? (*He hands her ice in soda cup in bag.*) Napkins? (*Wraps ice in napkin, gives it to him. He puts it up to his ear.*)

HARLON: You smell good.

FRANNIE: I smell like manure. And mint, there's mint around here, too. You excited?

HARLON: Huh?

FRANNIE: Nervous?

HARLON: . . . yeah.

FRANNIE: (*Looking at the sky.*) Look at all those stars. Did you know that every atom in your body comes from a star? You have atoms in you, stardust atoms, that have memories you aren't even aware of; memories of events that happened in outer space.

HARLON: You sure you can do this?

FRANNIE: Do what?

HARLON: Pierce my ear.

FRANNIE: Sure. Matches? (*He hands her matches. She lights a match to sterilize a needle.*) You know how when people almost die, they see light at the end of a tunnel? They're just remembering their own light, from when they were a star. (*She holds up the lit match and blows it out.*)

HARLON: Would you care for a Certs?

FRANNIE: (*Still sterilizing needle.*) No thanks. How's that ice doing?

HARLON: Cold. So. You don't have a boyfriend.

FRANNIE: (*Touching his ear lobe.*) Can you feel this?

HARLON: Do it again. Yeah. I can feel it.

FRANNIE: We'll wait.

HARLON: Can I kiss you?

FRANNIE: No. (*Looking at the sky.*) Last month I watched the Pleiades passing through a day old crescent moon. It was the most lovely romantic thing I've ever seen.

HARLON: You think that's romantic?

FRANNIE: Yes, I do.

HARLON: You think that's romantic?

FRANNIE: Yeah. What do you think is romantic?

HARLON: Kissing. (*There's a noise inside.*)

FRANNIE: Shh!

HARLON: What?

FRANNIE: I thought I heard her moving, inside.

HARLON: She's gonna be your step-mother?

FRANNIE: That's the plan.

HARLON: Do you like her?

FRANNIE: She's okay. She's too paranoid. And wimpy, with my dad. Look!

HARLON: What?

FRANNIE: A shooting star. Oh my God. Oh God, look it's still going, Jesus, it's still going, it's still going, it's still going, still . . . oh. Wasn't that great?

HARLON: Yeah.

FRANNIE: I love shooting stars.

HARLON: I like them too. I don't think I like them as much as you do. (*Pause.*)

FRANNIE: I love summer nights. Soft, warm, summer nights, just a little breeze. Crickets, cicadas. The smells—mint, manure, the linden tree, I even love the smells in the garage, the oil, the grease. It's heavenly. Celestial. (*Pause.*) You looked really good out there, in center field.

HARLON: Thanks.

FRANNIE: You made some really nice catches.

HARLON: Thanks.

FRANNIE: There was one I was sure you were going to miss, but you got it.

HARLON: Thanks.

FRANNIE: Can you feel this? (*Touches earlobe.*)

HARLON: Do it again. Do it again. Do it again. I don't think so. Do it one more time. No.

FRANNIE: Good. Ready?

HARLON: Uh. . .

FRANNIE: I've got the cork. (*Getting cork out of her pocket. She moves around in front of him, straddling his right leg, her right knee up* *over his groin. She holds the cork behind his right earlobe.*) Okay. Let's fly this baby.

HARLON: You can leave your knee there.

FRANNIE: Here we go. You relaxed?

HARLON: You can leave your knee there.

FRANNIE: All right. I may not get all the way through in one go. But don't worry.

HARLON: 'kay.

FRANNIE: Here we go. (*Pause as she prepares.*) You're kind of moving around.

HARLON: 'kay.

FRANNIE: I have to get the right angle. I don't want the front hole to be higher than the back hole.

HARLON: 'kay.

FRANNIE: (*Pausing.*) This is harder than I thought it was going to be.

HARLON: (*Beginning to approach orgasm.*) Yeah?

FRANNIE: I'm not sure I can do this.

HARLON: Really?

FRANNIE: I'm afraid I'll hurt you.

HARLON: You won't hurt me.

FRANNIE: You're breathing awful hard. Try not to move around so much. Are you okay?

HARLON: Yeah.

FRANNIE: Okay. Here goes. Here goes. (*She jabs it.*) Did you feel that?

HARLON: I. . .heard. . .it.

FRANNIE: It's not all the way through. You can't feel it? Can you feel it?

HARLON: Uh . . .

FRANNIE: Try to hold still.

HARLON: 'kay. (*Climaxing.*) Ohhh. . .

FRANNIE: Oh God. . . there.

HARLON: Ah.

FRANNIE: You've got a hole in your ear. (*He nods, smiling.*) Can you hand me that napkin? (*He hands her napkin that had ice in it. She puts napkin on his earlobe, gets him to hold it. She gets off.*)

FRANNIE: Did it hurt?

HARLON: No.

FRANNIE: It'll probably hurt a little when it thaws. You okay?

HARLON: Yeah.

FRANNIE: Sure? So. Now you've got a pierced ear. How's it feel?

HARLON: Good.

FRANNIE: You okay?

HARLON: Yup.

FRANNIE: You want the diamond stud or the little gold ball?

HARLON: The diamond.

FRANNIE: (*Pretends to take it from her ear.*) Good choice. (*Drops it.*) Oops, in the manure. Lee would have a heart attack over this whole procedure. Little spit. (*Pretends to put it in his ear.*) There. Listen to this little bit of carbon closely, you'll hear tales from the dusty nebulas of space.

HARLON: No.

FRANNIE: No?

HARLON: When I listen to this diamond that I'll hear all the time 'cause it's in my ear, I'll hear your voice, Frannie. That's all. Your voice. And that's all I'll wanna hear. (*Pause.*)

FRANNIE: Harlon?

HARLON: Yeah?

FRANNIE: You can kiss me if you want to.

HARLON: I do.

FRANNIE: I have to tell you though.

HARLON: What?

FRANNIE: I'm not very clear about it. The mechanics.

HARLON: Huh?

FRANNIE: Should I hold my breath?

HARLON: You never did it before?

FRANNIE: No.

HARLON: You never did it before? You?

FRANNIE: Harlon, just tell me. What should I do?

HARLON: What should you do? Simple. Just. . . (*He leans toward her slowly as lights fade.*)

SCENE 5

> It is 5:30. There's a soft early morning light. The car horn starts beeping, a steady tone that doesn't stop. Lee and Frannie both get up—Lee from the couch, Frannie from her sleeping bag outside (Harlon has gone). Lee goes into the garage and takes Ron's foot off the horn. Frannie looks in from the outside.)

FRANNIE: Lee? Lee?

LEE: Frannie. I want to talk to you.

FRANNIE: Okay.

LEE: (*Lee is in the doorway. Takes in Frannie's sleeping bag.*) You slept here? I won't waste words. I'm going back to Chicago as soon as my car is running. I'm not going on to Jay and Suzanne's. I'm sure you can find someone—Harlon, Mary—to give you a ride to St. Joseph. If not, your father can come and pick you up. That's all I have to say. So. Now I'm going to try to get some more sleep. (*Lee goes back into waiting room. Frannie pauses, follows her.*)

FRANNIE: Why?

LEE: Why? Because I didn't get very much sleep because I was worried about you.

FRANNIE: That's not what. . .

LEE: I was also worried about how angry your father was at me for not getting the car checked out before we left and for not arriving in time for the wedding which I know you're glad about and because you didn't call him last night which he asked you to do which message I couldn't relay to you because I didn't know where you were.

FRANNIE: I called you.

LEE: When?

FRANNIE: I don't know when it was. I did call.

LEE: Well, it doesn't matter. I'm not worried any more. I'm going back to Chicago. I'm breaking up with your father you'll be pleased to hear So. Now let's both get some sleep.

FRANNIE: I'm sorry. I didn't mean to worry you.

LEE: You probably didn't. You probably didn't give it a second thought. So. I don't know what you were doing, but I know you didn't get back until after 2:00. You must be tired. I've lost an earring. (*She starts looking for her earring, on the couch, the floor.*)

FRANNIE: I was. . . I was. . . (*Starts to tear up.*). . .

LEE: (*Looking under the couch.*) A magazine. Porn magazine. Empty oil can. A phone bill.

FRANNIE: It was . . .

LEE: (*Still looking.*) Damn, I don't want to lose that earring. (*Getting up, seeing Frannie.*) What? Frannie. Are you all right?

FRANNIE: No.

LEE: What's wrong? Frannie. What?

FRANNIE: (*Verging on crying.*) I'm upset because. . . I'm upset because . . .I felt really good, and now I feel bad like. . . I did something wrong. . .it's supposed to be nice . . . but now it feels bad. . .

LEE: Frannie. . .

FRANNIE: He's going to be so disappointed.

LEE: Who?

FRANNIE: My father. And it's my fault.

LEE: I don't know that he will be. And it's not your fault.

FRANNIE: He will be. He had high hopes.

LEE: Frannie, don't cry. It's not your fault. It's not because you disappeared last night.

FRANNIE: You were nice to him. You put up with him. I was starting to feel like I could. . . I could. . .

LEE: You could what?

FRANNIE: I could stop. . .worrying about him.

LEE: Oh, Frannie. Here, sit doom. Sit down. Frannie. Don't cry. I'm sorry. Here, use this. I didn't mean to be so I just . . .I was worried is all. I've never seen you be upset before. Frannie. So . . .tell me. Tell me. What was nice? You had a good time with Harlon?

FRANNIE: He kissed me.

LEE: He did?

FRANNIE: (*Still crying.*) Here I have this major event in my life I can't even feel good about.

LEE: You should, Frannie, you should, feel good. Forget what I said. Just forget it. So, he kissed you.

FRANNIE: I finally let someone.

LEE: And it was nice?

FRANNIE: It was pretty straight forward.

LEE: Well, that's great. That's wonderful.

FRANNIE: I was glad to finally get it out of the way.

LEE: Here, let's celebrate. What'll we have. (*Looking in Mary's bag.*) Bagel chips. Oranges. Would you like an orange? I'll peel an orange for us. Well, that's big news.

FRANNIE: Kind of ridiculous. I don't have one friend who's a virgin.

LEE: It's not ridiculous at all. Here, wrap this blanket around you. Cover your legs.

FRANNIE: You're the only one I'm telling.

LEE: I'm honored. I won't tell anyone.

FRANNIE: You won't tell my father?

LEE: No.

FRANNIE: Sure?

LEE: I won't tell him.

FRANNIE: Please don't.

LEE: I won't. You know, Frannie, sometime your father is going to have to face the fact that you're growing up. You're very nice to him, you're an exceptionally nice daughter, but your life shouldn't revolve around him.

FRANNIE: No?

LEE: No. He's lucky to have you, very lucky, but you have to figure out what your needs are and not just tend to his.

FRANNIE: I don't want to abandon him.

LEE: It's not a question of abandoning him. You should be dating, you should be doing more things with your friends. Have you ever been to a movie with anyone but your father? He'll get used to it. You should stop doing his laundry.

FRANNIE: It's a habit.

LEE: You shouldn't do it.

FRANNIE: You wanted to do it.

LEE: Only because of you. It didn't seem right that you were doing it.

FRANNIE: Really? (*Pause.*) I'm sorry I made you worried.

LEE: I was worried anyway.

FRANNIE: That's what I figured.

LEE: Frannie, I know it hasn't been easy, having me around. You're used to having your father all to yourself.

FRANNIE: I don't like having him all to myself. I don't think it's healthy.

LEE: Well, it seemed you. . . weren't all that thrilled about me being there. I don't think it's healthy either.

FRANNIE: I don't think he realizes.

LEE: No.

FRANNIE: He's pretty self-centered.

LEE: Yes, he is.

FRANNIE: You think he is?

LEE: I do.

FRANNIE: I think I'll go back to Chicago with you.

LEE: No, don't do that.

FRANNIE: I think I will. You don't want me to go with you?

LEE: It's not that I wouldn't like your company. I would.

FRANNIE: Thanks. (*Pause.*) You know what my saying was in my grammar school year book? You know, when they put a quote next to your picture?

LEE: What was it?

FRANNIE: Ly.

LEE: Lee?

FRANNIE: L y. I used to correct people's adverbs all the time. Someone would say "slow," "it moved slow," I'd say, "slow-*ly*." Didn't make me very popular. (*Takes piece of orange from Lee. Sees earring on floor. Picks it up.*) Here's your earring.

LEE: Oh, thanks, I do like these earrings. My husband gave them to me.

FRANNIE: Your husband. I always forget you were married.

LEE: Mm.

FRANNIE: What did he do?

LEE: You mean profession wise? Not much. He didn't like jobs. He hated money, was terrible with it.

FRANNIE: What was he like? Tell me.

LEE: He was . . . extraordinary. He had such a vigorous mind. I loved just staring at his head, watching him think; read. He was like a kid, you know, he would throw himself into things, get so excited, it was like there was always this *wind* around him. This gust, messing up his hair; he couldn't get a comb through his hair. Most women would think he was homely, but. . .He had this weather station up in the attic, kind of an observatory, with a skylight. For a couple of years he had homing pigeons up there, it was a mess. They'd roost on his telescope. You'd think you were watching an eclipse and it was just a wing, fanning down. He was obsessed with the weather, he would call up local TV stations and argue with the weathermen, tell them they were full of shit, make fun of their graphics, he was always right. His senses were so. . . acute; he could kiss me and tell that I was about to get my period, just from the taste on my lips. I liked that. I think his mind was too much for his body. He was actually quite frail. But that didn't stop him from anything, trekking, playing soccer with the eighth graders. He liked rock climbing, he used to take me rock climbing in the Grand Tetons, everywhere.

FRANNIE: Rock climbing? You? That's hard to imagine. No offense.

LEE: That's okay. Believe it or not, I used to be pretty brave. I didn't always drive under 45 all the time.

FRANNIE: What happened? Were you in an accident or something?

LEE: No. I honestly don't know what I'm afraid of. I'm just afraid. I don't like being this way. I'm hoping it's a phase that will pass. Orange? Do I seem fearful to you?

FRANNIE: Yeah.

LEE: I do?

FRANNIE: Mm.

LEE: Is it very noticeable?

FRANNIE: No.

LEE: It is.

FRANNIE: No.

LEE: It is. I'd like to read your poem, the one you were working on yesterday. The one with the carburetor.

FRANNIE: Okay. It's got a pygmy in it, too.

LEE: A pygmy?

FRANNIE: A pygmy in a rainforest. You were talking about it. How he understands his world and we don't.

LEE: He's in your poem? Does he understand the world of your poem?

FRANNIE: He is the poem.

LEE: (*Chuckles.*) Frannie. We could have been pals all this time.

FRANNIE: Yeah.

LEE: Well, we'll be pals now.

FRANNIE: I think you're really good for my dad.

LEE: You do?

FRANNIE: Yeah.

LEE: The problem is, I don't think he's good for me.

FRANNIE: You're really breaking up with him?

LEE: I think so.

FRANNIE: Why?

LEE: I don't like to let people down, and that's all I seem to do with him. I can't really tolerate it. I let my husband down.

FRANNIE: How?

LEE: I did.

FRANNIE: How?

LEE: It's hard to talk about. It had to do with his death, his illness, what I could have done. What I should have done. He was misdiagnosed. I can't talk about it. You can see, I can't.

FRANNIE: Here. (*Gives her towel and puts arm around her.*) I'm sure it wasn't your fault. Look, someone who's as nice to my dad as you shouldn't feel guilty about anything.

LEE: Maybe that's why I'm nice to him. (*Laughs.*) That's a thought. (*Pause.*) Now, that is really...(*Struck. Pause.*)

FRANNIE: Why don't we try to fix the car ourselves? Lee? Let's try to fix the car.

LEE: We can't do that.

FRANNIE: Why not? There's a bunch of manuals in there. There's a Volvo manual.

LEE: There is?

FRANNIE: They can't be any worse than your med school textbooks. Or organic chemistry.

LEE: Don't you think it's dangerous, working under the hood?

FRANNIE: No.

LEE: The battery might explode; I've heard of batteries exploding.

FRANNIE: Nah.

LEE: Nah? Okay. Okay.

FRANNIE: I'll get it. (*Exits into garage, wrapped in blanket.*)

LEE: Get it. (*Pause; revelation.*) I get it. I get it. (*Pause. Frannie comes back with a manual and a pair of pliers. She hands Lee the pliers.*)

FRANNIE: Here. (*Frannie sits down and they look at the Manual. Reading the cover.*) "Volvo, 240 Series, 1974 thru 1990, all gasoline engine models." What year is your car?

LEE: '89.

FRANNIE: Good. (*Opens to table of contents.*) "General dimensions; weights and capacities." "Tools and working facilities." "Recommended lubricants and fluids."

LEE: That's the X-rated chapter. Turn to the "Fault diagnosis." (*Frannie turns to that page. They both read together.*)

SCENE 6

It is 8:20. Ron is lying on the couch, seemingly asleep. There's evidence of an eaten breakfast—waxed paper, rolls, orange juice carton, Dunkin Donuts box, whatever. Mary enters with four or five mugs she has washed in the ladies room. Chuckling to herself, she puts them down on a tray near the Mr. Coffee machine, takes one and fills it up with coffee.

MARY: (*Chuckling.*) Silvie, Silvie. Tsk, tsk. You take cream in your coffee, hon? (*No response.*) You want that black, white or battleship grey?

RON: Black. Please.

MARY: Well, this is black all right. Mr. Coffee here could use an oil filter, here you go. Diesel espresso, house specialty.

RON: Thank you.

MARY: Make the little hairs on your chest stand up and do the hokey pokey, don't get up, don't get up! Relax, lie back: it's Sunday, breakfast in bed day. Jackson, my third and last I don't say final husband, always brought me breakfast in bed on Sundays, our place of worship, wore a dish towel for a loin cloth, care for a donut? 'Fraid they're all whole wheat, AMA approved. Couple aspirin.

RON: (*Taking aspirin.*) Thank you. You're very kind.

MARY: (*Looking into cardboard box.*) What do you know? Drank up all his orange juice, good boy Captain RV. I'm just catching up on bills here, 'bout three months overdue, finance charges up the yin yan, tell you what it's a strange kind of math, a finance charge, voodoo economics.

RON: This is a very nice garage.

MARY: Thank you. We like it.

RON: (*Sipping his coffee.*) It's very homey.

MARY: Had a lot of history traipse through. Added another chapter this morning, yup, gonna be one of Bonnie and my all time favorites. All girl fixing team. Ooo Silvie. Should I call him? Don't want to rain on Audrey's second honeymoon.

RON: I like this comforter.

MARY: Won it in a raffle.

RON: Really? It's very comforting.

MARY: So, what's your name, hon?

RON: Ron.

MARY: Where you from?

RON: Chicago.

MARY: Not Ron Patrick Maguire from Chicago?

RON: Yes.

MARY: Mm. (*Chuckles*.) Mine's Mary. (*Tosses him wallet.*) Here. Don't wanna get caught in a storm without your raincoat. Good Christ, Ma Bell is turnin off the phone 5 p.m. tomorrow. Three hundred and forty dollar phone bill - Bonnie's charging calls from Mexico. Would I love to call her up right now.

RON: Do you think I could stay here another night?

MARY: You want to stay another night?

RON: Yes.

MARY: You want to sleep here on the couch another night?

RON: I do.

MARY: Your car working okay?

RON: Yeah.

MARY: You need a place to stay?

RON: No.

MARY: You can stay.

RON: Thanks very much.

MARY: Well lookee here, according to this, we lost our electricity a week ago last Tuesday. That explains a lot. Been running on less than full capacity a while now, that's for damn sure. So. What's got you down?

RON: My girlfriend moved out last week.

MARY: Your girlfriend moved out. Tsk. That's tough. That's tough.

RON: It is.

MARY: Course, Jackson would tell you women are like buses. You miss one, another one'll be along in five minutes.

RON: That's the problem. I seem to spend my life at the bus stop, waiting for the next one. Before the one I've got has even pulled away.

MARY: Why don't you try being alone for a while?

RON: Alone? I don't think I'm capable of it.

MARY: All the more reason to do it. Hang it up for a while, give it a rest. I think it'd do you a world of good.

RON: You do?

MARY: Yeah. (*Denny enters.*) Well, lo and behold. It's Mother Nature's son. What're you doing here of a Sunday morning?

DENNY: I came to look at that Volvo.

MARY: That Volvo's long gone. In Illinois by now, Chicago bound.

DENNY: She left?

MARY: Yup.

DENNY: (*Disappointed.*) She left? Dang.

MARY: Fixed the car themselves, just the two of 'em. All girl fixing team, I gave 'em each one of Steve's old shirts says "Steve" above the pocket. And you better not tell Silvie cause I want to see his face when he hears the news.

DENNY: What was it?

MARY: Auxiliary fuse to one of the fuel pumps. Frannie was looking for the fuses in the glove compartment, found a box with masking tape said, "auxiliary fuses to fuel pump," different size from the others. Lee tracked a wire to back behind the seat under the rug, stuck in the fuse, started right up.

DENNY: Huh. Didn't leave the factory like that.

MARY: Well, they left in the highest of moods, gabbing away. Guess heading east suited them better. Denny, you coming down with something? I told you after the game you might should spend a few days in bed. Look like you been sortin' cats and dogs all night. Be right back. Nature calls. (*Mary takes key to ladies room and exits.*)

DENNY: Doggone.

RON: (*Eatting a donut.*) What's the matter?

DENNY: I wanted to see her.

RON: I wanted to see her too. Have a donut. (*He gets one, trying to keep his balance.*)

RON: You're Denny?

DENNY: Yeah.

RON: You don't have a brain tumor.

DENNY: Who are you?

RON: Did it come on suddenly, about three days ago?

DENNY: Yeah.

RON: You feel nauseous, like you're walking on a rolling ship?

DENNY: Yeah.

RON: Did you lose your hearing?

DENNY: No.

RON: Do you have a headache?

DENNY: No.

RON: You don't have a brain tumor. You have benign positional vertigo. I had it a couple of years ago.

DENNY: You did?

RON: Scared the shit out of me. I thought I had a brain tumor, too. There's a test I can do. (*Ron gets up with the comforter wrapped around him.*) Sit down. Shake your head back and forth. (*Denny does so. Ron studies his eyes.*) Yup, your eyes are moving, adjusting. It's fluid, something in your inner ear. Form of vertigo. It's a simple thing, you'll be over it in a week. (*Ron goes back to couch, lies down, eats donut, coffee.*)

DENNY: A week? Really? Really? You sure?

RON: Positive. You may as well get it looked at, but I'll guarantee it's not a tumor.

DENNY: If I had a tumor I'd have a headache?

RON: Yeah.

DENNY: I'd lose my hearing?

RON: You might.

DENNY: Huh. Thanks. Whew. Thank you very much. What's it called now?

RON: Benign positional vertigo.

DENNY: Could you write that down?

RON: Sure. (*He gets up, still wrapped in comforter and writes it down.*)

DENNY: When you had it, would you just suddenly fall down, collapse?

RON: Yup.

DENNY: What causes it?

RON: They don't know.

DENNY: Huh. Well, thanks again. Thanks very much. You can't imagine . . .

RON: I can.

DENNY: Do you have a problem with your car?

RON: No.

DENNY: Too bad. (*Pause.*) You spent the night here?

RON: Yeah.

DENNY: (*Nods.*) Well, I guess I'm going. Thanks again.

RON: Take care. Wait. . could I just ask you. . . have you ever spent time alone?

DENNY: Alone? Yeah.

RON: Not being in a relationship?

DENNY: Sure. I'm alone right now.

RON: How is it?

DENNY: It's okay. Course I got Red, my dog.

RON: Maybe I'll get a dog. I think I'll get a dog and be alone for a while.

DENNY: Good luck. (*Denny heads toward exit.*)

DENNY: There's nothing I can do for you?

RON: No. Thanks. Wait a sec. I wonder could you . . could you show me how to fix that gumball machine?

DENNY: Gumball machine?

RON: It doesn't work. I'd love for you to show me how to fix it.

DENNY: Okay. Sure.

RON: Should I get some tools?

DENNY: No, let's just have a look here.

RON: No gum comes out.

DENNY: No? Do me a favor, be ready to catch me, okay?

RON: Okay. (*Denny puts in penny, slides lever over and back.*) I would love to do the actual fixing, if you could coach me through it.

DENNY: Sure thing.

RON: Should I get a screwdriver? Pliers?

DENNY: Nope. You might could do it with your finger but . . . just grab that pencil there. Okay now, open the flap, stick the pencil up, jiggle it around.

RON: Jiggle it?

DENNY: That ought to do it. (*Ron takes out pencil. A gumball rolls out.*)

RON: That's it? That's all? What did I do? What happened?

DENNY: I'd say two balls got jammed up inside there, and you freed them up.

RON: How did you know that?

DENNY: Well, there's nothing wrong with the mechanism. The lever wasn't stuck. When you're analyzing a problem, always go for the simple things first. Eliminate the simple before you go on to the complex.

RON: Huh. Eliminate the simple. I'll remember that. Thank you so much.

DENNY: You fixed it.

RON: I fixed it. Would you care for a gumball?

DENNY: Sure. (*Taking it.*) Thanks. Can I buy you one?

RON: Great. (*Denny puts in penny. Gives gumball to Ron.*)

RON: Thanks. (*They both chew their gum.*)

DENNY: Old.

RON: What did you say?

DENNY: Old. This gum is very old. But I like it. I like it. (*Pause.*) Okay, well I'm heading out. It was my pleasure.

RON: Same here.

DENNY: Live in the moment. Life is short.

RON: Okay. I'll do that. Thank you. Bye. (*Denny hugs Ron. Exits. Ron goes to couch, sits. Mary enters. Goes back to paying bills.*)

MARY: What a morning. Haven't had so much fun since the hogs ate my brother. (*Mary pays bills.*)

RON: Do you think there are any dog stores open today?

MARY: Dog stores?

RON: You know. Where you buy a dog.

MARY: You mean like a pound?

RON: A pound. That's it, a pound. Do you think there are any open today?

MARY: Might be. We'll take a spin later on.

RON: I'd like that. I'd like to take a spin. Oh, Mary.

MARY: Yeah?

RON: In case you want some gum, I fixed the gumball machine.

MARY: Handyman, huh? (*Mary resumes paying bills. Ron wraps comforter around him, still chewing gum, smiling.*)

END OF PLAY

DEADLY VIRTUES

by Brian Jucha

Playwright's Biography

Brian Jucha is an actor and director. As a director, his recent works include BROWN DOG IS DEAD with the Talking Band at the Theatre for the New City, MEN IN GRAY/WOMEN IN BLACK at Downtown Art Co., R.W. Fassbinder's THE BITTER TEARS OF PETRA VON KANT, WOMEN IN BLACK and IN TIME'S COURSE (MEN IN WHITE) at HOME, and THE RIVER RUNS DEEP, SAVETTKA SINGS THE BLUES and DARK SHADOWS at Dance Theater Workshop. As an actor, he recently appeared in Anne Bogart's IN THE JUNGLE OF CITIES at The Public Theater and Robert Woodruff's BAAL at Trinity Rep. He has worked with Anne Bogart since 1979, creating original roles in 13 productions. Mr. Jucha is co-artistic director of VIA Theater and the director of VIA's resident acting company. He has a BFA from New York University's Experimental Theater Wing and currently teaches at the Playwrights Horizons' Theatre School.

A Note from the Playwright

Deadly Virtues was developed during a 7-week residency at Actors Theatre of Louisville as an original collaboration between myself and a company of five extremely talented performing theater artists. We began working on the piece using the seven deadly sins and the seven moral virtues as the basis for material. The actors chose characters, both fictional and real, who they would use as the sources for their individual journeys through *Deadly Virtues* and were instrumental in finding the material and texts that would later become part of their character illuminations. Much of the text for the piece was quoted, referenced, or de-constructed from "found" sources: literature, plays, film scripts, newspaper articles, etc. This re-cycling of words and images was part of the intended overall impact of the work—a means to wake up the audiences' collective memories and hopefully allow them to see the familiar in a new context. This way of working is becoming an increasingly popular form of creating original theatrical performance works, but also poses a unique problem when trying to publish a script version of a work that is as much about the movement and action as it is about the text. The words are simply another element in the overall "composition" of the piece. Therefore, we have chosen to present the structure and two original excerpts from *Deadly Virtues* rather than the entire script.

Characters

MR. Y Porphyria's Lover, the young man from Poe's "The Tell Tale Heart," The Boston Strangler
MADAME L Persephone, Joan of Arc, Melinda Loveless, Frances Farmer
MR. Z Dante, Rick from Casablanca, Fatty Arbuckle/Silent Film Icon
MADAME X Eva Perron, Josephine Baker, Cleopatra, Carolyn Warmus, St. Mary of Egypt
MR. X (Originated by Steven Skybell), Marie Antoinette, Romeo, Massenet, Dr. Kevorkian

MADAME X	Regina Bird Smith
MADAME L	Tamar Kotoske
MR. Y	Barney O'Hanlon
MR. X	Steven Skybell
MR. Z	Andy Weems
Scenic Design	Paul Owen
Costume Design	Laura Patterson
Lighting Design	Marcus Dilliard
Sound Design	Darron L. West
Props Master	Mark J. Bissonnette
Stage Manager	Lori M. Doyle
Assistant Stage Manager	Emily Fox
Dramaturgical Assistant	Sandee K. McGlaun

Setting

The Seven Deadly Sins threaten damnation, the Seven Moral Virtues promise transcendence. Brought together as the Deadly Virtues, this high-energy performance work combines theater, dance and music to define the battleground of human conscience. Five 'souls' are waiting in Purgatory for their ascent into Paradise. As Penance, they are forced to re-live their past lives and crimes.

Deadly Virtues Structure

1. a. Assembly
   b. Prologue (Mr. X's Liturgy)
   c. Preparation
   d. Presentation
2. A Regrettable Intervention
3. Character Illumination/Solo Turn #1   Mr. Y
4. These Lies They Tell
5. Character Illumination/Solo Turn #2   Madame L
6. Stifled Unrest   7 Deadly Sins/Virtues
7. Character Illumination/Solo Turn #3   Mr. Z
8. Character Illumination/Solo Turn #4   Madame X
9. Interruptus
10. Character Illumination/Solo Turn #5 Mr. X
11. Epilogue

DEADLY VIRTUES

Excerpt One

PART 4   THESE LIES THEY TELL

*The souls play a game of "mass-murderers' poker/charades"
while awaiting the next illumination. Each soul in turn "acts
out" the crime of the mass-murderer they are trying to get the
others to guess. The conversation and physical score are performed as separate entities.*

L: Well, I can't help it if I care for him, can I?

Y: No, I suppose not.

L: Then what are you going on about?

Y: Nothing. Only I was fool enough to think that you cared for me.

L: Oh, I do. As a friend. Not in any other way.

Y: But you do care for him in—the other way. But you're, you're rather
cold. That sort of thing doesn't mean anything to you.

L: That's what you think. It's no use going on about it. You said yourself I
couldn't help it if I'm in love with him.

Y: I once read that the basis of all love is death.

X: That is correct. But man has given a false importance to death.

L: I'm sorry. I didn't want it to end this way. Harry's waiting for me.

Y: What do you intend to do?

L: We're going to Paris.

MDE. X: Did you see that blue hat she was wearing? What was she thinking?

Z: Any animal, plant or man who dies adds to nature's compost heap and
becomes the manure without which nothing could grow, nothing
could be created.

MDE. X: It made her look like a chipmunk.

MDE. L: I think she looked good,

Z: Death is simply part of the process.

MDE. L: And she looked happy.

MDE. X: Why didn't she at least take it off when she removed her match-
ing coat?

Z: Every death - even the cruelest - drowns in the total indifference of na-

L: ture.

L: Maybe there was no time to get her hair into shape since it seemed to be just pulled back into a tail.

Z: There's a few more things to look at. We're not leaving any stone unturned.

MDE. X: I'm for the ban and she's against it.

Z: Nature herself would watch unmoved if we destroyed the entire human race.

MDE. X: They can stay out. The way I feel about it is, I don't like them.

Y: What about her father?

MDE. L: I don't know who he is. I was just out drinking one night and—well, it just happened. *(She strikes an ax to one of the other players heads.)* 1, 2, 3, 4, 5, 6, 7, 8, 9, 19, 20. So crucify me.

X: Lizzie Borden.

MDE. L: Yes.

Y: I'll put it to you like this. In combat areas, you've got people living in extremely close quarters. You've got community showers.

X: How would you feel about being in a shower with one of them?

MDE. X: Obviously these were emotionally disturbed young women irreparably scarred by abusive childhood's.

L: As long as they do the job, I couldn't care less. I don't think it will make a whole lot of difference.

X: A victim of abuse is more likely to abuse others.

MDE. X: She just lost her conscience. The angel on her shoulder was absent.

L: We're not going to be walking around wearing pink BDV's.

Y: If they come in, I'm going out. *(Mr. Y 'acts' out the crimes of George Hennard.)*

Z: People are going to go after them physically.

MDE. L: Is it child abuse for my parents to force me to go to church?

X: Who's going to be thinking of anything like that when you're in a foxhole and someone's shooting bullets at you? It's not going to happen.

Z: You have to take what they do with a grain of salt. George Hennard.

Y: I would agree that both girls had borderline personality disorder.

Z: Clearly coming up with sympathetic opinions is what they were paid to do. *(Mr. Z picks a revolver up off the table and shoots the other players.)*

L: I think people often use race and a lot of other things as a cop-out.

Y: . . . An inability to take the middle ground on any issue and a lack of self-esteem.

L: I don't see a problem at all.

Y: We're all crammed together in the showers, and I don't want to worry that some guy is staring at me.

X: Fundamentalism is a breeding ground for borderlines. You have to believe in a certain way in order to be considered good.

Z: The problem is that arrogant son of a bitch, he's so insensitive, but I've got it figured out.

X: If you act differently you are evil.

Z: Either his wife's a lesbian, or he's a homosexual.

MDE. X: I get the impression that she's one of those kids who got her ideas from watching too may horror movies and listening to heavy metal. Perry Smith. If I can't trust you in the shower, I sure can't trust you in the foxhole.

Y: I'm just worried that they're going to decorate the dormitories with magazine photographs of scantily clad men.

X: It's enticing to some teen-agers because it places no limits sexually or physically on pleasing yourself.

Z: Now how am I going to feel if I walk into a dormitory and see pictures on the wall from *Playgirl* magazine?

MDE. L: If you want to hurt someone, go for it.

Y: That appears to be the kind of behavior exhibited here.

MDE. X: *(Mde. X takes a dagger off the table and stalks the other players.)* Sometimes when viewing a traumatic event, it becomes like an out-of-body experience.

Y: I couldn't sleep at night. I'd be worried that one of them is going to sneak over and make a pass at me.

MDE. X: You are there, but you are not there. You disassociate so that you don't have to deal with it.

X: People should be disqualified from serving based on something they do, not based on who they are.

Z: They each crossed a personal line that night where there was no turning back.

Y: For one it might have been the kidnapping.

X: For another the beating.

MDE. X: *(Putting down the dagger and picking up the ax and using it as a phone.)* 'There's been a murder. Someone's been murdered.' *(Putting down the ax and returning to stalking with the dagger.)*

MDE. L: I like to release stress by cutting my wrists with a knife and bleeding slowly.

X: I have no problem with them serving, but I don't think they should run around screaming, 'I'm queer, I'm queer, I'm queer'.

MDE. X: This is all people are talking about, and everybody—

X: But there was a point where each of them should have said, 'Oops, I messed up.

MDE. X: I mean everybody is against it.

X: I made a mistake in getting involved. This is enough.

Y: But they didn't.

MDE. X: *(Killing one of the other players.)* When children kill, they tend to overkill. The violence they inflict is extreme, much more than is necessary to accomplish the murder. *(Using the ax as a telephone again.)* 'There's been a murder. Someone's been murdered.'

Y: Squeaky Fromm?

MDE. L: Squeaky Fromm?

X: David Berkovitz?

Z: Son of Sam?

MDE. X: The Zodiac.

ALARM BELL RINGS

Excerpt 2

PART 9   INTERRUPTUS

> *The following scenes are performed simultaneously. Mde. L and Mr. Y carry on a phone conversation from opposite sides of the stage. The telephone receivers are miked and heard through the sound system. The 'Opera Quiz' is played out center stage. ('Overlap' indicates that the texts are played simultaneously— 'In the Clear' indicates that the text is played by itself.)*

MUSIC: Soft Classical music is heard. Adagio for Strings.
TAPE: Phone rings.

PHONE CONVERSATION #1   IN THE CLEAR . . .

Y: It's me. I just thought I'd wake you up.

L: Hello.

Y: Hi, how are you?

L: Good. How are you doing?

Y: I figured you were there, like, screening your calls.

L: And I am.

Y: Is there somebody you don't want to talk to?

L: Not particularly.

Y: Are you lying in bed?

L: Yes, I am.

Y: I should have brought some, like, uh, hot muffins over or something like that . . . (*laughter*). . . .coffee. Are you smoking?

L: No, I'm not.

Y: It's not good to smoke in bed, you know?

L: I know.

Y: How you feeling?

L: I'm feeling very good. How are you feeling?

Y: Good. Good.

L: I had a good time last night. It was like a dream.

Y: I know.

L: I don't think it happened.

Y: (*Laughs.*)

L: I just imagined it.

Y: Yeah. It was great. I sort of feel the same way. It's sort of like, slow motion or something.

L: Yeah. So you're not real.

Y: I'm not. This is just a continuation of the dream here. You're sleeping. You're like in and out of sleep. Just lie back in bed, hang up the phone and I'm gone. It's funny, you're like, so close and yet this connection sounds like you're in . . .

L: I know it does.

Y: Bangkok. (*Laughs.*)

L: It doesn't seem like you're only two blocks away.

Y: No. No, I'm in dreamland. Well. (*Pause. Laughter.*)

L: Okay. Well. Take it easy.

Y: Thanks. All right. Mmmm. (*Clears throat.*)

L: Okay. We'll talk again.

Y: Yeah. Definitely. I'm, um, so . . . all right. I'm sorry, I'm like really bad at like, um, at um, I'm bad at, um, leave taking sometimes.

OPERA QUIZ #1   OVERLAP BEGINS . . .

L: Leave taking?

Y: Leave taking, like, getting off the phone or saying good bye or something.

L: Well, don't say good-bye.

Y: Huh?

L: I said, don't say good-bye.

Y: All right.

L: Say I'll see you later.

Y: Talk to you later.
L: Yeah.
Y: How's that?
L: It's better.
Y: Bye.

ALARM BELL RINGS

OPERA QUIZ #1

> *The "opera quiz" sections are underscored by tape loops and sounds scores from famous operas, some that are mentioned in the text. The soft classical music is restored for the phone conversations.*

X: So Madame X and Gentlemen, our first question is about leading ladies and the dreadful fate they usually have in serious opera. Uh, they usually die, among other terrible things that happen, and Hazel W. Babcock of Falls Church, VA, would like you to be quite specific about some of these leading ladies deaths. Tell us, first, the cause of their death, and second, if you can remember, their last words before they depart this veil of tears. First, Rigoletto, the heroine, how she, what is the cause of her death, Madame X?

MDE. X: Well, the cause of her death, of course, is love, primarily, but she substitutes herself for her adored object, the evil Duke of Mantua, uh, not, in the sense that she knows that he's to be murdered . . .

X: Yes.

TAPE: Phone rings. Messrs.'s X, Y, Z, and Mde. X run to get phone.

PHONE CONVERSATION #2   IN THE CLEAR

L: Hello? Mr. Y.

MDE. X: Mr. Y.

L: Hi! I was very bad at lunch. And I nearly started blubbering. I just feel really sad and empty . . .

Y: You don't need to. 'Cause there are people out there, and I've said this before, who will replace emptiness with all sorts of things. Kiss me, darling. *(Sound of a kiss being blown over phone.)*

L: *(Sound of laughter as she returns kiss.)*

SIMULTANEOUS TEXT ROUND 1

OPERA QUIZ #1 CONTINUES . . .

X: Madame X.

MDE. X: —uh, and that the Balkan murderers are going to murder the first person who shows up at the inn, so she's stabbed and put in a bag, in order to be dropped in the river by the Dark of Night, but she does manage to stay alive long enough to utter a little moan when her Father shows up to pay off the murderer. I don't remember what the moan consists of, but they do have a—a rather hearty duet before she—actually there's—it's an ensemble before she dies.

X: It becomes a little ethereal toward the end, doesn't it?

MDE. X: Yes.

X: Anybody remember what her very last words in that duet are? Mr. Z?

Z: I'm pretty sure it's 'Addio'.

X: Well, there are other sopranos who end with 'Addio', but this one doesn't.

Y: She breaks off in the middle of a phrase, the duet is 'Lassu In Ciel', and she says, "I'll be waiting for you up there with mother".

X: Yes.

Y: And—uh—in the middle of that phrase, she expires.

X: Yes, yes she does. She says, "I will pray for you—Preghero," and the last syllable is lost as she chokes.

PHONE CONVERSATION #2 CONTINUES . . .

Y: I can't tell what a smile that has put on my face. Do you know, darling,I couldn't sort of face the thought of not speaking to you every moment. It fills me with real horror, you know.

L: It's purely mutual. You don't mind it, darling, when I want to talk to you so much?

Y: No, I LOVE it. It's so nice being able to help you.

L: You do. You'll never know how much.

Y: I just feel so close to you. I'm wrapping you up, protecting.

L: Yes, please, yes, please.

Y: Oh, Squidgy.

L: Mmm.

Y: Kiss me please. *(Sounds of kisses.)*

L: *(Giggles.)*

Y: I tell you darling, she is desperate to tag on to your coattails.

L: Well, she can't. If you want to be like me, you have got to suffer.

Y: Oh Squidgy!

L: Yeah. You have to. And then you get what you . . .

Y: You get what you want.

L: No. Get what you deserve, perhaps.

Y: Talk to you later?

L: Bye.

OPERA QUIZ #2   IN THE CLEAR

X: Uh, how about Carmen? What is the cause of her demise and her final words? Madame X?

MDE. X: Another victim of love I'm afraid. A stabbee. Knives are very popular in opera—today anyway. Um, I think her last words, after she's stabbed, or before she's stabbed by her ex-lover Don Jose are "You go ahead and kill me."

X: She does say that, but she has some words even after that. Mr. Z wants to help us out . . .

Z: I know this one well, she takes the ring that Jose has given her and says 'Here's this ring you gave me—Tiens", so she has a last word and she throws it in his face—

X: Yes.

TAPE: PHONE RINGS. Merrs.'s X, Y, Z, and Mde. X run to get phone.

PHONE CONVERSATION #3   IN THE CLEAR

L: Mr Y.

X: Mr. Y.

L: I can't bear a Sunday without you.

Y: What about me? The trouble is, I need you several times a week.

L: Mmm. So do I. I need you all the week. All the time.

SIMULTANEOUS ROUND #2

OPERA QUIZ #2   CONTINUES . . .

Z: —and then some Carmen's are silent and some carry on with—after they've been stabbed for minutes rushing around the stage moaning and groaning—and then some die instantly, its up for grabs I guess.

X: How 'bout Desdemona, as we call her in Italian opera? Madame X?

MDE. X: Love. But not stabbed. Smothered. By a pillow. Actually, I think she's strangled—uh—it depends on the production, in any event, the air is taken out of her, I suspect she'd be more likely to be strangled because Otello is suppose to be a large burly man and prone to violence—brought to violence by the evil Yago.

X: You are certainly right, she is deprived of breath, but I think she is actually smothered . . .

MDE. X: She, oh God, she asks, prays for help. 'Help me. Muoio innocente. Muoio innocente.' It's one of the wonderful, tragic, 'I'm dying innocent, I've done nothing wrong'.

X: And it's after being smothered, isn't it?

MDE. X: Oh, yes of course.

X: She comes to and sort of says she's innocent and forgives her husband.

BELL—PREVIEW OF MR. X'S ILLUMINATION

Z: Prisoner Number 280.

X: Yes.

Z: Have you any last words?

X: Yes. I'm dying innocent, I've done nothing wrong.

MDE. X: When you wish to go, let your hand fall, this will release the pin and activate the air flow. Breathe through your mouth and nose.

L: Remember your seat cushion may be used as a flotation device.

X: I am alive. I may tell you that I love you and have only time to do this. I embrace you with all my heart.

Restore to opera quiz/phone conversation. . .

SIMULTANEOUS ROUND #3

PHONE CONVERSATION #3   CONTINUES . . .

Y: Oh, God. I'll just live inside your trousers or something. It would be much easier.

L: What are you going to turn into, a pair of knickers? Oh, you're going to come back as a pair of knickers. Why don't you?

Y: I daren't.

L: I do love you, and I'm so proud of you.

Y: Oh, I'm so proud of you.

L: Don't be silly, I've never achieved anything.

Y: Yes, you have.

L: No, I haven't.

Y: Your great achievement is to love me.

L: Oh, darling. Easier than falling off a chair.

Y: You suffer all these indignities and tortures and calumnies.

L: Oh, darling, don't be silly. I'd suffer anything for you. That's love. It's the strength of love.

Y: Don't want to say good-bye.

L: Neither do I, but you must. Bye.

Y: Bye, darling.

L: Love you.

OPERA QUIZ   IN THE CLEAR

X: How 'bout Mimi in La Boheme. What does she die of? Mr. Y?

Y: Well, she dies of, um, of starvation and deprivation and the cold. Uh, and Rudolfo has brought her a muff and uh . . .

Z: The muff has been brought to her . . .

Y: Oh, pardon me, it's been brought by Musetta whose says that Rudolfo has given it to her, and the last words are something about how cold it is, er, how lovely and fluffy it is and then how warm it is and she apparently drops off to sleep and in fact she dies, usually we see her hand fall—and the muff fall off her hand.

PHONE RINGS. Mr Y. picks it up.

PHONE CONVERSATION #4

Y: Look, I told you, I had a life before I, before I came here, before I met you.

L: It's another woman.

Y: Now listen to me. WAIT!

L: *(Laughs.)* Oh, that's silly of me. There, there must be dozens of women ready to throw themselves at you. Just like I did.

Y: Oh, do you think I want *(Breath.)*—just to say good-bye to you *(snaps fingers.)* like that? *(Pause.)*

L: But you must. And it's hard isn't it? Well, let me make it easy for you.

Y: Wait.

L: Because if that's all it was to you—that's all it is to me. Good-bye.

Y: Wait!!!!

OPERA QUIZ RESUMED   IN THE CLEAR

X: Yes, yes, and speaking of dropping off to sleep, Yes, Madame X . . .

MDE. X: Well, I believe she died of love, not of just starvation and cold, I mean the cold and, and bad diet no doubt sped her along, but I believe it was love.

Z: Consumption was a favorite death of the 19th century heroines.

Y: Yes, I've always assumed it was love, but I'm not sure that I could find anything in the libretto that specifically says that.

X: Does anyone remember the very last word?

Z: Is it 'her hand'? 'Le Manni'?

X: No, it's 'E dormire', well, it's 'La Manni, Al Caldo', and the last is 'E dormire'. So she knows she's dropping off to sleep, but not for the final sleep.

ALARM BELL RINGS

SHOOTING SIMONE

by Lynne Kaufman

Playwright's Biography

Lynne Kaufman's *Shooting Simone*, which premiered in 1993 in the Humana Festival at Actors Theatre of Louisville, is her sixth full-length play. She made her playwriting debut in 1985 with THE COUCH at San Francisco's Magic Theatre. THE COUCH received numerous awards including the Glickman, Drama-Logue≥, San Francisco Chronicle and the Bay Area Critic's Circle Awards for "Best New Play." SPEAKING IN TONGUES won a Kennedy Center/American Express/Fund for New American Plays Award and was produced by the Magic Theatre in 1989. OUR LADY OF THE DESERT was produced by Theatreworks of Palo Alto, California and received their "Best New Play Award" for 1990. ROSHI and DOTTIE AND THE BOYS were premiered at the Magic Theatre. Her plays have also received stage readings and/or productions at the Oregon Shakespeare Festival, the Sarasota Festival of New Plays, Northcoast Repertory in Solana Beach, California and the Fountain Theatre in Los Angeles. She has also written short stories for many national magazines. She received an M.A. in Dramatic Literature from Columbia University and is currently Director of International Studies at U.C. Berkeley Extension. She is married, has two grown children and lives in San Francisco.

A Note From The Playwright

"I was nineteen when I read 'The Second Sex'. It changed my life," says my character Kate Berman as she explains to her lover why she has come to Paris to shoot a documentary about the great feminist. My own fascination with Simone de Beauvoir began when I was riding the subway to Hunter College in the Bronx. I dreamed of living in Paris, making art not babies, hanging out with Existentialists, having an 'essential' but not an 'exclusive' love. For me, Sartre and Beauvoir were the essence of glamour, 'the Bogie and the Bacall of the Intelligentsia.' They were part of my psyche, of my personal mythology, but the idea lay dormant until the publication of Deirdre Bair's biography of Beauvoir in 1990. In it she revealed the human flaws of 'the mother of us all' and that this leading feminist, this 'independant woman' may have actually subordinated her own needs to those of Sartre. Bair's biography brought forth a barrage of letters from angry feminists who had modeled their lives on Beauvoir's and felt betrayed. In their disappointment, they rejected her writings as well as her life. Beauvoir had died in 1986. I longed to see her answer her critics and in Act Two of *Shooting Simone* she does. Although all the dialogue in the play is imaginary, I believe that I am true to Beauvoir's spirit, when she says, "No one lives a philosophy, it's hard enough to write one."

Act One of *Shooting Simone* is set 40 years earlier and deals with a love triangle of Sartre, Beauvoir and Simone's young country cousin Olga. It tests the "writing couple's" premise that theirs is the essential love and all others contingent. The affair with Olga almost destroys the couple but they are able to transform that trauma into art; Sartre writes "No Exit" and Beauvoir writes "She Came to Stay". Olga, on the other hand, feels exploited and it's the publication of her letters that inspires Kate's journey to Paris, to discover what really happened. The truth turns out, as it often does, to be equivocal and subjective.

Shooting Simone explores Sartre and Beauvoir's fifty year relationship. We see them first as young lovers as they deal with the tempestuous Olga and then in the year of Sartre's death as they give their last interview to a feminist film-maker. The play examines the changing face of feminism, the joys and perils of a relationship and the hard won virtues of continuity, commitment and compassion.

Production Note

The Louisville production used a single set of a Paris cafe with windows overlooking the street and doors on each side. Booths pull out on each end to suggest a bed in hotel room scene and a couch in Simone's apartment. Three cafe tables and several chairs provide the rest. Light fixtures can be flown in to suggest change of locale. Two actors dressed as French waiters are helpful for removing props and scene changes. Musical excerpts from Piaf and Josephine Baker can be used to end and begin scenes. It is best to have scenes move quickly and fluidly - no black-outs - and therefore while action is happening on one side of the stage, the characters in the next scene can be already seated on the other side, dimly lit (as in Act One, Scene Seven, as Simone crosses after strangling Olga, Sartre is already sitting there or in Act Two, Scene Seven A, the hotel scene with Rick and Kate, Sartre and Simone can already be seated drinking, in Simone's apartment, ready for Scene Eight.)

Characters

Cast: two men and two women.
Simone young/old
Sartre young/old
Kate/Olga and Alphonse/Rick are double roles.

Simone de Beauvoir: a strong handsome woman, 70
Simone de Beauvoir: a strong handsome woman, 35
Jean-Paul Sartre: a short, sickly man, 70
Jean-Paul Sartre: a short, homely-charismatic man, 35
Kate: a confident, energetic woman, 35
Olga: a sexy beauty, 20
Alphonse: a sailor, 30
Rick: a film maker, 25

Directed by László Marton

Cast of Characters (in order of appearance)

Jean-Paul Satre	Fred Major
Simone de Beauvoir	Janni Brenn
Olga/Kate	Kathleen Dennehy
Alphonse/Rick	Brett Rickaby
Garçons	Christopher Murphy*
	Brian Worrall*

*Member of the ATL Apprentice Company

Scenic Designer	Paul Owen
Costume Designer	Laura Patterson
Lighting Designer	Karl E. Haas
Sound Designer	Darron L. West
Props Master	Ron Riall
Stage Manager	Craig Weindling
Assistant Stage Manager	Carey Upton
Production Dramaturg	Val Smith

Additional casting in LA by Pagano, Bialy, Manwiller

Setting

Act I - Paris, 1937
Act II - Paris, 1980

The time: Paris, 1937, 1980. Place: A Paris cafe, Simone's apartment, a t.v. studio, a Paris hotel room, an Awards ceremony.

Summary

It is Paris, 1937. Jean-Paul Sartre and Simone de Beauvoir the Bogie and Bacall of the Intelligentsia, make a vow to always be each other's "necessary love." They will have "contingent" love affairs but nothing will threaten their primary and equal relationship. Olga, Simone's young country cousin bewitches Sartre, undermines Simone, and nearly destroys the "writing couple." Simone kills Olga, at least on paper.

The second act is set in Paris in 1980. Kate, a documentary film-maker, is attempting to resurrect the details of the affair and to find the true Simone, the great feminist, upon whom Kate has modeled her own life. Through her disillusionment, Kate finds her own individuality. *Shooting Simone* explores sexual jealousy, the changing face of feminism and the subjective nature of truth.

SHOOTING SIMONE

PRELUDE TO ACT ONE

> *Note: this brief scene is an imaginative recreation of the last scene of SARTRE's* No Exit. *The stage is empty except for three chairs and a table. Perhaps there is a red glow. SIMONE and OLGA sit at a table, staring straight ahead. SARTRE paces. A long tense silence. Finally SARTRE moves towards OLGA, stands behind her chair, caresses her shoulders.*

SARTRE: Will this never end?

SIMONE: Never.

SARTRE: You will always see me?

SIMONE: Of course.

SARTRE: (*He moves away from OLGA*) This is Hell. We don't need devils, burning oil, pitchforks. Hell is . . . other people.

OLGA: (*Runs towards him.*) My darling, please. . .

SARTRE: (*Thrusting her away.*) I cannot make love to you when she is watching.

OLGA: In that case I'll kill her. (*She picks up knife from table, rushes to SIMONE, stabs her several times.*)

SIMONE: (*Struggling and laughing.*) You stupid girl. Can't you see I'm already dead. (*OLGA drops knife: SIMONE picks it up and jabs herself with it regretfully.*) Dead. We are all three dead. Trapped in this room forever.

OLGA: (*Laughing.*) Forever. How absurd.

SARTRE: (*Looks at the women, joins them in the laughter.*) Forever! (*Their laughter dies away and they gaze at each other.*) Well, then let's get on with it. (*Black out.*)

ACT ONE

SCENE 1

> *It is spring, Paris 1937, early afternoon. A sidewalk cafe, SIMONE sits writing intently, papers strewn about on the table. Enter SARTRE, excitedly brandishing manuscript.*

SARTRE: My dear Castor (*Kisses her on both cheeks.*) Here it is. I can't wait for you to read it.

SIMONE: Of course, my darling, but let me just finish this page.

SARTRE: Please, this is important. I've said something outrageous. I need to test it.

SIMONE: In a minute.

SARTRE: Castor, I've taken on Freud.

SIMONE: You always take on Freud.

SARTRE: This time I've kicked him in the balls. (*Sits down, moves her papers aside, replaces them with his own.*) Listen, I've proven there is no unconscious.

SIMONE: What?

SARTRE: There is only consciousness. . . nothing else.

SIMONE: But what about repression?

SARTRE: Bad faith. I call it bad faith. Look, you can't repress something until it comes into consciousness; if it comes into consciousness, then it can't be unconscious.

SIMONE: But what if it's so traumatic that we forget it?

SARTRE: Forgetting is self deception. An excuse not to accept responsibility for our own lives. Don't you see man isn't driven by mysterious forces? To hell with Freud. We are responsible for all our thoughts, for all our actions. We're in control here. Well, what do you think, will it hold up?

SIMONE: In theory, yes, but I'll have to read it.

SARTRE: Of course, oh my darling, what a good day's work. I'm exhausted. When can you have it for me?

SIMONE: (*Flips through pages.*) It's long.

SARTRE: Just edit it, then. I'll send it to a typist.

SIMONE: They make so many mistakes. No, I can do it.

SARTRE: You are too good to me. I don't know what I'd do without you, my darling. How is your book coming?

SIMONE: Slow. I don't know if I'm cut out to be a novelist. The book is so dry.

SARTRE: Tell me about it.

SIMONE: Well, it's about what it means to be a woman.

SARTRE: And?

SIMONE: The thing is . . . I'm not sure.

SARTRE: You are one. Write about yourself.

SIMONE: I don't think I'm typical. I need to do some research.

SARTRE: And I want to read every word of it, but not before this.

SIMONE: Of course not. It sounds wonderful.

SARTRE: I hope so. I count on you, my Castor, my other self, to tell me if it isn't. My angel, my judge. We're one. One soul in two bodies.

SIMONE: I'll have it for you tomorrow.

SARTRE: Do you suppose you could have it tonight, so that I could work on it. To keep the flow going. You know I can't write anything without showing it to you first. (*SIMONE nods.*) Oh, thank you, darling. Let's order I'm starving.

SIMONE: Let's wait a bit; we're expecting a guest.

SARTRE: Who?

SIMONE: My cousin Olga.

SARTRE: Olga?

SIMONE: From Rouen. You met her once, when she was a little girl. Well now she's all grown up and driving her mother wild. She won't go to university. She wants to live in Paris and I've promised to find her a room.

SARTRE: We don't want a child around.

SIMONE: She won't interfere with us.

SARTRE: She's already interfering with my lunch. (*Looks about.*) Where is everyone? This place is empty.

SIMONE: Come and gone.

SARTRE: Who?

SIMONE: Aron. Levi-Strauss. Picasso. Camus said the crayfish is excellent.

SARTRE: Crustaceans! They look like insects. And they're hard to eat. You have to attack them and they cling to their little morsels of white flesh. It's like mining.

SIMONE: How about steak then?

SARTRE: Red meat! Definitely not. . . too raw.

SIMONE: It's broiled.

SARTRE: Even so. It retains its thickness, its texture, its blood. Too obvious. I hate meat.

SIMONE: Nonsense, you love sausages.

SARTRE: Ah, well, sausage is something else entirely. . . all pink and white, neatly tied on both ends with bits of string. Yes, sausage is all right. Now why do you suppose I like sausage?

SIMONE: Because you're from Alsace.

SARTRE: No, I think because it's civilized.

SIMONE: Man made.

SARTRE: Yes, that's it. Take fruit for example. It has no appeal for me. It grows by itself; it ripens; it falls from the tree; it's finished. It needs nothing from us. It's a mere accident. Now, on the other hand take a chocolate eclair.

SIMONE: So you like your rawness concealed, transformed.

SARTRE: We are not savages.

SIMONE: Do I detect a dislike for what is simple, natural, fleshly? A distrust of the body?

SARTRE: An elevation of the mind.

SIMONE: A mind must be embodied, otherwise it belongs in a petri jar, floating in alcohol.

SARTRE: Mine floats until it is embodied in you, my darling Castor. What would I do without you? I only feel my body when I am in the arms of a woman. You are very beautiful tonight (*Takes her hand.*) and I, your ugly little frog, am fortunate to be with you.

SIMONE: Why do you call yourself ugly?

SARTRE: Because others have called my attention to it.

SIMONE: Who? Who was the first?

SARTRE: A girl, of course. She was in my form at school. I had loved her for two years. I used to follow her home. One day she tripped right in front of me. I ran to help her. I put out my hand and she slapped it away. 'Don't touch me, you ugly-ugly, you four eyed monster.' I ran home and smashed my spectacles.

SIMONE: And you've been making up for it ever since.

SARTRE: Things change, thankfully. Women are different than little girls. You can talk to them.

SIMONE: Women like to listen.

SARTRE: Yes, especially when you talk about them. Explain their souls to them, something no one else sees or understands.

SIMONE: Still, I should think you would have learned about compassion. Yet every woman you're drawn to is attractive. Why haven't you ever been with an ugly woman?

SARTRE: What would it prove? Two ugly people! An overstatement. Where is your cousin? Why are the young always late?

SIMONE: Because they never think about anything but themselves.

SARTRE: They're so shallow really.

SIMONE: Yet so fresh. What attracts you to a woman?

SARTRE: It can be anything at all really. . . a dimple, a walk, the way she brushes her hair back with the inside of her wrist. They are free to provide so little because with you I have everything. The others are secondary. . . contingent. Ours is the essential love. We are forever.

SIMONE: Totally honest. Totally open. Transparent to each other.

SARTRE: They're so shallow really. We are one, you and I, Tiresias, man and woman in one soul.

OLGA: (*enters, breathless, carrying suitcase*) Cousine Simone! Hello. Hello. Hello. Oh, I am so happy to be here. It's so exciting. It's so beautiful. So romantic. It's just what I thought it would be. Exactly.

Exactly. Monsieur Sartre, may I call you cousin? It's wonderful how you and Cousine Simone are lovers and don't marry and don't even live together and never cook and clean. Oh, Rouen is so bourgeois, I hate it. This is the life. I love it here. I love Paris. (*Car horn honks.*) Oh, it's the cab driver. I couldn't walk all the way from the station, not with these new shoes. (*She shrugs off high red heels.*) I bought them especially for Paris. (*Turns to Simone.*) May I have some money to pay him? (*SARTRE gives her some bills.*) Thank you Cousin Sartre. I'll pay you back. As soon as I get a job. I'll pay you right back. (*Runs off, barefoot.*)

SARTRE: Job? She's planning to stay.

SIMONE: Just talk. You know the young.

SARTRE: She's really something. She reminds me of you.

SIMONE: Me?

SARTRE: When we met. All that energy. I must have had it, too.

SIMONE: (*Ironic.*) Once upon a time.

SARTRE: How are they so cheerful?

SIMONE: They wear silly shoes and don't carry money.

SARTRE: Maybe she'll be good for us, the little one. We're getting too serious.

SIMONE: It might be amusing.

OLGA: (*Rushes in, sits down.*) I want to know everything about you two. Everything, from the beginning. Tell me how you met.

SIMONE: At the Sorbonne.

OLGA: But how?

SIMONE: I looked at him longingly for a few years. He was the leader of the 'in' crowd, wild; they were drunk, dirty, they cut class; they were bad.

SARTRE: Then one day we heard about this little girl who was an expert on Leibnitz. We were too busy to read Leibnitz, so we told her to come to our rooms and fill us in and she talked for six hours. She wore braids and she was brilliant. The youngest agregee in all of France.

OLGA: Number one.

SIMONE: No, Sartre was number one. I was second.

SARTRE: But it was my second try at the exam. I failed the first year.

SIMONE: Because his paper was so original the judges couldn't grade it. They wanted their lectures chewed up and spit back, but Sartre wouldn't do it. He created his own philosophy. 'Existence precedes essence'.

OLGA: What does it mean?

SIMONE: Read his books, Olga.

OLGA: Say it simply.

SARTRE: Simply. . . one. . . we are the sum total of our actions. Two. . . there is no absolute truth. Three. . . there is no god. Four. . . there is no meaning. Five. . . we must act anyway. So you see, nothing we do matters, but it is of the utmost importance that we do it.

OLGA: I don't get it.

SIMONE: Read his books, Olga. Start with 'Nausea', it's short.

OLGA: My head hurts from reading books. Books aren't life. Books are instead of life.

SARTRE: That's very interesting.

SIMONE: How is that interesting? We write books.

SARTRE: What do you mean, little one, books are instead of life.

OLGA: Life is what you feel, not what you think and plan. It just comes on you and you do things like. . . (*Seizes SARTRE's hat and puts it on her head.*) or this (*Grabs SIMONE's wine and downs it.*) or this (*Leaps up on chair and lifts skirt high.*) Now (*To SARTRE.*) you do something.

SARTRE: Well, I don't know what to do. Do something spontaneous, irregular, irrational. . .

OLGA: Don't talk, do something.

SARTRE: All right then. (*He grabs OLGA's hand, puts it into his mouth and pretends to be a bear, gobbling her arm, all the way to her shoulder.*) That was fun. (*To SIMONE.*) I really felt carried away, like an animal.

OLGA: What kind of an animal?

SARTRE: A bear.

OLGA: What kind of a bear?

SARTRE: A black bear with yellow teeth and a red prick.

OLGA: Yes, with ivory claws and shaggy fur and a big bum and beady eyes and a long tongue that smells of fish. Take me to the zoo, cousin, I want to see the bear.

SARTRE: We've never been to the zoo.

OLGA: You've lived in Paris all your life and you've never been to the zoo? What do you do for fun?

SIMONE: Think.

OLGA: Ooof! Nothing good comes of thinking. All you do is get confused. It doesn't change anything. Animals are great. . . they just sleep and eat and play and make love. That's what we're supposed to do. You never see a bear rushing for a bus.

SARTRE: That's true, you don't.

OLGA: They're too smart for that.

SIMONE: Maybe they don't have the change.

OLGA: You know what I mean. They have their priorities straight. They follow their true nature.

SARTRE: Yes, authentic actions. Animals are the true existentialists.

SIMONE: Animals behave by instinct.

OLGA: I want to go to the zoo.

SARTRE: We'll go Sunday.

OLGA: Sunday! It might rain on Sunday. I might have a belly-ache. Why not today?

SIMONE: Because Sartre and I have work to do today.

OLGA: What work?

SIMONE: Writing.

SARTRE: Well, actually I can't get on with it until I get your corrections.

OLGA: Then you can go.

SARTRE: What do you say, Castor, shall I take the child to the zoo?

OLGA: Why do you call Cousine, Castor?

SARTRE: I've always called her that. Beauvoir sounds like beaver in English and beaver in French is castor. . . so she is the Castor.

SARTRE: And what does she call you?

SIMONE: Sartre.

OLGA: You have no pet name. I'll give you one. You'll be my bear. My big, black teddy bear. Come on, teddy, let's go see your brothers at the zoo.

SIMONE: What about lunch? Shall we order?

OLGA: No, Cousin Sartre and I will have a picnic at the zoo. Right, Teddy? We'll go marketing. . . first to the cheese shop and buy a round little chevre with basil and thyme and then to the bakery for a fresh baguette and to the patisserie for a tart au fraises and a chilled bottle of sancerre.

SARTRE: And the charcuterie?

OLGA: Of course.

SARTRE: Duck sausages. . . a whole string of them. . . like a fat pearly necklace. Yes, a picnic, what a breath of fresh air she is. . . your little country cousin.

SIMONE: (*Lights cigarette.*) A tonic.

OLGA: Oh, a Gauloise. . . may I have one?

SIMONE: Smoking is a bad habit.

SARTRE: It stains your teeth.

OLGA: But you smoke. Simone smokes.

SARTRE: We were never as beautiful as you.

SCENE 2

The cafe, two weeks later. SIMONE, SARTRE and OLGA sit at separate tables.

OLGA: (*Downs drink, shudders.*) Absinthe! Will it make me blind?
SIMONE: Blind drunk.
OLGA: But I read absinthe makes you blind.
SIMONE: That was ages ago; it's quite safe now.
OLGA: I'm always too late for everything.
SARTRE: You don't want to ruin your health.
OLGA: I want to do something exciting.
SARTRE: Poor Olgachken, how shall we keep you amused?
OLGA: I want to go someplace. Someplace exciting. Someplace famous like Closerie des Lilas or Moulin Rouge or La Coupole.
SIMONE: What's wrong with right here?
OLGA: Here! Nothing but writers. Boring.
SIMONE: There'll soon be music. Sartre will dance with you.
SARTRE: I don't dance. I talk. Shhh, Olgachken, (*He pats her hand.*) I'll talk to you.
OLGA: All day long I have to be quiet while Simone scribbles and then this. . . I'll go mad.
SIMONE: (*Takes chocolate from her purse and pops it in OLGA's mouth.*) There, that's better.
OLGA: You treat me like a child. I hate hazelnut. (*Spits it out on the table.*)
SIMONE: (*Picks it up and puts it into the ashtray.*) Your manners are atrocious.
SARTRE: Don't be hard on the little one. She's a child of nature.
OLGA: (*Angrily.*) Stupid.
SARTRE: Unrehearsed. Primal. Sublime.
SIMONE: Since when are you such an advocate of nature?
SARTRE: One can always learn, Castor. And the children shall be our teachers.
OLGA: I am not a child.
SARTRE: Not literally, my flower. Of course not.
OLGA: I know my way around.
SARTRE: Of course you do. You're very wise.
OLGA: (*Leaning in.*) Am I?
SARTRE: Your breasts are like twin fawns. (*Strokes her arm.*)
OLGA: (*Pulls away.*) Don't.

SARTRE: But it's from 'The Song of Solomon'.

OLGA: I don't care. It's dirty. And stop looking at me that way.

SARTRE: But yesterday I didn't notice your new dress and you sulked all day.

OLGA: That was different.

SARTRE: Why?

OLGA: If you don't know, I can't tell you.

SARTRE: But they've both to do with your beauty, my love. You dazzle me and I praise it.

OLGA: There's no winning with you. You twist my words. You're just interested in my body. I know it.

SARTRE: No, no my darling little flower. I'm interested in your soul. Tell me what you did today.

OLGA: I went looking for a job.

SARTRE: Did you? And what happened?

OLGA: There was nothing. Nothing but waitresses and shop girls. I didn't come to Paris to do that.

SARTRE: Of course not.

OLGA: Not that it's beneath me. It's just what would I learn? How would that help me to be an artist?

SIMONE: It might help you to pay your rent.

OLGA: Maman will pay.

SIMONE: She won't, Olga, she's had enough.

SARTRE: What sort of an artist, ma petite?

OLGA: I'm not sure yet.

SARTRE: A writer, perhaps?

OLGA: There are too many writers already.

SARTRE: A painter then.

OLGA: Why bother? There are cameras. And don't tell me photography is an art form, I don't accept it. I'd be a dancer but my feet hurt; I already have huge bunions. So I'll have to be an actress.

SARTRE: That's a good idea, Olga, you can take a class.

OLGA: I don't need lessons. I want to be an original. Great art is unique!

SARTRE: Of course it is. I have friends in the theatre. I'll get you an audition.

OLGA: When?

SARTRE: Soon, Very soon.

OLGA: Good. I don't want to do stuffy classics. I want a modern play. Do you think I have talent?

SARTRE: It depends on what you mean by talent.

OLGA: You're born with it. Do I have it or don't I?

SARTRE: I think you have great potential.

OLGA: You're patronizing me.

SARTRE: Olga, please, it's just that acting isn't my field.

OLGA: Then don't talk about it anymore. It's too depressing. I want to go dancing.

SARTRE: Yes, let's go dancing.

OLGA: Not you. Just Simone and I. You can't come.

SIMONE: Why not?

OLGA: Because tonight is just for women. No uncles allowed.

SIMONE: Sartre is not your uncle.

OLGA: He might as well be, the way he watches over me.

SARTRE: I thought I was your big black teddy.

OLGA: You scare everyone off.

SARTRE: Well, I never meant to.

SIMONE: Of course not, she's just being difficult.

OLGA: I am not. The way he puts his hands all over me like I belong to him. Well, I don't. I want someone young with muscles in his arms. I'm going to change. I'll wear my red dress. (*Flounces off.*)

SIMONE: Oh, now, she didn't mean anything by that.

SARTRE: I'm old and ugly.

SIMONE: You are a great man. You are a genius.

SARTRE: So what?

SIMONE: Are you going to sulk?

SARTRE: Don't you think I know how foolish this is? This stupid little girl has me crazed. One minute she's wild about me, hugs and kisses and cousin, explain this, cousin tell me that. And the next minute I've got the plague. I'm a leper. Tell me, is my nose rotting off?

SIMONE: You shouldn't let her get to you like that. You give her too much power.

SARTRE: There's something so fascinating about her. She's so authentic. She moves directly from feeling into action. She's so alive. Oh, Castor, we think too much. This one is the antidote. We can learn so much from her, It's just that she's driving me mad. Should I praise her or shouldn't I? I think she likes me even though she protests. She touched me when she left. I think she's still interested. What shall I do, advise me.

SIMONE: I think you're acting like a fool.

SARTRE: She's like some kind of magnet.

SIMONE: It's only because you can't have her. If you could, you'd lose interest very quickly.

SARTRE: Let's try it.

SIMONE: Try what?

SARTRE: Help me win her, then we can go back to normal.

SIMONE: I will not.

SARTRE: Why not? You've done it before. We tell each other everything. Remember our pact.

SIMONE: This feels different. You're on your own with this one. (*Stands up.*)

SARTRE: Where are you going?

SIMONE: Dancing, remember? Maybe you'll be lucky. She'll meet some young 'muscle' and you'll be off the hook.

SARTRE: Wait, what will I do tonight? Who will I eat with? It's only eight.

SIMONE: Go home and write, Sartre. I haven't seen a word of yours in weeks. (*Exits.*)

SCENE 3

> *A cafe. Music is playing. Two tables. A young, handsome sailor is sitting at one. Enter OLGA and SIMONE. He whistles as they enter. OLGA smiles. SIMONE ignores him. They sit at adjacent table.*

SAILOR: Good evening, ladies. You're looking lovely tonight. Are you two sisters?

OLGA: Yes.

SAILOR: Don't tell me such beauties are alone. It's my lucky night.

SIMONE: Don't count on it.

OLGA: Don't listen to my sister. She's overworked and a bit cranky.

SAILOR: Well, maybe we can help her to relax. How about a drink, my lovelies. What'll it be? Nothing is too good for you two beauties. I'll get a bottle of the best champagne. (*He exits.*)

OLGA: Sartre buys us house white. A half carafe at a time.

SIMONE: We dine with Sartre every night.

OLGA: An obvious mistake. Oh, how I love champagne. I adore the bubbles. Do you know why angels fly, Simone?

SIMONE: Why?

SARTRE: Because they take themselves lightly.

SIMONE: Who told you that?

OLGA: The parish priest in Rouen. Isn't that sweet? He was a dear old man, enjoyed looking up little girls' dresses. He stood at the bottom of the church steps and waited for the choir to come down. He kissed us on the tops of our heads and grabbed a little feel.

SIMONE: Well, at least he liked girls.

OLGA: Girls are nicer.

SIMONE: You were certainly nicer when you were a little girl. You've become quite disagreeable.

OLGA: We came to have a good time. I don't need another lecture.

SAILOR: Now, girls. (*Sound of champagne cork being popped.*) The second most beautiful sound in the world.

SIMONE: And the first?

SAILOR: This. (*He kisses her on the mouth, a loud smack. He joins them.*)

OLGA: I knew this was going to be a good night. What's your name sailor?

SAILOR: Alfonse.

OLGA: We will call you Alfie. Alfie, you are in the company of two famous women. I hope that does not scare you.

SAILOR: The French navy is not easily frightened.

OLGA: Good. I am Olga Kolowitz. If you have not seen me on the stage you will recognize me from my many motion pictures. And my companion, the famous author, Simone de Beauvoir. Her books sell by the millions in thirty-four languages.

SAILOR: Forgive me. I've been at sea.

OLGA: You're saying you don't know our work. Oh, well, dear boy, you'll be forgiven this time for your glorious eyes. Look at the boy's eyes, Simone. Couldn't you just dive right in? And what about that hair, so thick and luxurious? Like the pelt of a wolf. And those teeth, those sharp white teeth? Makes me want to bare my throat. But mostly it's his mouth, those soft, red lips. What do you say, Simone? Is he pretty or not?

SIMONE: He looks healthy enough.

OLGA: Oh, such faint praise. It's not patriotic. Alfie is keeping the waters safe for us. Surely, you can do better. You're a writer. Pretend he's your hero, describe him so the reader can taste him.

SIMONE: Stand up, young man. Shoulders back. Make a muscle. (*He flexes arm.*) Good. Now turn around. Make a muscle. (*He flexes butt*) Very good.

OLGA: Nothing like a tight butt, Simone. Now you think of Sartre, Mr. Flabby Ass. Can you picture him in those pants. Roll up your sleeve. (*SAILOR reveals formidable muscle, OLGA is delighted.*) Feel this. (*She places SIMONE's hand on Alfie's muscle.*) Now squeeze. Doesn't give way. Doesn't get soft. It flexes. Up and down. A thing of beauty. What did you do to get that muscle?

SAILOR: Nothing. It just grew.

SIMONE: It's a simple by-product of hard physical labor.

OLGA: It didn't come from sitting at a desk and wrestling with sentences. (*Pause.*) Can you dance Alfie?

SAILOR: A little.

OLGA: Will you dance with Simone? She's a wonderful dancer.

SIMONE: (*Protesting.*) I haven't danced in years.

OLGA: Once you start, it will all come back. (*SAILOR pulls SIMONE up and into the tight apache position. Music. Black-out.*)

SCENE 4

The next morning. The cafe. SARTRE sits reading. SIMONE enters. SARTRE looks at watch.

SARTRE: You're late today.

SIMONE: What time is it?

SARTRE: Nearly two.

SIMONE: Really?

SARTRE: Are you all right?

SIMONE: Excellent. I just took a long walk.

SARTRE: You look different.

SIMONE: My hair. Olga's doing. Do you like it?

SARTRE: I can't see your eyes.

SIMONE: Today it's just as well.

SARTRE: Late night? How was it?

SIMONE: Noisy. Crowded. Smoky. Wrong kind of people. You would have hated it. But then something extraordinary happened; this morning I had a break-through on my novel. The young girl, Xaviere, I see her in a whole different light. She'll become the catalyst for the older woman's transformation.

SARTRE: I thought she was a silly little hedonist.

SIMONE: Well, yes, she appeared that way because Valerie was so defensive. But once Valerie opens herself to new ideas, the novel can really take off.

SARTRE: Sounds a bit contrived, but as long as you're pleased. At least you're working. I can't write a word. I'm completely blocked. It all seems so pointless.

SIMONE: Really? And I was feeling particularly cheerful today.

SARTRE: It's Olga. She's driving me crazy.

SIMONE: Olga plays favorites. She's like a clever child pitting one parent against the other. You can't take it seriously.

SARTRE: That's easy to say because you're in favor.

SIMONE: Nonsense.

SARTRE: Nonsense yourself. Look at the spring in your step, the sparkle in your eyes. You're positively glowing.

SIMONE: One night.

SARTRE: One night what?

SIMONE: Nothing.

SARTRE: I never made you so happy.

SIMONE: You give me more than happiness.

SARTRE: What could be more than happiness?

SIMONE: Continuity. . . now shush. I'm starving. Let's order. They have duck sausage.

SARTRE: I have no appetite.

SIMONE: Once you smell it, you will.

SARTRE: I am morose. Who would have thought? What is there about her?

SIMONE: If we knew that, we'd be cured.

SARTRE: We? We?

SIMONE: You then. . .

SARTRE: What went on last night?

SIMONE: Demi or a whole carafe. . . what do you think?

SARTRE: We promised we'd tell each other everything.

SIMONE: It's embarrassing.

SARTRE: All the better.

SIMONE: We went dancing and I danced with a sailor. . . tight.

SARTRE: How tight?

SIMONE: I felt every button on his fly.

SARTRE: Good! Then what?

SIMONE: We came home. Olga brushed my hair.

SARTRE: And?

SIMONE: And. . . we went to bed.

SARTRE: And?

SIMONE: And this morning Olga made coffee with her very own hands. The child is getting decidedly helpful.

OLGA: (*Enters carrying red geranium. She skips to the table, greets SARTRE, embraces SIMONE, hands her flower.*) See what I've brought you for your hair.

SIMONE: (*Sniffs flower.*) Fire-engine red.

OLGA: To match the color in your cheeks.

SIMONE: Where did you find such a big geranium?

OLGA: From Madame Clais' pot.

SIMONE: Olga, you shouldn't have.

OLGA: She'll never notice.

SIMONE: You shouldn't take things that aren't yours.

OLGA: No one owns flowers.

SIMONE: But Madame Clais owns the pot.

OLGA: I left the pot. Don't be cross with me. I only did it for you. (*To SARTRE.*) You wouldn't be cross, would you, Cousin Sartre? You like it when I bring you presents.

SARTRE: I wouldn't know. I haven't had any in a long time.

OLGA: Well, if I lived with you, I'd bring you presents.

SIMONE: What?

OLGA: I moved my things in this morning. And Madame Clais isn't raising the rent.

SIMONE: I don't believe this.

OLGA: Neither did I. She's so stingy.

SIMONE: You can't move in with me.

OLGA: It's not the best solution, but what else can I do?

SIMONE: Go back to Rouen.

OLGA: Never.

SIMONE: I live alone, Olga.

OLGA: But last night?

SIMONE: We had too much to drink.

OLGA: You liked it.

SIMONE: It's impossible. Forget it!

SARTRE: Forget what?

OLGA: Then what'll I do?

SIMONE: Get a job.

OLGA: Doing what? I'll sell myself. Yes, become a whore. That's how you treat me anyway. After all I've tried to do for you.

SARTRE: Now, now, Olga.

OLGA: Simone, you're forcing me to do something very difficult.

SIMONE: Good.

SARTRE: I'll move in with Sartre.

SIMONE: What?

SARTRE: Olga, that's not a good idea.

OLGA: Then I'll kill myself.

SIMONE: Nonsense.

OLGA: (*Throws herself into SARTRE's arms.*) Save me.

SIMONE: Don't fall for this.

SARTRE: (*Comforting OLGA.*) Olga, please, surely. (*OLGA cries harder.*) Well, just for a week or two.

OLGA: (*To SIMONE.*) See.

SIMONE: (*To SARTRE.*) It's your life. If you want to disrupt it, go ahead.

OLGA: I am not a disruption. I am a collaborator. Sartre and I are writing a play together, aren't we?

SARTRE: Well, it's nothing really.

SIMONE: A play. You don't write plays.

OLGA: It's my idea actually. These three people, a man and two women. . . one young and beautiful the other old and bitter are stuck together. . . in hell. . . forever. It'll make me a star.

SIMONE: How far along is this play?

SARTRE: Not far.

OLGA: A first draft.

SIMONE: And you haven't shown it to me?

SARTRE: I was going to. It wasn't ready.

SIMONE: You show me every word. Where is it?

OLGA: Right here. (*Pulls it out of her purse.*) I was going to show it to you. We could have worked on it together, the three of us. But now, what's the point?

SIMONE: Let me have it, Olga.

OLGA: (*Clutching manuscript to her chest.*) No. It's mine. I'm going to your apartment to pack my things. Come for me there, Sartre, in one hour. (*Exits.*)

SIMONE: Can this be happening?

SARTRE: Castor, it's nothing.

SIMONE: (*Stunned.*) What?

SARTRE: It's just temperament. You know actresses.

SIMONE: She is not an actress. She is a silly schoolgirl.

SARTRE: This will all pass.

SIMONE: You hid your manuscript from me. Why?

SARTRE: I didn't think you'd be objective.

SIMONE: Don't let her move in.

SARTRE: She has no place to go.

SIMONE: She'll destroy us.

SARTRE: I know. I have all these resolves, but then I touch her. . . and I'm gone. Help me!

SCENE 5

SIMONE's apartment. OLGA is packing furiously. SIMONE is pacing. OLGA is putting a jacket into her suitcase.

SIMONE: That's my jacket.

OLGA: You gave it to me.

SIMONE: I said you could borrow it.

OLGA: (*Tosses it to her.*) Here, take it. So I'll freeze.

SIMONE: (*Tosses it back.*) Keep it. Olga, go home. Go home to your nice warm house in Rouen, to your nice warm clothing. Stop torturing everyone.

OLGA: Everyone tortures me. You think you're so much better than me. But I'm an artist, too. I'm an actress.

SIMONE: Then learn to be an actress, Olga. You don't just get up on the stage and play yourself. You need to train. It's like playing the violin. It takes time and patience. You'll make a fool of yourself and Sartre.

OLGA: You're jealous.

SIMONE: Of what?

OLGA: Of him and me. Of our closeness. Now it's us. . . Sartre and Olga. . . the new "we."

SIMONE: If that's what Sartre needs, I can accept it.

OLGA: All he needs is pussy. Young, fragrant, hard-to-get pussy. Don't glorify that smelly old man.

SIMONE: He loves you.

OLGA: He makes me sick. I don't understand half of what he says. I'm not what he thinks. He keeps asking me questions. He keeps giving me books. I hate him. I only said I'd go to make you jealous.

SIMONE: What?

OLGA: It's you I love. I've always loved you. When you came to spend holidays at Rouen, I'd go into your room after you left and bury my face in the sheets, just to have your smell, your perfume, your black cigarettes. I'd lie in your sheets and touch myself and pretend I was touching you. . . that I was you.

SIMONE: Oh, Olga, go home. You don't belong here.

OLGA: You can't send me home now. You'll never get rid of me. I'm too strong for you. He'll never let me go. He's a philosopher but he's ruled by his cock. And you? You're like every woman I know. You need a man to feel complete. And that man is a piece of shit!

SIMONE: Stop it. Don't say that.

OLGA: He'll leave you for me. He's already done it. I have him and I don't even want him. I want to see him squirm, that's all. It's fun. He likes being humiliated, Simone. It makes him hot.

SIMONE: You bitch. You heartless, conniving bitch. He can't help it. He feels ugly. He suffers. I won't let you destroy him.

OLGA: You really need him, don't you? You're pathetic.

SIMONE: Get out of here, Olga. Get out of Paris.

OLGA: The hell I will.

SIMONE: (*Takes money from her purse, gives it to OLGA.*) Here, take this.

OLGA: Not enough. (*Stuffs it into her pocket.*) It's too late, Simone, your life is over.

SIMONE: Never. (*Lunges at her.*) I hate you, Olga. (*They fall onto sofa bed.*) I'll kill you. Get out of our lives.

OLGA: You're living a lie, Simone. There's nothing left. It's finished.

SIMONE: Stop saying that. I'll kill you. I swear I will.

OLGA: He lied to you. You've been betrayed. Abandoned. You're nothing. A doormat. A fucking housewife.

SIMONE: (*Faces audience as she chokes OLGA.*) I can feel her struggle as she squirms and thrashes beneath me, my arms grow stronger. My fingers like tree roots breaking the soft clay of her neck. I can feel the tendons pop, my fingers like spades digging up the winter ground so I can plant my love, our love. Our necessary love can bloom again. . . in freedom. . . open and honest. . . forever. She has to be destroyed. Her breath is leaving. . . she is moving less. . . just a harsh gasp like air escaping a wound . . . . . I feel the sweat on my back, on my scalp. . . it's my own breath heaving. . . not hers. . . she is silent.

SCENE 6

SIMONE joins SARTRE who is sitting at cafe

SARTRE: You killed her.

SIMONE: I had to.

SARTRE: That's exciting. Why doesn't she kill the man though? Why the rival?

SIMONE: Women are more practical. They don't kill for revenge. They kill to get what they want.

SARTRE: So she gets the man.

SIMONE: Actually, yes. Symbolically she gets herself. She kills the Other and chooses herself. A great achievement for a woman. (*Enter OLGA. She sits at another table and listens.*) Which title do you prefer, "The Guest" or "She came to stay"?

SARTRE: "She came to stay." It has a nice sense of menace. And for my play?

SIMONE: "No Exit". It has the same feeling. . . of being trapped. There shouldn't be an intermission. You don't want people running out for chocolates in the middle. No, they have to be caught just like the actors. Can you imagine making love while someone is watching. So undignified. So ludicrous. All that moaning and thrashing and slobbering while you're being critiqued. Oh yes, people can relate to that.

OLGA: You used me. You sucked me dry and threw me out, You turned my blood into sentences. (*She tugs at SIMONE's arm; SIMONE brushes her away.*) You saw me fall apart and you took notes, Vultures!

SARTRE: (*This speech which he reads from his manuscript to SIMONE plays under OLGA's ranting.*) This is Hell. I'd never have believed it. You remember all we were told about the torture chambers, the fire and brimstone. Old wives' tales! There's no need for red-hot pokers. Hell is . . . other people.

OLGA: You have your imagination. I only have my life. It's not fair. (*To audience.*) To hell with them. Listen to me. "When I came to Paris I wore red shoes and I wanted to be an actress."

ACT TWO

SCENE 1

A television studio. This can be suggested by a boom mike and a pool of light.

KATE: This concludes tonight's presentation, 'Georgia O'Keefe: a woman on paper.' Next week's program comes to you direct from Paris, thanks to a special grant from the National Organization for Women. . . an in-depth interview with the leading feminist of the international community. . . the mother of us all. (*As KATE continues to talk we might see a series of slides of Simone de Beauvoir...Simone as a girl with her family, at the Sorbonne with Sartre, as a young teacher, with Sartre and Castro, with Sartre and Krushchev, marching for abortion rights.*) She is the author of one of the most influential books on the condition of women, 'The Second Sex'; a tireless fighter for women's rights; for birth control; for abortion; for political, social and economic equality. France's sacred monster, Simone de Beauvoir. Two weeks ago a book of letters was published posthumously by a one-time acquaintance, Olga Kolowitz. This book makes a number of damaging allegations regarding Ms. de Beauvoir's personal life and her commitment to feminism. We have been granted an exclusive full day interview with Ms. de Beauvoir and her longtime companion, philosopher, Jean-Paul Sartre. Join us next week from the Boulevard Edgar Quinet as we investigate these and other issues. Meanwhile this is Kate Berman of 'Women's Lives' wishing all of you out there. . . a life of your own.

SCENE 2

A hotel bedroom. KATE and RICK are asleep. Room is pitch black. Sound of an alarm beeping.

KATE: What time is it?
RICK: (*Sleepily.*) Huh?
KATE: (*Leaps out of bed.*) Where's the light?
RICK: No, don't. (*Too late; light floods the room.*)
KATE: (*Studies clock.*) It's seven.
RICK: Seven! We don't have to be there till noon.
KATE: I know. I forgot to re-set the alarm.
RICK: Come back to bed, Kate.
KATE: We're up now. We might as well get started.
RICK: Doing what?
KATE: Where's the shower?
RICK: Down the hall. Remember, we're saving money.
KATE: They put a bidet in the room but a shower down the hall.
RICK: Priorities.
KATE: There isn't even a sink. The pillows are like lead. It's dusty and noisy and there aren't any hangers.
RICK: Nervous?
KATE: Maybe. It's a big break. It could really be something. I've had this dinky little low budget show forever. . . All I've been able to do is raid the archives. And they've all been dead. . . Dickinson and Bronte and Woolf and George Eliot and George Sand. I've had dead Georges up the whazoo. And now I have a live one. The most important feminist in the world. I was nineteen when I read 'The Second Sex'. It changed my life. I threw away my lipstick. I stopped shaving my legs. I dropped out of teaching and switched to journalism. I wanted to be Beauvoir. I wanted to move to Paris and wear black. I wanted to live next door to my lover in a hotel and never cook and never clean and make art not babies. I wanted to hang out with no one but existentialists. . . but I wanted them all to look like Albert Camus. (*Pause.*)You're too young to remember all that, Rick. Beatnik poetry. Bongo drums. Marijuana.
RICK: You're right. Must be time for my nap. (*Reaches for her.*)
KATE: Not now.

RICK: It'll help you relax.

KATE: I don't want to relax. I want to go over my notes. I want to take a shower. I want a cup of coffee.

RICK: I bought you something. (*Hands her a red lace teddy.*) Well?

KATE: It's a teddy.

RICK: Try it on.

KATE: Now?

RICK: We're in Paris.

KATE: Well, frankly, I've always felt silly in these things.

RICK: Why?

KATE: They're so obvious. Like high heels and garter belts.

RICK: Sounds great.

KATE: Thanks, Rick, it's sweet. (*Puts it back in box.*) Can we get dressed now and get some breakfast? (*Scene continues from Rick's speech...Moment. Bonjour madame, etc.*)

RICK: Moment. (*Speaks into phone.*) Bonjour madame. Ici chambre cinq. Deux petit dejeuner sil vous plait. Cafe au lait, croissants, avec beurre et marmelade. Je vous en prie, madame. (*Hangs up.*)

KATE: Not bad but I wanted mine with onions.

RICK: Junior year abroad. I guess they didn't have it in your day.

KATE: They had abroad. I just wasn't there. I rode the subway and ate at Nedicks. You were a privileged youth, Rick, Ralph Lauren to the max.

RICK: Is that bad?

KATE: Au contraire, that's why you're here, chatting up the boss.

RICK: I thought I was here because I was a good camera man.

KATE: And a good cocksman to boot.

RICK: Why do you do that?

KATE: Do what?

RICK: Cut me down.

KATE: Oh, come on, don't be so sensitive. Can't you take a compliment.

RICK: It didn't feel like a compliment. It felt like a jab. Like a way to keep your distance.

KATE: I just want to keep things straight. We work together. We sleep together. And we're doing this shoot together. But it's my shoot. I call it from beginning to end.

RICK: Sure, sure, but why get so up tight?

KATE: Because a film has room for only one point of view. In this case it's mine, okay?

RICK: Okay. so what's it going to be?

KATE: Beauvoir wrote four volumes of her autobiography claiming to tell the truth about her life. Full disclosure. Setting an example for the world of how to be an independent woman. How to be free from needing a man, from being oppressed by men. Now Olga writes her account and says it was all a lie.

RICK: Who's Olga?

KATE: Simone's country cousin. (*She shows RICK OLGA's picture on on the back of her book.*)

RICK: She looks a lot like you.

KATE: Oh please! So Olga claims that Beauvoir found her identity through Sartre. That she always puts him first. . . his work, his needs, his life. That the great feminist is a goddamn bourgeois housewife.

RICK: So what does Beauvoir say?

KATE: Nothing. She hasn't given any interviews.

RICK: Then how did you get this one?

KATE: I told her she was the most important influence in my life and I was mad as hell.

RICK: At whom?

KATE: At whomever is lying. (*A knock at the door. RICK gets breakfast tray.*)

RICK: Look at this. They really do things beautifully here. Real china, real linen, real silverwear. A pot of apricot jam, not those horrible little plastic squares. (*Pours generous amount of coffee.*) The French take their pleasures seriously.

KATE: Hey, leave some for me.

RICK: This is for you.

KATE: Sorry. I am uptight. Still interested?

RICK: Not right now.

KATE: Oh, don't sulk sweetie.

RICK: Tell me about Simone. Tell me why she means so much to you.

KATE: You don't want to hear all that.

RICK: I do, Katie. I want to understand you.

KATE: Half the time I don't understand myself. I get so feisty. Look, you are my best friend. You're the best man I've ever been with. The best company. The most decent. It's just.

RICK: Just what?

KATE: I don't trust it.

RICK: You don't trust me.

KATE: I don't trust me. Us. Everytime I get too close it gets claustrophobic. It's like I can't breathe. Like if I love you, I lose me.

RICK: You're the most self-sufficient woman I know.

KATE: It's not that I can't be, it's that I stop wanting to be. I stop wanting to take risks, to think things out on my own. Instead, I'm part of a couple and I don't know where I end and you begin. I want to get along more than I want the truth. I want to stay home and rent movies instead of make them.

RICK: Can't you do both?

KATE: I haven't.

RICK: I'm here to help you, Kate. We're going to make the best goddamn feminist movie if we have to bust our balls to do it.

KATE: You dick-head. (*Laughter as they tumble on the bed.*)

SCENE 3

SIMONE's apartment. SIMONE is sitting on the couch. SARTRE is in a wheelchair.

SARTRE: When is she coming?

SIMONE: Any moment.

SARTRE: Why?

SIMONE: For American T.V. I told you.

SARTRE: Why did you agree?

SIMONE: We haven't done one in a long time.

SARTRE: They misquote us.

SIMONE: This will be on film. They can't.

SARTRE: They'll edit us out of context.

SIMONE: There has to be a point of view.

SARTRE: But why hers. . . this. . . who?

SIMONE: Kate Berman.

SARTRE: You turned down Walter Cronkite for a nobody.

SIMONE: I liked her letter. It was honest. And I wanted pictures of us together. It's getting late.

SARTRE: Not for you. You'll live forever. You'll have a bigger funeral. More flowers, more tears, more people following your coffin. You'll have all the women in France falling on your grave. And me, who will I have? Existentialism is out.

SIMONE: It'll come back. Fashions change.

SARTRE: And feminism is in. And so virulent. Who would have thought it? A philosophy that hates half the human race. At any rate, she's not coming because of the women's movement. She's coming because of Olga.

SIMONE: Olga! We never should have written those letters. She kept every foolish word.

SARTRE: (*Pause.*) It's hard to remember feeling such passion for anyone.

SIMONE: Passion decreases with blood supply.

SARTRE: If we're going to talk about Olga I need a drink.

SIMONE: With lunch.

SARTRE: Now.

SIMONE: It's bad for you.

SARTRE: Just one. (*SIMONE pours him a drink.*)

SARTRE: (*Sips.*) Watered!

SIMONE: A bit.

SARTRE: One of my few pleasures and you dilute it. Now you'll have to pour me a double.

SIMONE: (*Pours a bit more.*) It goes right to your bladder.

SARTRE: I'll let you know.

SIMONE: Do, Sartre, otherwise. . .

SARTRE: I know.

SIMONE: There's an odor already. What is it? (*SARTRE wheels away.*) Have you been using the salve? Soaking your legs? (*She attempts to peek under his lap blanket, he moves away.*)

SARTRE: This is undignified.

SIMONE: I'm sorry, my darling.

SARTRE: It's hopeless, Castor. My body is a corpse. Only my mind is alive, beating its wings against the cage.

SIMONE: Shall I read to you?

SARTRE: No, put on some music. No melody. I want dissonance. Schoenberg or Satie. Did you know, my darling, that Eric Satie once ordered ten identical grey suits. There's a man who knew how to simplify his life. (*Door bell rings.*)

SIMONE: There she is. Do you want to go to the toilet?

SARTRE: I'll use the cat box. (*Indicates bedpan. Enter KATE and RICK.*)

SIMONE: Bonjour.

KATE: Good morning.

SIMONE: Sartre, this is Miss Berman. . .

SARTRE: The inquisitor. (*KATE holds out hand for a handshake, SARTRE kisses it instead.*) Enchanté. So you will torture us into admitting all our little secrets. Light matches under our fingernails, drip water on our heads. dip our genitals in honey and throw us on an ant hill. I've read about you investigative reporters.

SIMONE: . . . and Mr. Saviano.

SARTRE: Light me from the left. It's my good side.

KATE: (*To RICK.*) We'll start with Ms. de Beauvoir on the couch and then a long shot of her working at the desk. (*To SIMONE.*) Until Rick's ready, why don't we just chat a bit? (*RICK sets up mike and camera.*) Let's start with the present. Are you working on something right now?

SIMONE: Always.

KATE: And that is?

SIMONE: A series of dialogues with Sartre. I ask him questions, record his answers on tape, transcribe and edit them.

KATE: And the topics?

SIMONE: Same old stuff. . . freedom, will, desire.

KATE: And he asks you questions as well?

SIMONE: No.

KATE: Why's that?

SIMONE: He has enough to say on his own.

KATE: But what about your thoughts?

SIMONE: Mine can wait. Sartre is the philosopher.

KATE: But your work has been a model for millions of women. Why do you put his first?

SIMONE: I didn't realize there was a competition.

RICK: Ready when you are.

KATE: (*Speaking to camera.*) We are in Paris, in the apartment of Simone de Beauvoir, author of "The Second Sex" and "The Mandarins". Also here today is Ms. de Beauvoir's close friend, philosopher Jean-Paul Sartre. I'm Kate Berman. Welcome to this special edition of 'Womens' Lives'. (*SIMONE nods; SARTRE grins and waves.*) Miss de Beauvoir, your current project is a series of interviews called. . .

SIMONE: 'Conversations with Sartre'.

KATE: Can you tell me why you've picked this particular topic?

SIMONE: It was a simple choice. My relationship with Sartre is the most important thing in my life.

KATE: And Mr. Sartre, would you say the same?

SARTRE: Yes, certainly. Our relationship is the most important one in my life.

KATE: That's a touching sentiment, but it's somewhat different from Miss de Beauvoir's.

SARTRE: Is it?

KATE: She said your relationship is the most important thing in her life; you said it's the most important relationship. That implies that other things. . . your work, your self. . . are more important.

SARTRE: I cherish our love beyond measure.

KATE: In its place. How do you feel about that?

SIMONE: I accept it.

KATE: You accept an inequity.

SIMONE: There's always inequity. It's oppression I oppose.

KATE: In all your books you talk about being independent. About not needing a man. 'One isn't born a woman, one becomes one.' Wasn't that the point of 'The Second Sex'?

SIMONE: One of them.

KATE: But you didn't live it.

SIMONE: No one lives a philosophy. It's hard enough to write it.

KATE: But you set the standards. Don't get married, you said. Marriage is economic and sexual slavery. Don't have children, you said. Motherhood is martyrdom. Children are parasites.

SIMONE: So you didn't have children?

KATE: We're not talking about me.

SIMONE: We're always talking about ourselves.

KATE: Look, that wasn't a novel you wrote. It was a manifesto. I took it seriously. So did millions of other women.

SIMONE: I chose to tell some things. I chose not to tell others.

RICK: What about Olga? Was there a triangle?

SIMONE: We were young. We thought if two people in love were good. . .

SARTRE: Three people in love would be better. (*He begins to laugh. SIMONE joins him. He laughs harder, then...*) Quick, Castor, the cat box. (*He attempts to get up.*)

SIMONE: Wait, I'll help you.

SARTRE: Too late. Sorry.

SIMONE: Never mind.

SARTRE: No warning at all. It's getting worse.

SIMONE: (*Takes his hand.*) It doesn't matter. Where were we?

RICK: We were talking about your life with Sartre.

KATE: We were talking about the condition of women.

RICK: After the break with Olga, were things different?

SIMONE: Yes, we knew what we could lose.

RICK: So you were stronger.

SIMONE: We all got hurt on that one. But Sartre and I transformed it into art. My first novel. His first play. And now Olga has hers. A best seller. Her version. Well, why not? That's all we ever get to know, our version. What about you, Miss Berman, what's your version?

KATE: I'm a reporter. I'm interested in the truth.

SIMONE: Which truth? There are so many. If it's beautiful, it's true. If it has meaning, it's true. If enough people believe it, it's true. If it helps you, it's true. The more you collect, the more truths you have. Your world becomes truer and truer. Unless, of course, you believe in a solitary truth. Then life is quite simple and quite dull.

KATE: I believe in objective truth. I believe it can be discovered and passed on.

SIMONE: Hmmm. (*To SARTRE.*) What is that story, my darling, the one about God and the Devil?

SARTRE: God and the Devil are walking along the Seine. God sees a shining mass of tangled gold. He stops to pick it up. "What is it?" the Devil asks. "That is truth," says God. "Give it here," says the Devil, "I'll organize it for you."

SIMONE: (*Laughs.*)

SARTRE: (*Laughs with her.*) You've heard it a million times.

SIMONE: Yes, but I always forget the end. (*Pointedly to KATE.*) I'll organize it for you.

KATE: Look, if you don't want to discuss what really happened, why did you agree to the interview?

SIMONE: I liked your letter. It was full of fire and outrage and so wrong headed. It reminded me of Olga. A chance to talk to Olga again. So, if you like, Miss Berman, I have something to show you, an exclusive. No one from the press has been there. You may even bring your camera.

KATE: What is it?

SIMONE: A school. The Beauvoir School for Unwed Mothers. You'll like it, Miss Berman. Two courses are required, public speaking and karate.

SCENE 4

The cafe. KATE sits at a table reading menu.

KATE: (*Tries to signal waiter repeatedly.*) Garçon. Garçon. S'il vous plait. Garçon. Garçon.

RICK: (*Enters.*) You don't call them garçon.

KATE: I read that you did.

RICK: Not since Hemingway. You call them monsieur and they still ignore you. I just ordered for us inside. You would have enjoyed it. A foray into the black hole of language hell. (*RICK does both voices; RICK speaks French, the waiter sneers in bad English. 'Deux croque monsieurs, s'il vous plait'. "Two sanweech am chiz." 'Une carafe d'vin blanc'. "Ze ouse wine." 'Je vous en prie, monsieur'. "No sweat."*)

KATE: Serves you right, smart ass.

RICK: You're just jealous.

KATE: Junior year abroad.

RICK: I got us fed.

KATE: I can manage by myself. And by the way what were you trying to prove today?

RICK: When?

KATE: You interfered with my interview. You brought up all kinds of dumb tangents. I'm not interested in gossip. I'm going for ideas.

RICK: How about the idea of a relationship lasting fifty years? How did they do it? It's a miracle. . . loaves and fishes. . . Everyone's starving and they've got the secret.

KATE: What secret? It's a given. Women have known it since the cave. Put the guy on a pedestal, he'll stick around. Did you catch my Virginia Woolf show. . . 'Every man wants to see himself mirrored in his woman's eyes. . . twice as big as life.' Tell me about it. . . the colossal male ego.

RICK: Katie, get off the soap box. This is a chance to do a great film, a universal film - not another polemic about feminism.

KATE: It's always a polemic to a man. How many white males opposed slavery?

RICK: Abraham Lincoln.

KATE: An exception. The ruling class never gets the picture. Who's writing about the Holocaust? The Germans or the Jews?

RICK: There are a lot of ways to get across a message.

KATE: This film is about Beauvoir, about her work, about what she's accomplished and what's left to be done. If she's lied, she needs to be discredited, if she's told the truth she needs to be exonerated. Either way this is not about relationships. Why is it every time we talk about women we talk about goddamn relationships?

RICK: Sartre's dying, Kate. This may be the last interview he gives. Let's spend some time with him.

KATE: Then spend it. But not on my dime.

RICK: Our dime.

KATE: The hell it is. This is my shoot. Don't mess with it.

RICK: Come on, we've worked on things together before. You've never been like this. What's eating you?

KATE: Nothing.

RICK: She's really important to you, isn't she? You feel betrayed.

KATE: Can we get some bread? I'm starving.

RICK: You're the independent one. Order it.

KATE: Garçon. Christ, monsieur. Some. . . how do you say bread. . . hell. . . some croissants. . . merci.

RICK: What survival skills. Outward Bound would be proud.

KATE: Oh, shut up!

RICK: I love you, Kate. I want to take you back to bed and kiss away those dark circles.

KATE: I look lousy.

RICK: You look tired. When we get back, move in with me.

KATE: It would never work.

RICK: Why not?

KATE: You're too young.

RICK: I'll get older.

KATE: And you're a man.

RICK: Some of my best friends are men.

KATE: Well, mine aren't. Not when they mess with my film.

RICK: I'm just trying to open it up a little. It doesn't have to be so linear. I mean it's good, Katie, but it can be better. It can be more than just a 'cast off the shackles' flick. It can be looser, more organic, more personal. Let the story tell itself. Like this morning with the cat box.

KATE: What about it?

RICK: When Sartre peed in his pants.

KATE: Oh, God, is that what it was?

RICK: She was so tender with him. It was like it was all right. Like everything was all right.

KATE: Well, of course it was; she worships him. He'd never do it for her.

RICK: Maybe once he wouldn't, but now I think he would. If he could. He's changed a lot. They both have. It could make a great film. Their life, their real life with all the confusions and contradictions and somehow. . . how they made it work.

KATE: Made what work?

RICK: A shared life. What's better? What's more important? Dropping the mask. Letting yourself be known. Needing someone.

KATE: It's Paris, isn't it: it addles the brain.

RICK: How about it, Kate? Putting someone else's welfare equal to your own. . . sometimes above your own. My shrink says that's the mark of an evolved human being. . .

KATE: Oh, please, it is so easy for you New Age men. You can have it both ways. You get to keep the old boy privileges and you get to be sensitive, too. Well I can't afford to be in touch with my feelings. And I don't have time for designer shrinks.

RICK: (*Stung.*) Too bad. It might do you some good.

KATE: What's that supposed to mean?

RICK: Anyone can benefit from therapy.

KATE: No, you meant something specific.

RICK: Well, you could lighten up, Kate. You don't always have to be on top.

KATE: Always?

RICK: Yeah, always. Even in bed.

KATE: You don't like it, you can leave.

RICK: That's the choice, isn't it. Okay. I'll get out. (*Picks up camera,*

starts to leave.)
KATE: Where are you going? That is completely unprofessional.
RICK: You're right.*(Returns, drops camera onto table.)*
KATE: What am I supposed to do with that?
RICK: Put it on automatic, Katie. You won't know the difference.

SCENE 5

SIMONE's apartment. SARTRE is siting on the sofa. RICK is taking still photographs of SARTRE. SARTRE poses, then RICK opens a travel flask and pours SARTRE a drink.

SARTRE: Ahhh, straight whiskey. The Castor waters it something fierce. That's why I'm always pissing. I have to drink a gallon before I get any alcohol. Don't get old my friend; it's tyranny.
RICK: What's the alternative?
SARTRE: Dying while you're young and handsome. Unfortunately I never had that option.
RICK: You were never young?
SARTRE: I always lived in my head. It made me old. Camus was the handsome one. I always hated him for that.
RICK: I thought you two were buddies.
SARTRE: We were until I gave him a bad review. He never forgave me. Said I was jealous. *(Pause.)* He was right.
RICK: Jealous of his writing?
SARTRE: No, his work made mine more important. Alone I was a philosopher; together we were a movement. No, I was jealous of his style with women. They were falling all over him. He would sit at a back table at The Flore, unshaven, unwashed, chain smoking Gauloises and the women would be unzipping their jeans as they raced to his table. Germans. Americans. Swedes. Me, I had to stick to the French. I needed language. I had to seduce them with words. Otherwise, no dice.
RICK: Even Olga?
SARTRE: Especially Olga. That one got too intense. We stopped that, Castor and I, after Olga.
RICK: Stopped having lovers?
SARTRE: Stopped letting them matter. . . so much. But we both liked having them. We needed the variety.
RICK: Beauvoir too?
SARTRE: Of course. Oh, she liked pretending it was my idea. But she

never wanted to get married. She refused me twice. She liked having a nice stable relationship and all those young 'muscles'. . . Bost and Landsmann and that American. . . Algren. He was a rough neck, called her 'Simon Bood-oir'. She liked that. But then she used his love letters in her novel, word for word. He didn't like that. . . being caught with his pants down.

RICK: Is that the way you felt about your letters to Olga?

SARTRE: No, I'm not ashamed of my passions. If I were, I wouldn't have let Simone publish them.

RICK: Simone?

SARTRE: Of course. Olga left them to us in her estate.

RICK: Let me get this straight. You owned the letters and you published them.

SARTRE: They're part of history.

RICK: But why now?

SARTRE: Timing. Castor thought it would help our next book.

RICK: But she wouldn't give any interviews.

SARTRE: That was my idea. It worked for Garbo.

RICK: So the whole thing is a game.

SARTRE: A strategy. We're still arguing about one. Simone thinks it'll hurt her reputation, but I think it would add complexity. . . modernity. . . panache.

RICK: What's it about?

SARTRE: Ah, if I told you that I'd be in big trouble. Women are funny. You step on their toes. . . they cut off your balls.

RICK: Tell me about it!

SARTRE: Lovers' spat?

RICK: Artistic differences.

SARTRE: That's not too bad.

RICK: And I told her she was bossy in bed.

SARTRE: Big mistake.

RICK: I don't know what's gotten into her lately. She's impossible.

SARTRE: You feel exploited.

RICK: Yeah, like a sex object.

SARTRE: It's what I've always wanted to be.

RICK: I've got some ideas about this film, too. Ways to make it better.

SARTRE: So?

RICK: More important.

SARTRE: To whom?

RICK: To me. To men. Look, Kate doesn't want to deal with the relationship at all. Just make the whole film about Beauvoir and the women's movement. It's like you don't exist.

SARTRE: Why, that's absurd.

RICK: That's what I say. (*Pours another drink.*) The most important philosopher of the twentieth century, author of 'Nausea', 'Being and Nothingness', 'No Exit', 'The Flies'. Everyone knows 'The Second Sex' is based on existentialism. It's a sacrilege.

SARTRE: I'm not in the film at all?

RICK: Nope.

SARTRE: Surely, you can influence her.

RICK: Believe me, I've tried. She's stubborn.

SARTRE: Well, then there's only one thing to do. I hoped it wouldn't come to this. But extreme times call for extreme measures. (*He removes a letter from his pocket and hands it to Rick.*) Journalists can never resist a scoop. It is 1937. My affair with Olga had hit a snag. Olga was restless. I was dejected. Simone was miserable. So one night the ladies went to a dance club and everything changed.

SCENE 6

SIMONE'S apartment, 1937. Sounds of laughter and running as SIMONE and OLGA burst through the door.

OLGA: 'Such beauties, are you two sisters?'

SIMONE: 'I am a famous author and my cousin is a famous film star, Alfie.'

OLGA: What a body he had. Well rigged, fore and aft.

SIMONE: With a cannon ready to fire. (*The women clown, maybe sing, or dance a sailor's horn-pipe.*)

OLGA: Oh, Simone, you should always wear your hair loose. It's beautiful that way.

SIMONE: It's too much trouble. I pin it up and it's out of the way.

OLGA: (*Takes brush out of her purse, brushes SIMONE's hair.*) 'A woman's hair should surround her face softly like petals on a flower.'

SIMONE: (*Disdain.*) Colette. . . all she writes is romance.

OLGA: All you write is philosophy. . . like Sartre.

SIMONE: I'm writing a novel.

OLGA: Filled with philosophy. You're not interested in love stories. They're too stupid. (*Pause.*) Why do you do Sartre's laundry?

SIMONE: I don't do Sartre's laundry.

OLGA: You bring it to the laundress every Tuesday.

SIMONE: So, a few more shirts to carry, what does it matter?

OLGA: Why doesn't he do it for you?

SIMONE: He would, if I asked.

OLGA: Then why don't you?

SIMONE: Because he would forget and then we'd both be wearing dirty underwear. What would it prove?

OLGA: That you're not his slave.

SIMONE: You don't know anything about it.

OLGA: I know what I see. You're different when you're not around him. You're funnier, softer. Look how tense you are. (*She begins rubbing SIMONE's temples.*) Too much thinking. I bet you don't even make love any more.

SIMONE: That's none of your business.

OLGA: You can see it.

SIMONE: How?

OLGA: By these little wrinkles around your mouth. You keep it so tight. When a women makes love her mouth is open, soft. Like a flower.

SIMONE: Colette again. That's enough (*Takes brush from her hand.*)

OLGA: I don't like Sartre. He looks like a toad. A big fat bull frog, squatting there on his haunches, making so much noise you can't hear anything else. (*Croaks and speaks at the same time, mimicking SARTRE.*) Absolute morality. Absolute truth. Absolute bullshit.

SIMONE: (*Laughs guiltily.*) Stop that!

OLGA: We don't need him. We had such a good time tonight dancing with that sailor. He was crazy about you, the way his hands kept slipping down your back, stroking your bottom.

SIMONE: He must have been all of twenty.

OLGA: At twenty, you can go all night.

SIMONE: I'm not interested in that.

OLGA: Why not? Sartre has lovers, why don't you?

SIMONE: I can if I choose.

OLGA: It would be good for you to be pleasured a bit. You've still young. Young and beautiful. Your skin is like marble. So smooth and silky. Let me give you a good back rub, a soothing one, all over. I have some oil in my room. I can warm it in my hands. It'll feel good. I can oil your body so it feels so sleek. Do you remember when you'd bathe me in Rouen, soap me all over and I'd be your baby seal. . . and you'd be my mother. I'd be all slippery under your hands and slide all over the tub.

SIMONE: (*Softly.*) I remember.

OLGA: Oh, Simone, I can do such nice things for you. I can take care of you. Yes, let me. You're so tired. Come my darling, my poor little sleepy seal. (*She kneels before her, starts to unbutton SIMONE's blouse.*) Let's take this off. (*SIMONE begins to protest.*) Oh, you're so warm. Shhh, there's nothing for you to do. I'll do it all.

SCENE 7

SIMONE and KATE are walking among the bassinettes in the nursery. They can walk behind the windows of the set where the baskets have been placed.

KATE: What a life. Nothing to do but eat and sleep.
SIMONE: Yes, every time the babies cry, the girls give them the breast.
KATE: The babies look happy.
SIMONE: So do the girls. It must feel good. Sexy. Like a lover.
KATE: Better. They don't talk back. (*The women laugh, exit the nursery, into the sunshine.*) God, it's hot.
SIMONE: It's summer.
KATE: It's better out here. At least there's a breeze. You really could use some air conditioning. (*SIMONE keeps fanning.*) It's expensive. I know. It's not the French way. I know. It's like asking for ice in your drink. If I wanted all that, I should have stayed at home.
SIMONE: Or at the George Cinq. Who doesn't like luxury, but we need other things first. Like computers. I want my girls to have a leg up. Freud got it wrong. Never mind hysteria. Cure math anxiety and women will be all right. (*Hands KATE a fan.*) I bought a gross of these from Hong Kong. Four francs each.
KATE: (*Begins to fan herself.*) Very feminine.
SIMONE: And they develop the wrist.
KATE: I got some great footage in there.
SIMONE: Well, you can hardly go wrong. Babes in arms.
KATE: Like shooting fish in a barrel.
SIMONE: Ah yes, the American idiom. So direct. I had an American lover once. He taught me about le jazz and the mean streets. He wrote— 'The Man—
KATE: (*Overlap.*) 'Man With the Golden Arm.'
SIMONE: Another American expression I like very much. So descriptive. So you enjoyed the nursing moms. The adolescent pietas.
KATE: It's amazing how the babies look up at their mothers with such trust.
KATE: Did you ever want a child?
SIMONE: I thought about it seriously, once or twice. Did you?
KATE: When I was pregnant.
SIMONE: And?

KATE: I ended it. It was a girl. Even at three months you could tell.

SIMONE: Do you regret it?

KATE: Sometimes. (*Pause.*) He was my college professor . . . romantic poetry. We were in love. I thought he would leave his wife. He said he couldn't; she'd fall apart. I did a terrible thing. I told her. She listened quietly, then she gave me the name of a doctor, someone reliable and cheap. (*Pause.*) And I vowed that would never happen to me again. I'd never be anyone's mistress or anyone's wife. But I didn't know what else to be. And then I found your book. And I thought someone on the other side of the world understands me. (*Pause.*) And you? Did you ever regret it?

SIMONE: I was never pregnant.

KATE: What? But you marched. You signed that petition. You were thrown in jail.

SIMONE: It was a principle I believed in.

KATE: But you said you had an abortion.

SIMONE: If I were pregnant, I would have.

KATE: But you weren't. You lied. You lied about everything.

SIMONE: Not everything. I did not lie about the choice.

KATE: I followed your example.

SIMONE: Did you want the baby?

KATE: No, I wasn't ready.

SIMONE: So it was your choice.

KATE: Yes, but you still lied. You only told what made you look good.

SIMONE: I have disappointed you. So many flaws. So many weaknesses. We women are so hard on each other. We demand perfection and when we don't find it, we tear each other down. When I was a girl, I was furious at my mother for making me bathe in my nightgown; it was a sin for me to look at my own naked body. So when I wrote "The Second Sex", I wrote three chapters on menstruation, masturbation and orgasm. She wouldn't read it, of course. Even the Minister of Culture flung it across the room, "We have seen quite enough of Simone de Beauvoir's vagina." When the book was a success, I forgave my mother. (*Pause.*) And she bought lots of copies for her friends.

KATE: That's not going to get you off the hook.

SIMONE: Then do me one better. Be braver. Be stronger. Be more loving. Put it together. Make it work. Perhaps I didn't discover the New World, but at least I drew a map. No-one sets sail without a map. Once you get there you can correct it.

KATE: I'm talking about right now.

SIMONE: 'One morning in the middle of my life, I awoke in a dark wood in which there was no path.'

KATE: Is that yours?

SIMONE: Dante. Same problem. And he was a man.

SCENE 7A

> *KATE's hotel room. KATE is listening to tapes of interview, when there is a knock on the door.*

KATE: Yes?

RICK: It's me.

KATE: It's open.

RICK: (*Enters.*) Hello. (*Formal.*)

KATE: Hi. (*Tentative.*)

RICK: Well, I just came to pick up my stuff. I'll only be a minute.

KATE: That's okay. No rush. No, I'm just listening to the last interview.

RICK: How did it go?

KATE: I don't know.

RICK: You got what you needed though.

KATE: Yes, I think so.

RICK: Good.

KATE: What did you do?

RICK: Hung out with Sartre.

KATE: And?

RICK: Nothing much. Personal stuff.

KATE: That can be interesting, sometimes. I was looking at the stuff you shot this afternoon. The story about the God and the Devil.

RICK: That was a great story.

KATE: It wasn't just the words. You caught the way they looked at each other. The way their hands touched. They way they laughed together. It was good.

RICK: Well, it's all yours. Use it anyway you like.

KATE: That's very generous. I'll make sure you get a credit.

RICK: Fine. Well, I guess that's everything. So long. (*He starts to leave.*)

KATE: So long. (*Pause.*) Wait.

RICK: Yeah?

KATE: Have a safe trip.

RICK: Thanks.

KATE: Don't change your money at the airport. It's a lousy exchange rate.

RICK: Right.

KATE: Rick. (*She strips off robe, is wearing teddy.*) Well, how does it look?

RICK: Pretty silly.

KATE: Good, (*She hands him a red lace jock strap.*) because I got this one for you.

SCENE 8

SIMONE's apartment. SIMONE and SARTRE sit, drinking.

SARTRE: Let's have another.

SIMONE: You've already had two.

SARTRE: This is a celebration.

SIMONE: Of what?

SARTRE: Of a masterful public relations coup. You must admit, my darling that young man. . . that. . .

SIMONE: Saviano.

SARTRE: Rick. . . did a fine job on our film. After all a documentary tribute isn't exactly news but a lesbian affair with "the mother of us all" is. Our books are flying out of the stores.

SIMONE: I could have just told her myself.

SARTRE: With all due respect, Castor, you have no nose for intrigue. Revelation by a jealous partner. The stuff of tabloids. The clink of cash registers.

SIMONE: It's demeaning somehow.

SARTRE: This is nothing demeaning about immortality. (*Pause.*) You never did tell me just what happened that night. Did you and Olga make love?

SIMONE: Not exactly.

SARTRE: What do you mean?

SIMONE: We held each other mostly.

SARTRE: Touched?

SIMONE: A bit.

SARTRE: Kissed.

SIMONE: Rather a lot.

SARTRE: Oh, I wish I could have been there.

SIMONE: Watching?

SARTRE: In the middle. How was it?

SIMONE: It made me uncomfortable.

SARTRE: You didn't enjoy it.

SIMONE: I liked it fine but it was. . . somehow too close. . . I lost all sense of boundaries.

SARTRE: Isn't that what love is?

SIMONE: No, with us, it was a fit. . . a click. . . like a key in a lock. With Olga it felt like quicksand.

SARTRE: It sounds wonderful.

SIMONE: In a way it was. But I didn't want wonderful. I wanted us.

SARTRE: (*Gets out writing pad.*) 'I didn't want wonderful. I wanted us.' That's good. I'll add it.

SIMONE: To what?

SARTRE: To my obituary. This is what you'll say. (*Reads.*) 'Last night Sartre died. I was with him at the hospital. I tried to climb under the sheets but the nurse stopped me.' (*Hands it to her.*)

SIMONE: (*Reading, deeply moved but concealing it.*) 'His death separates us, and mine will not bring us together.

SARTRE: Well?

SIMONE: It's fine.

SARTRE: What about, "He took my hand and said 'Thank you, Castor.'"?

SIMONE: A bit sentimental.

SARTRE: We can work on it tomorrow.

SCENE 9

Two high podiums, one on either side of the the stage. One is spot lighted. KATE stands behind lighted podium in evening gown.

KATE: Bon soir, mesdames et messieurs. I am delighted to be here at Cannes and honored that you have chosen 'Shooting Simone' as a finalist in the documentary film category. The film is in two parts, The first, 'The mother of us all' is about the work of Simone de Beauvoir and how she changed the world. It is about the fire in her mind which she passed on to us all, her spiritual daughters and sons. The second half of the film is produced and directed by my partner, Rick Saviano.

RICK: (*Enters behind second podium.*) 'A necessary love' is about Beauvoir's relationship with Jean-Paul Sartre, the man she called her double. They vowed to tell each other the truth. They vowed to tell each other everything. And they did it for fifty years.

KATE: An addendum to the film was shot just last week. We flew to Paris at Madame Beauvoir's request and filmed this short statement.

SIMONE: (*On film looking pale and weary.*) Last night Sartre died. I was with him at the hospital. I tried to climb under the sheets and hold him but the nurse stopped me. 'It's not safe, madame, the gangrene'. So I sat beside him and held his hand. Sometime before dawn, he let go of his life. I must finish 'Conversations With Sartre.' It is the first book of mine he will not see. His death separates us, and mine will not change that. Yet is it not fortunate that we were able to live out our lives for so long together. Not always wonderful. But we didn't want wonderful. We wanted us.

END OF PLAY

THE ICE-FISHING PLAY

by Kevin Kling

Playwright's Biography

Kevin Kling returns to the Humana Festival as playwright/performer with THE ICE-FISHING PLAY. His other Humana Festival credits include the one-act play 21A and LLOYD'S PRAYER. 21A (winner of the Heideman Award for Best Short Play) premiered in ATL's 1985 SHORTS Festival and went on to be performed at the 1986 Humana Festival, Sweden's Scensommar Festival, Australia's Festivals of Sydney and Perth, Scotland's Edinburgh Fringe Theatre Festival, New York's Westside Arts Theatre and Minneapolis' Guthrie Theater. LLOYD'S PRAYER was workshopped at the Sundance Playwrights Lab in 1987 and premiered in ATL's 1988 Humana Festival. Kling, a member of the Playwrights' Center since 1983, has most recently performed his monologue HOME AND AWAY at Seattle Repertory Theatre, New York's Second Stage Theater, Chicago's Goodman Theatre and at Minneapolis' The Jungle Theater. His play THE 7 DWARFS was workshopped at Sundance in 1988 and performed by Minneapolis' Theatre de la Jeune Lune. Mr. Kling is a recipient of a Bush Fellowship, an NEA grant, and a Jerome Book Arts Grant. He is also a member of the performance trio, "Bad Jazz." THE ICE-FISHING PLAY was developed at the Playwrights' Center in Minneapolis under a McKnight Fellowship.

Introduction to the Play

The *Ice-Fishing Play* explores collisions and near-misses of human relationships, and looks closely at how people struggle to relate to each other. The quest to catch "the Big One" isn't just about the biggest fish in the lake. It's about discovering the importance of human-to-human contact, of human-to-nature contact, of human-to-fish contact, before it becomes too late to do anything about it.

Michele Volansky

Characters

Voice of Tim
Voice of Paul

Ron
Shumway
Francis
Irene
Duff
Junior
Young Ron

Directed by Michael Sommers

Cast of Characters (in order of appearance)

Voice of Tim	Fred Major
Voice of Paul	Ray Fry
Ron	Kevin Kling
Shumway	Pepper Stebbins*
Francis	Victor Gonzalez*
Irene	Susan Barnes
Duff	Michael Kevin
Junior	William McNulty
Young Ron	Collin Sherman

* Members of the ATL Apprentice Company

Scenic Designer	Paul Owen
Costume Designer	Toni-Leslie James
Lighting Designer	Karl E. Haas
Sound Designer	Darron L. West
Props Master	Ron Riall
Production Stage Manager	Debra Acquavella
Assistant Stage Manager	Amy Hutchison
Production Dramaturg	Julie Crutcher
Casting arranged by	Marnie Waxman

Setting

Act I The present
Act II Three days later

The action takes place on a lake in northern Minnesota.

THE ICE-FISHING PLAY

The play takes place in an ice fishing house on a lake in northern Minnesota. The ice house is about an eight by twelve foot room. It has a stove, a small table, a cot that folds out of the wall; there are stuffed deer heads and other animals and fish on the walls. There are also trap doors in the floor for fishing. When it's day, light comes from them. When it's night, they are dark. The house is not high tech but very efficient, and comfortable. On the ceiling is a half finished fresco, very good takeoff on the sistine chapel, only God is reeling in a northern Pike with cherubs cheering him on. Ron enters the ice house. He is dressed for severe weather. As he opens the door a storm is heard outside. His face is bright red he has snow on his shoulders. In his hands are a bait bucket and a twelve-pack of beer. He stomps his feet. Sniffles stomp sniffle sniffle stomp sniffle sniffle stomp. Takes the snow off his shoulders, wipes the red off his face. Walks to the stove, turns it on, takes off his snowmobile suit. Goes to the door marked Refrigerator, opens it. We see outside through the refrigerator door and hear the wind blow. Ron throws the beer in. Then he turns on the radio. During Tim and Paul's show Ron flips open one of the trap doors in the floor, takes out his ice auger, drills a hole, cleans the ice out, gets out a tip up - an ice fishing pole that shoots up a red flag when you have a bite - then he takes out a minnow, gives it a kiss, puts it on a hook, and drops it down the hole. Then he opens a beer, lights the stove, and sits down.

PART ONE

TIM: (*Lets out a blood curdling scream.*) AHHHH . . . turn it off, turn it off . . .oWWWW.Turn it off Paul.. Ow. Ow stop it..Jeez well, folks, all I can say is if it hurts like that on me, a human, just think what this baby will do to the fish. This is gonna revolutionize the sport I tell you, Paul.

PAUL: Yeah, I'd say . . .

TIM: Whew, Well that little demonstration was courtesy of Junior Swansen's Fish Barn up there off Highway Ten and Lainont. You know, Paul, I was telling the wife last summer, I says Passion, you've been working what ten twelve hours a day this whole week: what do you say we knock off and go fishing? So naturally I take her down to Junior's for gear and bait. Old Junior is gone you know, he traded in his Bass Master and Graphite rod for a harp oh three years back now, but his boy Junior the third, pound for pound probly the nicest guy you're ever gonna meet, has got that store decked out with all kinds of these gadgets, and sonar, radar, bait all your angling needs. Well, me and the wife we set up by the shore in the shallows off this little weed bed till we seen some nice ones comin in under the boat on the radar screen. And before long Wham, bam, pow they hit like tuna, inside an hour we had our stringer crawlin with a limit of three, four pounders. All keepers!

RON: Yeah, right.

TIM: Another true life adventure brought to you by Junior Swansen's Fish Barn. You've tuned in to the Tim And Paul show the eyes and ears of the North. I'm Tim, that's Paul and together we're Tim and Paul.

PAUL: Yeah.

TIM: We're gonna have some fun today. No, not too much fun, Paul, just the right amount. So lets see what we got for news. Oh Jeez you hate to see this. What's this world coming to, Paul?

PAUL: I don't know.

TIM: Topping our news coverage today. Police are out looking for the suspect in the failed robbery attempt at Jensens Liquor store. Nothing was reported missing in the incident but the proprietor was shot three times in the chest. Police aren't releasing the name of the suspect but is reported in the area and is armed and dangerous. Jeez, what makes a guy do something like that? I don't get it, Paul, I just don't get it. Who would wanna shoot old Wiley Jensen three times in the chest, leaving his wife and two kids to run that liquor store by themselves, then not take anything not even a bottle of something? You could understand it if the guy came up from the city, but from what I gather he's a local boy for crying out loud - went to school with my own kid, was a track star, sung in the choir choir for Pete's sake. Now he's out shooting up the town his father was the Mayor of for twelve years. . .I don't know. The hackles on my neck are up, Paul, it's beyond me. (*Ron kisses his minnow and puts it on the hook.*)

TIM: Seriously folks don't take any chances though with this guy. He is a killer. He has killed. And he's around here somewhere. . .I tell you these stories never get any easier. (*Ron looks up at his gun rack.*)

TIM: Let's move on to the weather, Paul?

PAUL: You bet.

TIM: Well here we got some good news. There's a arctic express comin in from Canada. It should hit any time today. . . Oh jeez look outside Paul it's already coming down like crazy. Wooow look at that. It's been a while since I seen snow like this. Beautiful. Beautiful. Beautiful but deadly folks. Look we're in for a big one here - I mean I can hardly keep from squealing like a child when I look at the weather report, but we gotta keep our heads. Stay inside. Lookee there at Paul. . . Paul's outta the studio now catchin flakes on his tongue. Get in here ya nut. I gotta admit, though. I never seen it snow like this since I was a kid. Now if you're caught somewhere, stay put: if you have car trouble, wait by the vehicle till help arrives. . . Don't eat snow like Paul because, contrary to your thirst, it takes more energy than the liquid it provides. Pretend you're on the ocean and you can't drink the snow. Seriously. And be careful with alcohol - it'll thin your blood. I don't know about that really, but be careful because the dangers of hypothermia are real. Remember the rule "If it hurts you're doing fine, but if you start feeling good and you're happy with yourself and your life seems nice and smooth, seek help immediately - that's hypothermia talking, something is wrong and you don't have much time." Thanks Paul. Paul, our mobile command weather unit, just handed me a bulletin. Wooow, Heavens and earth they're already saying this could be another Blizzard of the Century. That is as opposed to the Blizzard of the Century we had a couple years ago. And Oh boy we've got some school closings coming up. Can you believe it? Paul, remember being a kid, all the family in the kitchen huddled around the radio for the school closings? And now here we are, the bearer of glad tidings. While I read the list here, Paul, why don't you cue up that tape my son borrowed me and let her play, once again reflecting our effort to serve the needs of the entire community, as if to say "Quit moving away you kids, there's a good life here." Well here we go, kids, listen up . . . Academy of the Holy Angel; Ada-Borup, private and parochial; Adrian, private and parochial; Atkin, private and parochial; Albany, private and parochial; Albert Lea, private and parochial; Albrook, private and parochial; Alden-Conger private and parochial; Alexandria, private and parochial; (*If needed*) [Alliance Christian Academy; Annandale, private and parochial; Anoka, private and parochial; Apple Valley, private and parochial; Argyle, private and parochial; Astlby, private and parochial; Atwater-Grove City, private and parochial; Austin, private and parochial; Babbitt, private and parochial; Badger, private and parochial; Bagley, private and parochial; Balaton, private and parochial; Barnsville, private and parochial; Barnum, private and parochial; Battle Lake, private and parochial; Beardsley-Valley, private and parochial; Becket, private and parochial; Belgrade-brooten-Elrosa, private and parochial; Belle Plaine, private and parochial; Bemidji, private and parochial; Benson, private and parochial; Bertha-Hewitt, private and parochial; Bethlaham Academy, Bigfork, private and parochial; Big Lake, private and parochial; Bold, private and parochial; Blackduck, private and parochial; Blaine, private and parochial; Blooming Prairie, private and parochial; Bloomington Jefferson, Bloomington Kennedy, Blue Earth, private and parochial. (*As Tim reads the list of schools, Paul puts on music with a driving beat. Ron's line goes under, the tip up jumps. Ron sets the hook and starts to reel in.*)

RON: Gotcha. I gotcha you bastard, haha. . . come on baby come on. Jeez what a hog. . .come on. . .yeah, that's right. You're in the pan, you son of a bitch, you're on the wall of the rec room. I'm gonna fix it up just for you, you bastard, that's right - put up some nice paneling and a piece of shag carpeting over the oil spot on the concrete and a pool table and a bar and beer lights and a keg meister. . .(*It's quite a fight.*) NO. NO. No. no. no. (*All of a sudden the line is slack: Ron pulls up a license plate. He looks at it. Throws it down. Stands and realizes something. Grabs the plate, looks at it again, and runs outside. He comes back in. His face is red and he has snow on him. He takes off the snow and wipes the red off his face. Takes his truck keys out of his pocket and drops them down the hole. Ron turns off the radio. Ron starts to bait another hook. Lights up on Irene.*)

IRENE: I told you, Ron, din't I?

RON: Don't start on me now, Irene, I'm upset.

IRENE: I says, "Ronnie, you know that ice by the dam is too thin." And I told you I don't want to see you going out there.

RON: I know, Irene.

IRENE: Don't give me "I know." I know what "I know" means and it doesn't mean "I know," it means shut up. Don't tell me to shut up Ronnie Huber - especially when you know I'm right. "I know". I want to see you get outta this one. You're dead this time, Ronnie. I swear. And I'll tell you another thing: if I find out you came out here, you can forget about coming home.

RON: Jeez, Irene. I come out here to be alone, so go on now. This is my place where I can go. I can have my peace of mind and listen to the radio, have a coupla beers if I want, and if something happens - say I sink my truck in the middle of a lake with maybe another Snowstorm of the Century movin' in - I can still look myself right in the eye and not feel like a dumb shit. That's why I got this place.

IRENE: All right. You want to be all alone, Ron?

RON: Yes.

IRENE: You want me to leave?

RON: Yes. I told you.

IRENE: All right, your wish is my command, Ronny. Poof, you're all alone. (*Lights out on Irene. Ron sets another line, turns on the radio.*)

RON: Good.

TIM: Braham, private and parochial; Brainard, private and parochial; Brandon, private and parochial; Breckinridge, private and parochial; Brooklyn Center, private and parochial; Bowerville, private and parochial; Brownton, private and parochial; Buffalo, private and parochial. . . (*There is knocking at the door.*)

VOICE OF FRANCIS: Hello, Hello is anyone home? Hello, I know you're in there, I can hear the radio. (*Ron turns off the radio.*) I heard you turn it off. Hello.

RON: Buonsville, private and parochial; Butterfield-Odin, private and parochial; Byron, private and parochial; Caedonia, private and parochial; Cambridge, private and parochial; and Campbell-Tintah, private and parochial; Canby, private and parochial; Cannon Falls, private and parochial; Carlton, private and parochial; Carlton, private and parochial; Cass Lake-Bena, private and parochial; Cedar Mountain, private and parochial; Centennial, private and parochial; Chandler-Lake Wilson, private and parochial; Chaska, private and parochial; Chatfield, private and parochial; Chief-Bug-O-Nay-Ge-Shig, private and parochial; Chisago Lakes, private and parochial; Chisolm, private and parochial; Chokio-Alberta, private and parochial; Clearbrook, private and parochial; Cleveland private and parochial; Climax, private and parochial; Clinton-Graceville, private and parochial). . . (*More knocking.*)

VOICE OF FRANCIS: Hello. (*Ron answers the door. The wind is blowing.*) Good day, brother.

RON: Hey.

FRANCIS: My name is Brother Francis and this is Brother Shumway. (*There is a loud sneeze.*)

RON: Bless you.

SHUMWAY'S VOICE: Thank you.

FRANCIS: Could we trouble you for a minute of your time?

RON: Well. . .

FRANCIS: Please, brother. It's a matter of the utmost importance Life and death. . .

RON: Well, yeah come on in. (*Brother Francis and Shumway enter. They* have red faces and cotton snow on their shoulders. During the next dialogue Francis takes the towel, wipes off the red and takes off the snow and puts it near Ron's. Shumway wipes his face but the red won't come off likewise the snow is sewn on his jacket and hat.) You boys are out on a pretty raw night. Where are your coats? (Shumway sneezes.)

RON: Bless You.

SHUMWAY: Thank you.

RON: Your buddy there seems to be in rough shape.

FRANCIS: Oh no, he's fine. He originally hails from a much more temperate clime and your winters take a bit of getting used to.

RON: Well, you know we feel when you freeze Paradise it lasts a little longer.

FRANCIS: Yes.

RON: I'd offer you boys something but all I got is beer.

FRANCIS: No, thank you, brother. (Pause. Shumway suppresses a sneeze.)

RON: Well. Whatya know for sure.

FRANCIS: The Grand Climax is at hand.

RON: Oh, You don't say. Now which Grand Climax is that?

FRANCIS: Brother, would you read this passage, please? (Francis shows Ron a passage in a book.)

RON: Happy is he who reads aloud and those who hear the words of prophecy, and who observe the things written in it: for the appointed time is near.

FRANCIS: Revelations 1:3. Can you tell me what that means?

RON: I gotta admit I don't have a clue.

FRANCIS: Because your soul is not at rest, ready to comprehend the words of the Lord.

RON: No, I don't know because when I read aloud I gotta concentrate on the words, not their meaning, so I can't tell you what it means. Now if you were to let me read it to myself I don't have to worry about all that. (Francis holds out the book. Ron reads to himself.) Well apparently you're happy when it's time for your appointment?

FRANCIS: Good. Right. You're happy about an appointment. Now, Brother, do you know who this is? (Shows Ron a photo in a book.)

RON: Yeah..Oh who is that? It's uh. . .it's oh shit. . . it's right on the tip of my tongue.. Godammit who is that.. Christ, I outta know. . .

FRANCIS: It's Moses.

RON: No, that's not it. I know, it's Charlton Heston, that's who it is. Bird Man of Alcatraz.

FRANCIS: No.

SHUMWAY: That's Bert Lancaster.

FRANCIS: It's Moses.

SHUMWAY: I mean who played Bird Man of Alcatraz.

RON: No, Bert Lancaster you're thinking of Barabbass.

SHUMWAY: That's Anthony Quinn.

RON: No, he's Spartacus.

SHUMWAY: Nope, Kirk Douglas.

RON: He's Sampson.

FRANCIS: It's Moses.

SHUMWAY: No, that's Victor Mature.

RON: No, Victor Mature, that's Hercules.

SHUMWAY: Joe Bonamo was Hercules.

RON: I'll bet that was Joe Bonamo. Then the Bird Man of Alcatraz was Bert Lancaster. But this here, that's Charlton Heston.

SHUMWAY: Right.

FRANCIS: IT'S MOSES. Moses, Moses. (*Francis glares at Shumway. Shumway sneezes.*)

RON: Bless you.

SHUMWAY: Thank you.

FRANCIS: All right. Now brother this time look carefully. Do you know who this is?

RON: Oh yeah, that's easy. That would be William Def. . .

FRANCIS: NO!

RON: All right, but I seen that one twice.

FRANCIS: Jesus. It's Jesus. Lord of lords, King of Kings, Jesus. You've heard of Jesus?

RON: Of course I have, but you asked me who he was, not who he was playing.

FRANCIS: This is the real Jesus. Those are characters in movies. Not real. Movies. Particles of light. Written by people, not God. You can't trust anything written by people. Human interpretations and publications are fallible. Like Joseph of old would say. . .

SHUMWAY: Do not interpretations belong to God?

FRANCIS: Shumway, please.

SHUMWAY: Genesis 40:8

FRANCIS: SHUMWAY. And please blow your nose. There are twenty six letters in Our Lord's alphabet not twenty four. (*Back to Ron.*) Brother, I happened to notice you enjoy the fine art of fishing.

RON: Does the Pope. . . I mean is a nun's. . .Yeah.

FRANCIS: Did you know Jesus was also a fisherman?

RON: It only makes sense.

FRANCIS: And do you also recall the parable of the loaves and fishes where Jesus fed five thousand people on two fish. . .

RON: (*To Shumway.*) I'd give fifty bucks to see the Game Warden's face when he heard that one. (*Ron and Shumway crack up.*)

FRANCIS: Shumway, would you please wait for me outside.

SHUMWAY: Outside?

FRANCIS: Yes, until were through here, please.

SHUMWAY: No.

FRANCIS: No?

SHUMWAY: No. I. . . I have a prayer.

FRANCIS: Very well, brother Shumway, you may lead us in a closing prayer.

SHUMWAY: (*Shumway loudly clears his throat.*) God, I don't understand. I know as God you cannot be understood except by yourself. So if we are to understand you we can only do so by being transformed into you, so that we know you as you know yourself. And since we will not know you as you know yourself until we are united into what you are. Faith seems to play a large role in this and. . . I ..I don't know if. . .if I. . . (*Shumway breaks down.*)

FRANCIS: It's all right brother. In his name we pray.

SHUMWAY: Amen.

FRANCIS: Thank you Brother. Now wait for me outside. I'll only be a moment. (*Shumway nods and exits.*) I don't think he's going to make it.

RON: Me neither.

FRANCIS: He doesn't have what it takes.

RON: Like a coat.

FRANCIS: Brother, am I not subjected to the same infirmities? Yet here I stand, strong and solid in my beliefs. Brother Shumway is weak because he doubts. Be that as it may . . . I will not quit his mission and soon he will be welcomed into the arms of Our Lord. I can guarantee Brother Shumway will have solace. Can you say the same? The apocalypse is near; there will be a judgement.

RON: It sounds more to me like the end of your bible is near. Now go on and get out there, you nut, and bring your buddy back in here til the storm is passed. (*Francis starts to exit. Stops.*)

FRANCIS: Brother Ron, I know why you are out here on this pristine lake void of life, this sanctuary.

RON: You do, huh?

FRANCIS: Yes. But you cannot escape, brother, for the devil you fear is not searching without, it lives within. The Lord sayeth "The more we are alone the more we are together." Remember that brother one day death will knock upon that door. . . and on that day, Brother Ron, may your debts be paid in full and peace be yours. Good day. (*Francis exits. The wind is blowing.*)

RON: WERE YOU BORN IN A BARN? (*Ron closes the door.*) That kid's about fifty yards short of a full spool. (*He turns on the radio. It starts up - right where it left off.*)

TIM: Cloquet, private and parochial, Columbia Heights, private and parochial; Comfrey, private and parochial; Cook, private and parochial; Coon Rapids, private and parochial; Cosmos, private and parochial; Cretin-Duram Hall, Cromwell, private and parochial; Crookston, private and parochial; Dassel, Cokato, private and parochial; Dawson-Boyd, private and parochial; (*There is a knock at the door. The radio stops on its own. Ron looks at the door. Tim resumes.*) Deer River, private and parochial; Delano, private and parochial; De La Salle, private and parochial; Detroit Lakes, private and parochial; Dover-Eyota, private and parochial; Duluth, private and parochial; Denfield, private and parochial; Duluth East, (*There is another knock. Silence. Ron looks. Tim continues.*) Eagan, private and parochial; Eagle Valley, private and parochial; East Grand Forks, private and parochial. . . (*Another knock. Radio is silent.*)

RON: Death?

VOICE OF DUFF: No it's me. Duff. (*Duff enters, the wind is blowing outside. He takes the towel and wipes the red off his face and puts his snow on top of Ron's and Francis'.*)

RON: Duffer, hey whatya know for sure.

DUFF: Takes a mighty big dog to weigh a ton.

RON: That's a fact. Cold enough for you?

DUFF: Yeah I'd wear a coat. Any luck?

RON: Yeah, all bad. I lost my truck.

DUFF: I seen the hole. What did you lose.

RON: Chevy ..

DUFF: You bought a Chevy truck? Ronnie! Slummin' it! How could you?

RON: What, I gotta good deal.

DUFF: I'd hope. (*Duff sets up a line, kisses a minnow, hooks it, and drops it.*)

RON: Beer?

DUFF: What?

RON: You want a beer?.

DUFF: No, thanks though. (*Long Pause.*)

RON: It's been a while, Duffer.

DUFF: Twenty seven years.

RON: Twenty seven years. Jeez. (*Long Pause.*)

DUFF: I ran into Irene. She says she's worried about you out here.

RON: She knows I am set up out here by the dam?

DUFF: Yeah, I guess. She told me right where to find you. (*Lights up on Irene reading a paper.*)

RON: Jeez, it's getting so I. . .

IRENE: Can't even finish a sentence without her knowing what I'm gonna say next.

RON: Seriously it. . .

IRENE: Really pisses me off.

RON: It's like. . .

IRENE: I don't have a mind of my own sometimes.

RON: Heavens . . .

IRENE: And earth. . .

RON: I..

IRENE: Tell you.

RON: Why din't she come herself ,.

DUFF: She don't think you want her out here. (*They look at Irene.*)

RON: Jeez.

DUFF: She's something Ronnie.

RON: Sure is.

DUFF: Not from around here.

RON: No, south of here a ways. By the Cities.

DUFF: It's obvious. She's. . .

RON: Special.

DUFF: Yeah, I'm afraid so. Why don't you quit staring at her and go talk to her.

RON: I will.

DUFF: Well go on then.

RON: I am. Irene?

IRENE: Yeah?

RON: Wanna go out with me?

IRENE: No.

RON: Goddamnit.

DUFF: Ahhh, Shake it off Ronnie.

RON: You din't see her up close, Duffer. If it gets any better I don't even wanna know about it. Jeez, she's a keeper, Duff.

DUFF: Then you gotta treat her like one. Present the bait, jig it a little. When you feel her tug set the hook in the boat. One two three. (*Ron approaches Irene.*)

DUFF: Be careful though, she's special.

RON: Irene? Excuse me, Irene Hobbs.

IRENE: Kripes, it's cold.

RON: Well you know how we feel when you freeze Paradise, it. . .

IRENE: They're already calling it the Storm of the Century. What is that, the third Storm of the Century this year?

RON: You wanna go out with me?

IRENE: No, Huber.

RON: Hey, she knows my name.

IRENE: Storm of the Century, Man of the Year, Day of the Dolphin. If it ain't one thing it's another. Bears live here in the winter.

RON: Yeah.

IRENE: How do they do it?

RON: Well you see, they eat pine bark in the fall and the sap plugs em up, then in the spring they eat dogwood and woosh. . . cleans 'em right out.

IRENE: No, how do they keep from going nuts up here.

RON: Oh. I don't know, maybe winter's the time they set aside to figure things out. So do you wanna. . .

IRENE: What is there to figure out?

RON: Well like this conversation. However it turns out - which I already think I know how that'll be - I can go on the lake into my ice house and sit and run through what you said and then what I said until it works out that I said the right things and you go out with me.

IRENE: Then what?

RON: Then I come back and try it again in person.

IRENE: What if I keep saying no?

RON: Then. . . well, then I guess sooner or later you gotta deal with my recessive gene.

IRENE: Your what?

DUFF: Not the recessive gene, Ronny, you're gonna yank the hook right outta her mouth.

RON: Well, for some reason all of us Hubers - me, my ma, my dad, my brother Duffer - we'll be going along like anybody like nothing bothers us when Bam. . .Like a time bomb the recessive gene will kick in, we'll be given to an act of passion.

IRENE: I think you could stand to eat some dogwood, Huber.

RON: No. I'm serious. Ask anyone - it can be ugly. It's there from our past. It's something like Latin or Chippewa, just lurking in our weed bed.

IRENE: But I like you got it. You got a good heater in your truck.

RON: It's a Ford.

IRENE: Then come get me after school, Friday.

DUFF: Hey, Ronnie, lookit this. Ronnie.

RON: What?

DUFF: They found two kids frozen to death already. Not ten feet from a house. I guess they were out doing missionary work and didn't see it coming. There's even a picture - look, the two of 'em frozen solid like a statue, one holding the other up like the Sands of Iwo Jima. Francis and Shumway. Poor guys - what were they thinkin'? Look, no coats or nothing.

RON: That's it - I knew I'd seen them before, they came up to the house on the last Storm of the Century. Francis and Shumway. Geez. (*Ron shudders.*)

DUFF: Schnapps?

RON: What? (*Duff takes out a bottle.*)

DUFF: I got some schnapps. Takes the chill off. Here.

RON: Thanks. (*Takes a swig.*) Agh. Duffer.

DUFF: You like it? Plenty more where that came from.

RON: What is it?

DUFF: Sauerkraut. I made it myself. You can make Schnapps out of anything, I found out. Just take your favorite flavor and add it in. (*Takes a swig.*) Ahhh. Perfect. I knew this guy once would put red pepper in his boots to keep his feet warm. Swore by it. Said if it worked in your mouth, it'll work on your feet. Tried to get me to do it, but no way. I figure he tried it once, word got out, so in order not to look like a dumb shit he did it the rest of his life.

RON: No.

DUFF: Yeah, believe me, people go to great lengths to not look like a dumbshit when it's probly in their best interest to fess up and move on. (*Pause.*)

RON: All right! So I parked my truck by the dam! There, are you happy?

DUFF: I wasn't talking about you, Ronnie.

RON: No?

DUFF: No.

RON: I thought you were.

DUFF: I think you're a genius.

RON: Oh yeah, right? How do you figure that, Duff.

DUFF: Lookit, talent is something you're born with. Godgiven. Can't do nothing about it. Smarts is something you gotta figure out on your own during life, but Genius is something somebody else has to call you. You're a fishing genius.

RON: I hate to break it to you, Duffer, but this lake we're sitting on ain't yielded so much as a crappie in five years now. I'm fishing on a dead lake, so don't make me out to be no genius.

DUFF: You know he's down there. That bastard's below us even as we speak, Ronnie boy, and you know it as well as I do. Why else would you sink your truck?

RON: That wasn't exactly on purpose.

DUFF: Sure, it's obvious, it's you or him and you're lettin him know it the only way you can. I'm proud of you, lad. . .

RON: Duff, what if maybe I'm out here to relax, get away from it all? Did you ever think of that ?

DUFF: Ronnie, people like you don't go fishing for no good reason. Do you think a man becomes a cop because he feels all is right with the world? Hell, no. Psychiatrists, you think they go into all that education because they wanna help other people? Hell, no - they got serious problems they need solving in their own heads. . .. So when you tell me you're out here just fishing, who the hell do you think you're talking to? I'll tell you, it's me, your brother Duffer, and there's a reason Dick Tracy is a cop, somebody is a psychiatrist and you fish. Besides. . .

RON: What..

DUFF: You met the Old Man of the Lake.

RON: Yeah. I was a little kid, though.

DUFF: Don't matter. You were the only one to see him alive, right here on this spot. You hold his legacy.

RON: Naw

DUFF: I was there when you came home, boy were you scared. And when Dad got off work, we were waiting for him at the elevator. Remember? He came out of the mine with his hard hat and the light still on.

RON: He had to squint just to see who we were. . .

DUFF: But that squint - it wasn't just the sunlight he was getting used to, it was the world.

RON: And with me yelling "A monster, a monster. . ."

DUFF: You said there was a monster lived in the lake and that an old man told you. And Dad says "Where'd you see that old man, son."

RON: Out by the beaver dam.

DUFF: The beaver dam!

BOTH: I thought I told you. . .

DUFF: And then Dad beat you good for coming out here.

RON: Yeah. Yeah, he did.

DUFF: If you pull a fish up from the deep - and I'm talking about one of those ocean fish with a lantern on its head . . . if you pull one of those babies up to fast they explode, Ronnie, and you know why. It's because they're used to a different kind of pressure, see, a continuous amount. I always wondered what dad was like in the mine, because the pressure of the outside world was not the one he was suited for. . .

RON: That's a fact: he went downhill fast when the mine closed up.

DUFF: Grampa got the trees, Dad got the iron ore, that left the fish.

RON: You should've stayed, Duffer. You could fish. Hell, you got the perfect build for it.

DUFF: You can teach a man how to bait a hook, but you can't teach him to fish. No. No, I had to get outta here. Face it, Ronnie, you're all we got left, Ronnie.

RON: We. . .

DUFF: And you gotta get that fish for me, you, Dad, Grampa, the Old Man of the Lake. . .All of 'em.

RON: All of who, Duff? (*Pause. Play #2 on Lights in a fat City.*) Duffer?

DUFF: We got on the ice at dawn. Cold. Cold to where your nostrils in your nose stuck shut if you breathed in through it. And quiet. Too quiet. We set up our portable canvas shacks, drilled our holes and hunkered down. Nobody saying a word, nobody making eye contact for fear somebody will know what you're thinking, or, worse yet, you'll be thinking the same thing. . ."Did we bring enough bait? What if we're skunked? Don't say it or you'll jinx everyone." And we know the bastards are down there. But where is the question. How deep, what are they hitting on? I go with a leech on a jig, I'm a live bait man, you know, always was and I ain't ashamed of it. I hear the guy next to me, freckle-faced kid from the cities praying, I think it's to come through this with a nice keeper, but as I listen I hear him ask for the feeling of his toes back. . . Poor kid, but did he ever mention it, or wanna go back and warm up in the truck? Hell, no, that's the caliber of the men I was with, Ronny. Then at O-three-hundred they hit. Oh God, did they hit. For most of us, it was the first tournament we'd ever seen. And here they come, school after school. Hitting one wave after another. All keepers. . . I think, no, no. What am I saying? There were Perch mixed in there, rough fish, little ones we shoulda been throwing back, but it came so fast Bam Pow there was no time to think, no time to identify.. throw em on the ice and re-bait the hook. We'll sort em out later. . ..No time to get the gloves back on, I couldn't feel my fingers, Ronnie. I know it sounds like utter chaos, but in the midst of it all there we were, a bunch of guys who a week ago didn't know each other from Adam, working together like a well oiled machine. . . And then I hear it like a hole in the confusion, a lone voice: "The bait's not gonna last..we're low on leeches and minnows both." Well, there's no time to go to the gas station and get more bait - the school will be long gone by then. Raymon Welsh looks up from the minnow bucket. "That's it," he says, "this is the last one". We draw straws and they give the last minnow to me. . . "you know he's down there Duff, we need the big one or it's no trophy. Come on Duffer" I baited up and lowered him down. . ..

RON: What happened, Duffer?

DUFF: Let's just say we forgot the number one rule, Never enter tournament you know you can't win. But I guarandamntee there's never been another one like it, and I guess there never will be. (*Duff takes a swig of schnapps.*)

RON: God, I wish I woulda been there.

DUFF: No you don't, Ronny.

RON: That wasn't really a fishing story.

DUFF: No, but I thought I'd put it in a way you could grasp.

RON: I miss you, Duff.

DUFF: Don't say that.

RON: I do, though.

DUFF: Yeah but you don't say it, jeez, Ronnie. Besides I'll be back.

RON: You said that last time.

DUFF: And here I am. (*Duff heads for the door.*) I'll tell Irene you're fine.

RON: Thanks.

DUFF: Later.

RON: Later. (*Duff exits. Lights up on Irene reading the paper. Ron doesn't notice her. Irene looks at Ron. He still doesn't notice. The radio starts*)

TIM: Irene Hobbs, private and parochial; Irene Hobbs, private and parochial; Irene Hobbs, private and parochial; Irene Hobbs, private and parochial; Irene Hobbs, private and parochial . . . (*Ron notices Irene.*)

RON: Irene? Irene.

IRENE: Hmmm.

RON: What ya reading?

IRENE: (*Straight faced*) The funnies.

RON: The funnies?

IRENE: Well, first I got in the habit of it because they sit there just above the horoscopes. And with you out fishing on the lake all the time, I'd get out the paper and read the horoscopes to see how your day is out there. What you're thinking and what you're doing, who you're having an affair with. . .

RON: I'm fishing. . .

IRENE: And then one day I seen an ad for this art colony that says I might already have talent. And they have this test where I can draw the famous head of Tippy the Turtle, Pete the Pirate, Carl the Carp or a split level condominium. So I go with the carp for luck and two weeks later I get back a letter, and lo and behold, Ronnie, I've got talent.

RON: I knew that. You coulda saved yourself a stamp.

IRENE: Yeah, but when it comes to art you like to hear it from a professional.

RON: I spose.

IRENE: Anyhow, since I have proven talent it turns out I am privy to a list of courses to take, like Secret Expert Tips of the Masters; Exploring New Art Methods; From Doodles to Dollars. And this whole other world opened up to me, Ronnie, I gotta tell you this excitement started welling up that I haven't had since I was in high school and did something on my own. You know, completely on my own. And look, here they give a list of graduates from the program. . .Some of these people are really famous.. like this guy here. He's a graduate of the art colony. That mountain looks real enough to climb, huh?

RON: I wonder where that mountain is.

IRENE: By the colony I guess. And that's not all. Look, here's a guy who does internal organs for medical journals, and heres somebody who draws fashion illustrations and another one who drew Mickey Mouse for forty-five years and this guy here is in the funnies every day. See, here he is in today's. So, anyhow, I was just lookin' at the funnies to see if maybe that's my particular area of expertise.

RON: I don't wanna pop your bubble Irene, but those things are scams. They just want your twenty bucks.

IRENE: Fifty.

RON: Fifty, that can't be right. Fifty bucks for art school?

IRENE: Ronnie, it's got a reputation, and besides, I figure if I even sell three or four paintings I'll make that back easy.

RON: Well alls I got to say is if you want to take up art take up a real art.

IRENE: Like what

RON: Christ Irene, like taxidermy.

IRENE: Taxidermy!

RON: Don't laugh, it's an ancient art that honors the hunt.

IRENE: I don't want to kill for my art Ron.

RON: I'll kill em. I'd be happy to if that will give you something to do. Look we'll set you up in the basement. I'll put up some nice paneling put a piece of shag carpet over the oil stain. . . besides if you get good we can set it up as a bonus for the people who hunt and fish out of the resort. Bring in some extra cash..

IRENE: I'm not sure about this one.

RON: Don't sell it short, Irene, vanity is a powerful thing. There was a guy come up here from the cities. Boat, motor, all brand new equipment. Says he sold make-up during the war, made a fortune. Told me that during good times or bad people want to look good, in fact often times they'll go without food before make up.

IRENE: I can see that.

RON: Well, a nice walleye over the mantel is to a guy what lipstick and eye shade is to a woman, you know, in that it revolves around the vainess of a man's masculinity.

IRENE: All right, so?

RON: So alls I'm saying is why mess around with the funny papers when you can have the real Carl the Carp. . .

IRENE: You'd have my ass if I put a carp on the wall.

RON: All right then, Nathan the Northern, William the Walleye, Mark the Muskie. Huh? I'll even sweeten the pot and throw you a big party for your first deer head.

IRENE: I don't want a deer head party. Lookit, Ronnie: I sit around here day after day while you're at least outside fishing. . .

RON: I don't know what to tell you, Irene. You should get out more if you want, or visit with Cookie Crumbfelter.

IRENE: Ron, I gotta tell you, I ain't all that fond of Cookie. We got different interests. Alls she cares about is . . . she says "Isn't this dress fun?" Fun? I was brought up thinking fun revolved around an activity but I go along with her and I says "That's a nice one, Cookie. It looks really fun, a blast." "Oh," she lets out a big sigh, "I don't know." Like it's gonna be a problem somewhere down the line. I swear, Ronnie, I don't think that woman is happy unless she's depressed. Or she says, "I seen a movie." Alright Cookie, what movie.. well she don't remember but it was about a man who was. . . oh, what's that actor's name, oh you know who I mean, he has a father, who had a friend, that lived in. . . oh what's that town's name.. oh who was he, he had the hair. . .

RON: That would be Joe Banamo in Hercules.

IRENE: How did you know that?

RON: It's obvious.

IRENE: Well then you should talk to Cookie. Don't make me.

RON: Alright Irene, geez. Join the damn art colony I just think it's a rip-off, and that's my honest opinion.

IRENE: BUT THAT DON'T MATTER. (*Pause*) When I was in high school I had this feeling. It was this sensation where I could step outside myself and look at how I fit in the world. And it didn't revolve around another human. It was pure, like a primary color like yellow. It was just me in the world. And then I met you and you sort of set up house in that feeling, but I didn't mind - that's right where I wanted you. Then we had Darlene and naturally it fell to me to do most of the raising, but I didn't mind that either because believe me, I love her with all my heart.

RON: God, she was a pretty baby.

IRENE: She looked like a boy, Ron, I had to scotch tape bows to her head so people dint call her little fella. Anyhow, over time I forgot I was getting older, and now in the winter Darlene's in school, the resort's all closed up, and you're out on the lake, and what do I do, Ron? I got so many colors mixed in there I don't know how to get yellow back.

RON: I don't know what to tell you, Irene.

IRENE: Well, what about you.

RON: What?

IRENE: Don't you want something Ron,

RON: Like what?

IRENE: Don't you have dreams?

RON: Sure I do. . .like what, though?

IRENE: Well, what would you wish different for your life?

RON: Let's see, I got this place, the resort keeps us above water, I gotta enuff help to where I can fish especially in the winter. The bar keeps us eating and I've only had two fights in there: I been in both of 'em. I gotta beautiful wife and daughter who sort of looks like me, but not enough to make me worry about her future.

IRENE: But that's what you already got.

RON: Yeah? I'm happy, Irene.

IRENE: Isn't there something you want to do or be or go?

RON: Yeah I guess I'd like to go somewhere, but where? I'm not missing anything by living out here, and even if I am, I don't know what it would be. I'm sorry, but I'm happy, Irene.

IRENE: What do you want? Then what is it that bothers you, huh? What, Ronnie. There must be something I do. What is it?

RON: Nothing, now don't try to get me upset just because you know how.

IRENE: Ronnie, what is it?

RON: There's nothing.

IRENE: What? Then what scares you?

RON: Irene, I'd just be making something up.

IRENE: What scares you then? What, Ronnie.

RON: Nothing.

IRENE: What, Ronnie? What, What . . ..

RON: One thing?

RON: Yeah. What. . .

RON: I'm afraid. . . let's see. . . I'm afraid to be alone.

IRENE: That's not it.

RON: It is.

IRENE: That can't be it. You're alone all winter, I hardly ever see you.

RON: That's not the same "alone." I always know where you are. I always know I can find you if I need to. So I'm not alone. Look, in the winter, how long am I on the ice in one stretch?

IRENE: You come in every four days. I could set a clock by it.

RON: That's how long I can last, four days, and then I gotta get in and see you and make sure you're here.

IRENE: Jeez, Ronnie, of course I'm here, where else would I be?

RON: I'm not saying it's realistic, I'm just saying it's a fear I got. When Duffer was serving overseas he wrote me this one time. He said when he'd go on leave, for R and R, they'd get to go into Hong Kong sometimes, in China. He said there's a custom there that if a woman dies before she's married her folks would take some of her things, her most prized possessions, and put 'em in a box, then leave the box by the side of the road. If you were a gentleman and unattached and you came upon one of these boxes, you had the option of picking it up and going to a church and marry the young woman. Your souls are then joined in heaven, and from then on you are never alone. He said sometimes he felt like taking one of those boxes and getting married just in case something happened to him, but he never did. He was killed shortly after I got that letter, and with the funeral and grieving and all it slipped my mind what he'd written. I found that letter a couple of years ago, and I took Duffer's chainsaw, his lucky hat . . . put 'em in a box left em off Highway 7. A week later I drove by, and lo and behold it was gone.

IRENE: That was a nice thing you did for your brother

RON: Sometimes I wonder though, if some old guy came by and seen it - "hey free chainsaw" - and little does he know now he's married off to Duffer.

IRENE: It don't matter.

RON: That's what I thought. Without sounding too liberal minded I figured a soul was a soul, and if Duff is pissed off he'll let me know soon enough. And on the flip side, it'd serve the old geezer right for taking a chainsaw that doesn't belong to him.

IRENE: Did you ever get the feeling Duff didn't like me?

RON: Why do you say that?

IRENE: Well, when we got married, what was his gift? A year's supply of bait at Junior's fish barn. And then he goes and writes "Just Married" on the car with bumper stickers that say "I'd rather be fishing."

RON: Oh, he was just joking, Irene, that was his way.

IRENE: Maybe to the naked eye, but there was always something with us.

RON: I wouldn't lose any sleep over it. (*She comes into Ron's ice house.*)

IRENE: Well, don't you worry, Ronnie Huber, you will never be alone.

Ever. That I can promise with all my heart.

RON: I think you should take that art colony.

IRENE: I didn't mean to go off on Cookie like that.

RON: I know, I thought you were going to make a comment on her lips, though.

IRENE: Why no, Ron, I wasn't gonna say anything about her lips.

RON: Oh.

IRENE: What about em?

RON: They always amazed me they're so. . . thin, looked like rubber bands to me. In fact, when we were little I used to pretend me and her were married and I would take a rubber band and practice makin out.

IRENE: Did you like it?

RON: No.

IRENE: Good. I'll tell you what, Mr. Huber, if you foot the bill for one week at the art colony. . .I'll give a whirl at stuffing the next Nathan or William or Mark you pull out of the lake. Deal?

RON: Deal. On one condition. No more talk of art tonight, all right, Irene?

IRENE: All right, Ronnie, no more art.

TIM: Ellsworth, private and parochial; Ely, private and parochial; Esko, private and parochial; Eveleth, private and parochial; Fairmont, private and parochial; Fairbault, private and parochial; Farmington, private and parochial; Fergus Falls, private and parochial; Fertile-Beltrami, private and parochial; Fisher, private and parochial; Floodwood, private and parochial; Foley, private and parochial; Fon Du Lac Ojibway, Forest lake, private and parochial; Fosston, private and parochial. . . (*Blackout. End of Part One.*)

PART TWO

Back in the ice house. Ron is asleep on the cot. The deer head has a party hat on and a cigarette in its mouth. The radio is playing a polka. Ron is sleeping with a smile on his face, but as the commercial progresses into tropical themes it turns into a nightmare.

TIM: (*There is the sound of a severe winter storm.*) Sound familiar? (*The sound of a car that won't start.*) Winter got you down? (*Tropical Hawaiian music plays.*) Hey, then give a call over to Backwoods Excursions for all your traveling needs. . .Hawaii; the Bahamas; Porta

Viarta; beautiful beaches; tropical foods; shopping; exotic floorshows; palm trees; the sun; friendly natives; fruit; swimming; scuba diving; snorkling; sightseeing; volleyball; horseback riding; surfing; hiking; dune buggies; coconut sculpture; (*Duff enters quickly so as not to make too much noise with the wind outside. He turns off the radio, Ron is in the throes of a nightmare saying "No, No" and repeating themes like "volleyball", and "snorkling." Duff takes a fish - a large, mounted Northern Pike - off the wall, pulls up Ron's line, puts the fish on the hook and lowers it down. Then he flips the tip up so the red flag is up.*)

DUFF: Ronnie, Hey wake up in there, wake up. . . your bobber's under. . . you gotta fish. . . (*Ron gets up, he is drowsy. He goes to the line as if on automatic pilot.*)

RON: What?

DUFF: You got a fish. Ronnie, set the hook. (*Ron sets the hook.*)

DUFF: You got him.

RON: I got him. Come on, you bastard, you're on the wall now. In the room with the paneling, and carpet, Woooo, He's a heavy one.

DUFF: Play him, Ronnie.

RON: Like a log, not much of a fighter.

DUFF: Don't give him slack.

RON: I know.

DUFF: You got him, that's for sure. They'll get sluggish in the winter.

RON: Yeah, that they will. Come on baby, come on, come on. . .(*Ron pulls up the mounted fish.*)

DUFF: Not a lot of meat on him, but he'll look nice on the wall. Here's a spot.

RON: Real funny, Duff.

DUFF: You shouldn't have been sleeping anyhow. If that was the real hog you woulda lost him.

RON: God, I had a nightmare. Volleyball.

DUFF: Hey, I got a surprise for you. (*Duff goes to the window and peeks out.*) Shhhhhhh. Look.

RON: Hey it's Junior! What the hell is he doing?

DUFF: Standing on his head

RON: Why? He looks stupid.

DUFF: I convinced him it would be funny if you opened the door and there he was standing on his head in the middle of the Storm of the Century.

RON: It does look pretty funny! (*Ron goes to open the door.*)

DUFF: Wait, let's see how long he can hold it.

RON: I never figured Junior to be so nimble. (*They observe Junior out* *the window. Long Pause.*) Woops.

DUFF: There he goes. Quick. He's gonna be madder than a bear with a sore ass. (*They go to the door, Duff swings it open.*) SURPRISE, JUNIOR. What you laying there for? Get in here, you doof. (*Junior enters. He is covered with snow and has a red face. He takes off the snow and wipes the red off his face. Ron and Duff hide behind the fridge.*)

DUFF AND RON: Surprise!

DUFF: Junior, is that a tube of Chapstick in your pocket or are you just happy to see me? Junior, I thought you were gonna be standing on your head.

JUNIOR: Thanks for holding out so long, Duff, while I'm out there freezing my ass off. You aren't as smart as you think either. I seen your little eye peeking out the window behind the curtain. Hey, Ronnie, news flash, your brother's an asshole.

RON: Tell me about it. (*He reaches out his hand.*) Put 'er in the vice, Junior. (*Junior shakes it.*)

JUNIOR: Here's the five I owe ya. Got a beer for me?

RON: There's a square in the fridge.

DUFF: It's nine in the morning, Junior.

JUNIOR: So? Run with the dogs or piss with the pups, Duffer.

RON: Grab two.

DUFF: Three. (*Junior goes to the fridge.*)

RON: How's the wife, Junior?

JUNIOR: Cookie? Fine. Irene?

RON: Fine.

JUNIOR: Think fast. (*Junior throws the can to Duff.*)

JUNIOR: She still doing taxidermy?

RON: Not much call for it anymore. So she's been painting. Always liked painting better, anyhow. She's good, too, boy - real good like a photograph.

JUNIOR: Let me know if she tackles another deer head. I swear, that deer head party was the best party of the year. (*Junior and Duff and Ron open up their beers and hold them high.*)

RON: Cheers.

DUFF: To your health.

JUNIOR: Pork chop in every can. (*They all take a swig*)

JUNIOR: Jeez, Pabst, Ronnie - give a skunk a job.

RON: You're welcome, Junior. (*Junior starts doing a strange dance.*)

DUFF: What are you doing, Junior?

JUNIOR: I got red pepper down my leg from standing on my head. So whatya know for sure?

RON: What's it look like, I'm sitting around practicing for when I get old?

JUNIOR: No luck, huh?

RON: Nope.

JUNIOR: What ya using?

RON: Jig and a shinner minnow.

JUNIOR: You guys and your live bait. I'm telling you, the fish are way ahead of you: they don't fall for live bait anymore.

DUFF: Junior, tell me: what do fish eat when we're not fishing?

JUNIOR: That's not my point. Fish are wiser now. They actually know when you're fishing, so live bait is basically ineffective. You gotta give 'em something they can't resist, that goes beyond their common sense. Something with a battery in it.

DUFF: Let me guess. Something that goes for fifteen dollars at Junior's Rip-off Barn.

JUNIOR: Have your fun, but you can't argue with genetics.

DUFF: You're so educated you're stupid.

JUNIOR: Look, it's simple evolution. All the fish that are moronic enough to get caught are nailed at two or three pounds. . . but the smart ones, the ones that live to spawn, create the future generations. . . Hey, they don't even know they're smart, it just gets passed on because they lived.

DUFF: You make me thankful I'm not a reader.

JUNIOR: Look. Here's an extreme case scenario. Lets say there's a fish that, totally by accident, when it is subjected to oxygen makes a noise that sounds like, "release me and I'll grant you three wishes." I'll bet my beer can collection that over an amount of time there's gonna be a lot of those fish, let me tell you. And they can't even give the three wishes. Hell, they don't even know what they said, but the fact they said it ensures the survival of their race. Here's a real example. Where are all the muskies? I'll tell you where. Gone. Why? Stupid.

DUFF: Junior, you're like Lake MiLacs - you're not very deep and you go on forever.

RON: What about pollution?

JUNIOR: There are fish they could introduce. . . they eat pollution, they love it like candy, can't get enough of it. Science has known this for years, but some bleeding heart purist somewhere got to em first. I'll tell you, though, any year now these lakes could be teaming again.

DUFF: You've been running a bait store too long.

JUNIOR: And I'm gonna keep runnin it. It's the same with humans: you have to evolve or die out, but I'm not talking physically now, I'm talking fiscally.

RON: Which holds by your same law of the jungle theory.

JUNIOR: Is a pig's butt pork? I was over at Wiley Jensens liquor store the other day and he's got a screen door leaning up against a stack of twelve packs. Next day a pile of screen doors. I ask, "What's going on, Wiley? Where'd you get all the screen doors?" He says they're from the people livin' in government housing. He's giving a twelve pack for every screen door and word got out: hell, he's gonna make a bundle sellin off come summer.

RON: I don't like that.

JUNIOR: Why? It's government housing, they got the doors for free.

DUFF: He shouldn't be making deals like that. He's gonna get his one day, that guy, somebody's gonna finally snap and take him out, mark my words.

JUNIOR: He's just making a living. Times are hard.

RON: Not that hard. Beside, the last time times were hard Wiley put on an addition on the store.

JUNIOR: Whereas you buy a resort and the fish stop biting, whatya got? You screwed Ronny. No offense, but I think you're just jealous.

DUFF: What about the Fish Barn?

JUNIOR: The Fish Barn will always be there because we diversify. We keep ahead of the times give people what they want before they know they want it, and that's why my kid Junior the 3rd is gonna be fine too. Genetics. He's like the son of that fish that survived even though it didn't know what it said. And while you Huber boys are mulling over that one, I'll be right back. (*Junior heads for the door marked with the sticker for unisex restroom.*)

DUFF: Wait up.

JUNIOR: What?

DUFF: I gotta go too. Sword fight.

JUNIOR: Then you go on. I'll be next. I was down in the cities one time with my old man. He was down there on some union business for the mine, so he took me along and when he was done we went to a ball game down at Miller's field. I'm in the men's room standing at the trough and I'm just starting to go when I look up and this old guy is staring at me. And he's smiling - just his lips no teeth - and for some reason I couldn't go and ever since I can't go in front of another human. It's a fact, and sometimes if I think somebody can hear me I have to make up mental games to get going.

RON: Like what?

JUNIOR: I have to pretend I enjoy it. Like I'll say over and over "I like to go in front of men. I like to go in front of men." Like a chant.

RON: And that works?

JUNIOR: Most of the time.

DUFF: I don't believe it.

JUNIOR: It's true.

DUFF: I believe it's true. I don't believe you told us.

JUNIOR: Hey, I got nothing to hide. (*He exits*)

RON: I think sometimes it's best to have a few things to hide.

DUFF: Yeah, me too. (*Pause*)

JUNIOR'S VOICE: Hey, cut it out.

DUFF: What.

JUNIOR'S VOICE: I know you're listenin' in there.

DUFF: Don't forget to dot the "i", Junior.

JUNIOR'S VOICE: Talk about something.

RON: Like what?

JUNIOR'S VOICE: I don't know: pretend I'm not out here. Hurry up. I gotta go.

DUFF: That Junior, what a dumb shit.

RON: I tell you, if stupid had weight he'd 've been through the ice a long time ago.

JUNIOR'S VOICE: No, something else.

DUFF: I like to go in front of Duff and Ron.

RON AND DUFF: I like to go in front of Duff and Ron.

JUNIOR'S VOICE: Come on.

DUFF: All right, Junior. (*Quieter.*)

DUFF: What is it with Junior.

RON: What?

DUFF: He seems his old abrasive self, but then he goes and admits something like this I get worried.

RON: Lost his dog.

DUFF: Ran off?

RON: Died.

DUFF: That big black lab? Happy, stupid old lab?

RON: It made the mistake of saving Junior's life . . . .. started barking the night the original Fish Barn burnt down. Junior got up to yell at it like he did every night and then saw the flames. He swore the dog warned him and then Junior was so grateful he set the thing up in the lap of luxury. I mean that dog had its own place setting at the dinner table, had its own bunk beds, a bean bag chair in front of the T.V. The poor thing started getting fat. I swear the only exercise it got was when it was dreaming. He stopped barking, started getting tumors like a human. I tell you the thing forgot it was a dog . . . .. and I told him, I says "Junior, you gotta let Tuffy be a dog. Get him outside." So he took it fishing, bought it gear and a sweater and even drilled it a hole. In under ten minutes Tuffy's bobber went under and the dog went in the hole right after it. Junior grabbed for him but just got the sweater.

DUFF: Tragic.

RON: Junior swears he heard the dog come up in another ice house and the people could tell quality and stole it, but I personally think Tuffy committed suicide. Anyhow, it's still a sore spot between me and Junior because I talked him into taking Tuffy fishing. (*Junior enters.*)

DUFF: All finished?

JUNIOR: Yep. (*Pause. They stare at Junior.*)

JUNIOR: What? Who needs a cold one?

RON: I do.

DUFF: I do.

JUNIOR: What are you two dumbshits fishing in a dead lake for anyhow? (*Junior goes to the refrigerator and gets three beers.*)

DUFF: It ain't a dead lake, Junior, there's still one left down there, a monster.

JUNIOR: Yeah, right.

DUFF: The one that got the Old Man.

JUNIOR: The Old Man, that's just a legend.

DUFF: Ronnie seen the Old Man on his last night alive right here on this spot.

JUNIOR: That so Ronnie?

RON: Yeah, I was little, though. I don't remember so good.

DUFF: Listen up Junior: this lake was formed by the glaciers and is by far the deepest in these parts, and combined with the beaver dam there are depths to this pool that can't even be hit with your sonar. There's an Indian legend that a creature lives in the center of this pit. A ravenous beast, eyes bulging with grief, a serpent's body, and a luminous beacon suspended from its forehead. Now, some demons can be bought off with prayers and gifts, but this one requires blood.

JUNIOR: Jeez.

DUFF: It's said the Old Man was half Indian, half French, big of bone, his face innocent in feature and expression. Poison Roy the Fisher King. Raised by the milk of wild beasts yet refusing to build with poplar wood because that was the tree they used to crucify Jesus, he was pure in all ways, in fact he had no scent, couldn't be tracked. Poison Roy, the last one to fish here by the dam, swore he would land this fish, and this is what Ronnie walked into that night.

JUNIOR: You don't have a choice, Ron. You hold his legacy.

RON: Yeah.

JUNIOR: Don't matter, Ronnie, you inherited the hog.

DUFF: He knows it. Ronnie?

RON: Why do you think I sunk my truck?

JUNIOR: Brilliant.

DUFF: All right.

JUNIOR: Hey, if anybody can bring that fish in, its the combination of these three great minds.

DUFF: I swear, Junior, you're an embarrassment to the man you think you are.

JUNIOR: Don't think you're so high and mighty, Huber. You get in your bass boat one leg at a time, just like the rest of us. I got smarts. I know every plug that's been invented. Now, I'll admit you got a talent to get people, fish, I don't care what, to do things they'd never dream of doing, and Ronnie. . .

DUFF: Is the fishing genius.

JUNIOR: If that bastard's down there we'll get him

DUFF: He's down there all right and Ronnie's gonna haul him in.

JUNIOR: Well If he hasn't bit a minnow and jig all these years, he's not gonna start now.

RON: Junior's right. (*Junior opens Ron's tackle box.*)

JUNIOR: Now for the perfect bait. Lemme see. What all you got here? Got a White Lightning Swedish - Pimple Mud Puppy Lady Luck Go for the Gold Touchdown Medusas Head Kiss Me I'm Irish Win Place or Show Chug-A-Lug Hula Princess Afterlife in the Weed Bed.

DUFF: What's this one, Junior?

JUNIOR: I'll be, that's an old Enticer. Jeez I haven't seen one of those in a while. A classic.

RON: Oh that was a gift from Irene when we first started going out. I'll never forget, I laughed at it and hurt her feelings so I hung on to it so she could see in my tackle box. I never used it. (*Junior and Duff look.*)

DUFF: That's the ticket.

RON: Naw, you guys.

JUNIOR: Look, over the years that fish has had a shot at everything in this box ten times over, but I guarandamntee one thing, it's never met up with an Enticer.

DUFF: Put a minnow on it.

JUNIOR: That's sacrilege. Live bait on the enticer? Look, you already got yer battery powered wiggle action. We'll spray on a little "scent away" human smell repellent, (*Junior sprays some on.*) don't get this stuff near your beer or you'll taste fish till you can get your teeth brushed. There, we're all set,

DUFF: Put a minnow on it

JUNIOR: A minnow, What the hell for?

DUFF: Look, I say we don't take any chances. (*Kisses the minnow.*)

JUNIOR: You kissed the minnow. Are you superstitious or what?

DUFF: No, but I don't wanna jinx it this late in the game. Its common sense.

JUNIOR: But you put the human smell on it. (*Junior sprays the minnow with "scent away" human smell repellent.*)

JUNIOR: There. All set.

RON: Looks good, Junior.

DUFF: No. Wait. We gotta face facts. There's a chance the lad is already freezing to death.

RON: I never felt better.

DUFF: Now you do but we need to give you an edge in case you get woozy. . .I got it. We'll make an adaption on this tip up. (*Duff gets down the shotgun and cocks the gun.*) We jerryrig it so when the hog bites it pulls the trigger, Bam, the gun goes off and wakes you from your slumber. . . You might miss a tip up flag, but if you got any consciousness you won't miss a gun going off. All right, Ronnie, I loaded in two shell so if the first one don't wake you up you got one more, then muster whatever strength you got left and haul him in. (*In the mean time Junior has added more hooks to the Enticer.*)

RON: What're you putting on there, Junior?

JUNIOR: Were gonna nail this bastard, I got everything on here but the kitchen sink.

RON: Isn't that gonna tear him up?

DUFF: Nope, he won't feel a thing.

JUNIOR: He's right - fish don't feel like people. Most animals don't. (*Duff is rigging the shotgun to the tip up.*) Fish don't feel like we do. Cut a fish in two it'll just swim along no pain on its face. They're not like. . . A monkey - they're smart. I seen this one show where this scientist taught a monkey how to smoke. Some of the apes are almost smart as a human, and there was this dolphin.

RON: Taught him to smoke?

JUNIOR: No. What good is smoking gonna do a dolphin? No they taught them a language, like radar, but a dolphin is not a fish, mind you. A mammal. A fish don't feel like us. Only monkeys and dolphins and some strains of dogs. A good dog not, yappy ones . . . ...

RON: Chickens?

JUNIOR: No. We eat chickens. Chickens.

DUFF: Now, all right we're all set. When he takes it you're gonna know it. . .Be sure to keep your head clear of the barrel. Keep an eye peeled, I'll be right back. (*Duff exits out the restroom door. Knock on the front door.*)

RON: Yeah?

IRENE'S VOICE: Ronnie? (*Irene enters. She is covered with snow and has a red face. She takes off the snow and wipes the red off.*)

RON: Irene, what are you doing out here?

IRENE: I did it Ronnie, I sold a painting.

RON: Hey, did you here that, Junior? Irene sold a painting. I told you she was good.

JUNIOR: Nicely done, Irene.

RON: Which one?

IRENE: The wooducks.

RON: Oh yeah, that's a good one.

IRENE: Oh Ronnie, I'm so excited.

RON: Me too. We gotta celebrate. Get out a coupla cold ones Junior. My wife just sold a painting. What'd you get for it honey?

IRENE: 20,000 dollars.

RON: What?

IRENE: 20,000 dollars!!!! Its gonna be made into a stamp.

JUNIOR: A duck stamp? you gotta duck stamp?

IRENE: And if it goes national I'll make five times that.

JUNIOR: You're famous Irene.

IRENE: Let's all go to Red Lobster, my treat.

JUNIOR: YOOOO, Red Lobster.

RON: 20,000 dollars.

IRENE: I owe it all to you, Ronnie. First you shot them ducks. And then you got me to stuff em and I gotta admit I hated every minute of it. But by the time I started painting em, I don't mean to brag or nothing, but there wasn't much about a duck I din't know, inside or out.

JUNIOR: Irene, if you want I'll set you up a corner in the bait store, a gallery. I can even maybe get you a guest spot painting on. . .

IRENE: I don't know about TV, Junior.

JUNIOR: I was gonna say the radio but painting on TV might even be better.

RON: 20,000 dollars. . .

IRENE: Ron, I was so worried with the resort going under. I could see the toll it was takin on you, but now we can afford to get out from under it, move into town if we want.

RON: Yeah. . .

DUFF: I warned you Ron.

IRENE: This is just the beginning, too. once you get a stamp you can sell em as fast as you can paint em.

JUNIOR: That's a fact. You'll never have to work again, Ronnie.

DUFF: I told you she was special but you didn't listen.

RON: What are you saying Duff? (*There's pounding on the door*)

VOICE OF FRANCIS: Brother Ron, Brother Ron!

RON: Yeah, come on in fellas. (*Francis and Shumway enter*)

FRANCIS: Thank God you're still here. The end of the world is not at hand.

JUNIOR: Hey, I think you got something here.

FRANCIS: The judgement day is a long way off.

RON: How 'bout that? Perfect timing.

SHUMWAY: Brother Ron, I can breathe through my nose. . .

FRANCIS: It's a miracle.

SHUMWAY: Hosannah, Hosannah, heavenly host, hosannah

RON: That's hypothermia breathing for you kid.

SHUMWAY: It feels wonderful. Naughty Nancy, nature's nymph nimbly nestles Ned.

FRANCIS: A miracle.

JUNIOR: Ronnie, your bobbers going under.

RON: Alright.

SHUMWAY: Mighty Maurice, man of men, meticulously masturbates mice.

FRANCIS: Saint Shumway.

RON: Now what are you doing Irene?

IRENE: Ron, I'm painting the ceiling like the Sistine Chapel only Adam is gonna be a walleye and God's finger is a Johnson cast master.

JUNIOR: Ron, your bobber.

DUFF: I warned you, Ronnie.

RON: What?

DUFF: You two are set for life

RON: You're right there, Duffer yooooo.

DUFF: Like Junior's dog.

RON: Duff, Irene's not gonna jump in no lake without her sweater.

DUFF: Not Irene - I'm talking about you, Ron. I told you she was special, remember? But you didn't listen. ..

FRANCIS: We're saved.

DUFF: You're sunk. Next thing you know. . .

IRENE: She'll be finishing your sentences for you.

RON: Stop it Duff. This..

IRENE: Ain't you talking, Ron. For one thing I don't look like this.

RON AND IRENE: I haven't for years.

RON: It's how I remember you.

IRENE: And your brother, look at him.

BOTH: He died when he was twenty five.

RON: He's my older brother, always will be.

DUFF: You gotta get him, Ronnie, for all of us.

RON: Duffer.

JUNIOR: Ron, your bobber: set the hook.

IRENE: Ron, we can move into town if we want.

RON: No, Irene I don't want that in here.

IRENE: But I'm over half done.

RON: No. Irene this is my place where I can go and be alone and think and if I want to remember you like this, I can, and my brother, I can, and Junior and even these two nuts, I can. . .

IRENE: You want to be alone?

RON: Yes.

IRENE: If I leave, Ron, I'm not coming back, here.

RON: Good. Go.

IRENE: But.

RON: I don't want your goddamn painting, none of it.

CRACK

JUNIOR: Hey Ron.

RON: Hey, Junior, pull up a chair.

JUNIOR: Naw thanks: once I set my ass down I never wanna get up, and Cookie's waiting for me. I just stopped out to see how you're doing.

RON: Fine.

JUNIOR: Sorry to hear about Irene.

RON: Yeah, thanks.

JUNIOR: She was something, boy.

RON: Yeah, she was.

JUNIOR:' You know, me and Cookie are trying out a new restaurant in town if you wanna go.

RON: No, thanks. though.

JUNIOR: We've been doing that. Went to one the other day "Peace Meal" it's called. I look on the menu, where's the four basic meat groups? And then you gotta ask for white bread. I got a plate of one of the terrible T's. I can't remember - tofu, tamari, tahini, tabouli, something. Washed it down with the swallows of cappacino and look, I got nothing against vegetarians, some of my favorite foodstuffs are vegetarians, but I left hungrier than when I walked in, cut my mouth on my coffee cup that had a sculpture of an endangered species on the rim of the mug, sea urchin got me. Made me hope the damn things do go extinct so they don't put em on the coffee mugs. No offense to Irene, but the artists ruined everything.

RON: You can't say that, Junior.

JUNIOR: Used to be there was no such thing as art. if there was a drawing it was to say how to kill something. . . or a song was to bring rain, people used to know why they beat on drums, now you get these income poops coming up from the cities with a new shirt and a twenty dollar bill and they don't change either, beat some drums in the woods for a week, don't even know why, go home have sex with their wives till they forget how, and have to wait another year to come up here again. And it was the Goddamn artists come up here and turned us all into metaphors, once you're a metaphor you can't do nothing without it meaning something. I got to hand it to Irene, though, she seen it coming. Was smarter than the rest of us.

RON: I think she just liked to paint, Junior.

JUNIOR: She turned your perfectly good resort into a artist colony.

RON: You know as well as I do there were no more fish to catch that's what saved the place. And I gotta admit the bar never did better. I'd put a artist down on his luck up against a thirsty fisherman any day of the week.

JUNIOR: Well alls I got to say is things have a habit of turning around. Coupla years ago I'm driving down Highway Seven, having a hell of a bad day, when all of a sudden there's a chainsaw laying there in a box all oiled up and ready to go.

RON: Duffer, oh no.

JUNIOR: Good old Duffer. There was a man knew his way around a chainsaw.

RON: I know that's right. Duffer used to go off in the woods and we wouldn't see him for days and then he'd come home exhausted and out of gas, not say a word. And then a story would come back how a hunter had got himself lost back in the woods somewhere he, swore had never been seen by another human eye, about to give up hope, when there carved out the tree was the image of a Viking or a Pirate or Alfred E. Newman.

JUNIOR: Now, see, that's the kind of art I can relate to. I hate to say it, because of how much he pissed me off, but I really miss Duffer.

RON: Yeah, I miss you too, Junior.

JUNIOR: Shut up.

RON: I do.

JUNIOR: Well don't tell me.

RON: How did you go, Junior?

JUNIOR: Heart attack, can you believe it?

RON: Same as Irene.

JUNIOR: Yeah. Look, I gotta get moving, Ronnie.

RON: All right, Junior.

JUNIOR: Good luck.

RON: What?

JUNIOR: With the hog.

RON: Oh yeah. Think he's down there?

JUNIOR: It's my job to think so. Later.

RON: Later. (*Junior exits. Lights up on Irene.*)

IRENE: Hey, Ronnie.

RON: Hey, Irene. How long you been there?

IRENE: The whole time.

RON: I'm sorry, Irene. Hey, I just got the new brochure from that art colony you went to. You're in there with the cartoon man and the mountain painter.

IRENE: Oh yeah? Which painting did they pick?

RON: They got your Mallards. Boy they look good enough to shoot.

IRENE: How's Darlene?

RON: She's down in the cities now, happy as can be, we talk every coupla weeks. She comes up for holidays. She's going into Fashion.

IRENE: Fashion.

RON: She's special, Irene.

IRENE: Yeah, I'm afraid she is. We used to have to scotch tape bows to her head.

RON: Still do, you should see her new haircut. It's a different world out there, Irene. We were kids and the family would go down to the cities for shopping or whatnot and on the way home we'd stop get a coupla burgers Dad yells, "Clean up the car kids." And we'd get all the wrappers and cups and whatever else was on the floor and hand it up to the old man and zing out the window with it. Then we'd quick look out the back to watch it hit and explode. "There's my coke cup, there's my french fries.. "Hey, goddamit," Dad yells, "who put the bottle in there? Now my case is gonna be one short" and we'd giggle flying up Highway 7 at 85 miles an hour past the farms. All of a sudden my dad says "Watch this kids, magic" and all the lights went out in all the farm houses like a power outage, and Dad says ten O'clock..without even looking at his watch I thought he was the amazing Kreskin when in fact he knew Cronkite had just finished the news and all the farmers were off to bed. We all had the same heartbeat then. Now it seems crazy.

IRENE: Why did you come out here, Ron?

RON: I wanted to find you.

IRENE: How did you know I'd be out here?

RON: Now don't get upset, Irene, but this was the one place I told you never to go.

IRENE: Well, I'm going to bed, Ronnie, you coming up?

RON: Yeah, I'll be up there in a minute. (*Irene Exits. Young Ron Huber* *enters the ice house.*)

YOUNG RON: Hey.

RON: Hey.

YOUNG RON: Any luck?

RON: No.

YOUNG RON: What are you after?

RON: A monster that lives down there.

YOUNG RON: Oh.

RON: Well, what do you know for sure?

YOUNG RON: I know your stove ain't on. And you sank your truck but it was a Chevy anyhow. I know when I grow up I'm gonna catch the biggest fish in this lake. Me and my brother. And I'll get a place on this lake and run it. No girls allowed except one, and I'm going to marry her. She's special but I don't mind, in fact I like it.

RON: You do, huh?

YOUNG RON: Yeah, I like it a lot.

TIM: So much for the Storm of the Century. Kind of petered out. I swore we were really in for one there at first. . . I'm afraid tomorrow it's a beautiful day. So here's the schools that are open. Class will resume at Frazee, private and parochial; Fridley, private and parochial; Fulda, private and parochial; Gary, private and parochial; Glencoe, private and parochial; (*During the school closings Young Ron is seated watching as Old Ron sits by the fishing hole and puts his mouth over the barrel end of the shotgun as the lights fade to black*)

END OF PLAY

(Glenville Emmons, private and parochial; Goodhue, private and parochial; Goodridge, private and parochial; Grand Meadow, private and parochial; Grand Rapids, private and parochial; Granite Falls-Clarkfield, private and parochial,; Greenbush, private and parochial; Greenway-Colleraine, private and. parochial; Grey Eagle, private and parochial; Grygla-Gatzke, private and parochial.)

WHAT WE DO WITH IT

by Bruce MacDonald

Playwright's Biography

Bruce MacDonald makes his ATL playwriting debut with WHAT WE DO WITH IT. His other plays include CLOSELY RELATED, REPLAY and THE NEXT CHAMPION OF THE WORLD, THE UNIVERSE, AND THE COSMOS. He has a new full-length play, THE LOVE OF YOUR LIFE, and is at work on an original screenplay, among other projects. Mr. MacDonald attended Williams College for his undergraduate degree and U.C. Berkeley for four years of graduate school. His acting career consists of work around the Boston area, and he appeared in local professional theatres in roles such as "Bluntschli" in ARMS AND THE MAN, "Delley" in OLD TIMES, "Nick" in THE AUTUMN GARDEN and "Burton" in BURN THIS. He is currently an actor and is living in Cambridge, Massachusetts with his wife and their three daughters.

A Note From The Playwright

A few years ago I heard a woman talk about having been sexually abused as a child by her father. The most astonishing thing I recall she said was that to this day she could not shake the feeling that he was still "the one" for her. That's where this play came from.

In production, the play works best if you try to achieve a real balance between the two arguments. I'd suggest beginning with the premise that both characters are telling the truth as best they can.

Characters

John, 70's
Cheryl, around 40, his daughter

Directed by Frazier Marsh

John	Ray Fry
Cheryl	Priscilla Shanks
Scenic Designer	Paul Owen
Costume Designer	Hollis Jenkins-Evans
Lighting Designer	Karl E. Haas

Sound Designer	Casey L. Warren
Props Master	Mark J. Bissonnette
Stage Manager	Craig Weindling
Assistant Stage Manager	Amy Hutchison
Production Dramaturg	Michael Bigel

Setting

A small, carpeted room with two chairs angled toward the audience. The present.

WHAT WE DO WITH IT

With lights up we discover JOHN and CHERYL seated in their respective chairs. Except where indicated, they generally look out toward the center of the audience (DC). He's had a few drinks, but he isn't drunk. She's very still.

JOHN: (*As though he's just been kicked in the stomach.*) Is she mentally ill? Because if that's what it is, I'll do absolutely anything, I'll do whatever I can. It happens to people, it's a disease, they can't help it. (*To her.*) Are you mentally ill? Cheryl? (*No response; DC.*) I don't know if you have children, but. . .(*Shakes his head, forces a pathetic laugh.*). . .this is where it gets you. (*Indicates his heart.*) Right here. (*To her, repeats the gesture.*) It gets you right here. God, we loved you. We loved you like you were the first child born to the world, like you were Jesus Christ. Worshiped you. Brought you gifts from everywhere I went. (*DC*) Tell me to shut up if I'm saying something wrong. But I'm not going to just sit here like a dumb old, you know, dumb old asshole. Excuse me. (*Stops, shakes his head; then to her.*) I was on the road all the time, weeks at a time, and your mother paid the price. I mean she did what mothers did in those days. She was a good woman, your mother. We were very happy, very happy. You may not believe it, but that's the truth. Children think they know the truth, but they distort it. They don't mean to, but they distort it. (*Blackout. Lights up again immediately.*)

CHERYL: (*She's trying to remember something; then, deliberately, without a hint of pleasure.*) The thing I remember most is driving to the country. It was in the summer. We had a favorite motel near a lake. It had a little golf game outside—miniature golf—and you could walk to the lake on a path through the woods. We'd get two rooms with a door that connected. Donny and I were in one, they took the other one. This was when I was. . .five? Six? In there somewhere. Before everything started. (*Beat.*) I was always counting the hours before we had to go home again, it drove Donny crazy. He and I would wake up very early and go into their room and wake them up and they wouldn't care and we'd talk about everything we were going to do that day. I remember. . .the smell of the bed. (*Beat.*) Then we'd get dressed and go out to a restaurant and have pancakes and bacon and whatever we wanted. That's all I want to say about it.

JOHN: (*To her.*) I'd forgotten about that place. (*DC*) I'd forgotten it was all that. . .as wonderful as she said. But I don't doubt it. We did lots of things like that, drove away on the spur of the moment as a family.

(*To her.*) You may not remember them all. I don't. (*DC*) I guess I wouldn't have mentioned that one first, that particular motel. Dumpy little place up in the White Mountains. There were lots of nicer ones over the years. We had picture albums, I wish I brought them.

CHERYL: I never saw any pictures.

JOHN: I took the pictures, I have the pictures.

CHERYL: This is one of those ways he tries to make us look normal, like any other family, like we have picture albums.

JOHN: There are picture albums. Pictures of the four of us standing together, smiling, being a family. (*To her.*) Would you believe me if I found the pictures? (*PC, forces a little laugh.*) I guess that's what it comes down to in this day and age, you have to provide the evidence. It's a sad commentary.

CHERYL: It really doesn't matter if there are pictures or not.

JOHN: Wait. Wait a minute. If the truth doesn't matter, what are we doing? Isn't that what she said? Can we just stop a minute and clarify that? That fact and not-fact are two different things, that we have to separate them? That we cannot rewrite history? I'll do whatever's necessary, but I have no intention of rewriting history.

CHERYL: Do you see what he's doing?

JOHN: (*To her.*) You know, I came twelve hundred miles to be here, Cheryl. Did you say how many years it was? Did you tell the truth? Was it my idea, all those years? *Nine years.* No, seven years, (*DC*) because she did come to her mother's funeral. Even though she wouldn't speak to me. Of course not. In front of our friends, in front of my oldest friends in the world at her mother's *fun*eral, she would not speak to her father. (*To her.*) Why are you doing this? Cheryl? Look at me. Cheryl, look at me. I'm an old man. I'm not that well. I don't have much. What do you want? If I can, I'll give it to you. (*Beat; DC*) I thought she wanted to make up. I swear to God, (*To her, breaking down.*) I swear to God I thought you wanted to make up. (*Blackout. Lights up again immediately. He's all recovered.*)

CHERYL: I think I must have called him Daddy. (*Beat; the voice of a young girl, as though trying it out.*) Daddy? Daddy? (*Normal voice.*) Then. . .I didn't call him anything. (*Beat.*) He called me Cheryl.

JOHN: (*To her, defensive.*) Well wasn't that your name?

CHERYL: Or Cherie (*Pronounced Sherry*).

JOHN: (*To her.*) Your mother called you that.

CHERYL: My mother. . . I can't remember my mother.

JOHN: Listen to this.

CHERYL: I don't know where she was. I never knew where she was.

JOHN: (*To her.*) She was home! Where else would she be? You make it sound like (*Interrupts himself.*) . . . Your mother *wor*shiped you! And when you went silent, when you refused her calls and returned her letters and even returned *Christmas* presents—(DC) did she tell you about that?— (*To her.*) she was crushed, she was devastated. You're imagining things, Cheryl! (DC) Have you considered the possibility that everything she says. . . the possibility that all of this *gar*bage is the product of her imagination?

CHERYL: (*Beat.*) Yes.

JOHN: (*To her.*) Yes she says. (DC) I want to know where on earth she *gets* these ideas. (*To her, helplessly.*) I don't know, TV shows? Some kind of magazines? What? It's like they infiltrated your mind, they poisoned your memory.

CHERYL: I wanted to be making it up. They were nightmares.

JOHN: (*DC, conclusively.*) They *were* nightmares. They were nightmares. (*Blackout. Lights up again immediately.*)

JOHN: (*To her, demanding, loud, almost threatening.*) What *happened*? For God's sake tell us what happened! Why won't you do that? Why are you afraid to do that?

CHERYL: I'm not going to.

JOHN: (*As before.*) Why? Why, Cheryl? Tell us why.

CHERYL: Because you want me to. Because it would give you pleasure. Because you want to hear me say the words. I know how you want me, I can feel it right now, I can *smell* it. It's still the same for you. After thirty-whatever years it's still the same. I can even smell his breath, it's just the same, it's his drinking breath disguised with a little mouthwash. What is it, Listerine? Was that the one?

JOHN: I have *not* been drinking, that is a lie, that is a *lie*, that is another complete and utter fabrication. Tell us what it was, Cheryl. Tell us. We're waiting. We want to know what your mind has concocted.

CHERYL: I think it would arouse him. I actually believe it would arouse him.

JOHN: Oh dear God. (*He closes his eyes, shakes his head a little. Blackout. Lights up again immediately.*)

CHERYL: (*DC*) What he's doing is a kind of reverse insanity defense, where you claim the victim is crazy. (*To him.*) What did you think? That I would forget? Could you have been so, I don't know, *drunk* that you thought I could forget? (*Beat.*) Or maybe you just convinced yourself it didn't happen because. . .because otherwise how could you live with yourself. That was it, wasn't it. You convinced yourself, and you figured I must have done the same thing. (*Beat, DC.*) Well I did. For the first, it was almost twenty years, that's exactly what I did, I convinced myself it didn't happen. (*Beat.*) I read about some of the people who survived the concentration camps. When they first got in, what kept them alive was remembering the lives they had before. But as time went on, and they knew they weren't getting out, they would come to accept the concentration camp as normal, as what life was. They learned how to expect nothing else, they forgot their old life, and so they survived. Are you *listening* to this? I came to accept what you did to me as *normal*. I've thought about that a lot. In a way it's the hardest thing to live with. Because my thinking it was normal must have helped *you* think it was normal. And I want to be very clear that I am not defending you. I was a child. I was a child. (*Beat.*) About ten years ago I started to remember. Something snapped and. . .I started to remember. It was like finding out I had a serious disease. All of a sudden it was what my life was about.

JOHN: I don't think she means to be lying. I believe she thinks she's telling the truth. I want to know what we can do for her, something to make her. . .(*Interrupts himself.*) Whether there's some kind of, I don't know, treatment? Medication? We used to call them delusions, things your mind makes up. I would guess it's out of her control. (*Blackout. Lights up again immediately.*)

CHERYL: (*Beat.*) One of the things I remembered. . .(*She battles with herself not to break.*) One of the things I remembered was sometimes I initiated it. I went to him. Sometimes I did that. I've tried and tried to understand (*To him.*) how you got me to do that, and I can't. I must have thought it would be easier that way, or safer, or something. What I know is I didn't have a choice. You made me think I liked it. (*Blackout. Lights up again immediately.*)

JOHN: (*Beat.*) It's easy to believe her, she makes you want to believe her. (*Forces a pathetic laugh.*) *I* want to believe her. But what we are witnessing is the result of. . .I don't know. Sickness. Some kind of sickness, I'm not the expert. She is so, she has so much anger, and the question is, what caused that anger? What caused her to turn against her father? With horrible, *horrible* lies. Turned against both her parents, really, because I hate to say this (*To her.*) but it shortened your mother's life, Cheryl. Returning those presents, not coming to the hospital. (*beat*) Do I know that for a fact? Of course not. I *feel* it. It took away her will to live. And she never said, Where's Cheryl? Where is my daughter? Not once. And I have to resent that, I do resent it. But she kept her dignity. I don't believe you intended it, I don't think you understood the impact your actions would have. As your mother said, She knows not what she does. I don't mean to be accusing you of something, but you pushed me, Cheryl, you have made me talk about *what really happened*. (*Beat.*) Because if the truth were known, I would have preferred to not speak. I would have preferred to not see you than to see you like this. Sometimes it is a question of decency.

CHERYL: (*Very still for a long moment; then, quietly, to herself and DC.*) What you want is freedom. Even a little is better than none. I feel. . . you know, this will sound strange, but I am freer to hate him. If he acknowledged everything and took responsibility and, I don't know, begged forgiveness and all that, well, that would be more complicated. I don't know what that would do. So I take what I get. (*Beat; she smiles.*) He asked if I was mentally ill. (*She can't help smile, she almost laughs, then stops.*) Am I mentally ill? Yes. Yes. Of course I'm mentally ill. I have a mental illness. (*Then, real slow, getting every word right.*) He told me once, "There will never be anybody who loves you like me, Cherie. Nobody. For ever and ever." (*She looks at him; then.*) That's what you said. (*He looks at her. They continue to look at each other as we fade to blackout.*)

END OF PLAY

KEELY AND DU

by Jane Martin

Playwright's Biography

Jane Martin's KEELY AND DU is her fourth play to premiere in the Humana Festival of New American Plays. Ms. Martin, a Kentuckian, first came to national attention for TALKING WITH, a collection of monologues that premiered at Actors Martin Theatre in 1981. TALKING WITH first played in New York in 1982 at the Manhattan Theatre Club, and since then it has been performed around the world, winning the Best Foreign Play of the Year award in Germany from Theater Heute magazine. Her other plays include CEMENTVILLE, which premiered in the 1991 Humana Festival and was subsequently performed at Australia's Festivals of Adelaide and Perth, and VITAL SIGNS, a collection of shorter monologues which premiered in the 1990 Humana Festival and has since been published by Samuel French and produced at several theatres around the country. CRIMINAL HEARTS premiered at The Theatre Company in Detroit in April of 1992. Other Martin plays include THE BOY WHO ATE THE MOON (1981), COUP/CLUCKS (1982 SHORTS Festival at ATL), SUMMER (1984 SHORTS), and TRAVELIN' SHOW (1987 ATL tour to Warsaw).

Introduction To The Play

"For your lifeblood I will surely demand an accounting. I will demand an accounting from every animal. And from each man, too -"

Pro-life. Pro-choice. Who is accountable, God or man? What man or woman can be accountable for a human life? What is the extent of individual freedom? What is a rape victim's right? What is a Christian's duty? These are among the infinitely troubling questions provoked by Jane Martin's drama *Keely and Du*.

The issue is abortion. But this is no schematized political view. Martin insistently works from the gut. Her characters confront the physical, emotional and spiritual realities of procreation.

Crucial to the dilemma of *Keely and Du* is the fact that when a child is born, a family is created. Not every mother has the resources to nurture. Not every father deserves his traditional authority. A child's existence cannot be completely separable from the lives of his/her parents. Martin rings fascinating changes on the definition of mother and father, resonating through the structures of family, church, and society.

While *Keely and Du* is a mind-probing "issue" play, it has a human face. The four characters' stories are deeply passionate. Like many of Martin's creations, they exist on the extreme edge of everyday reality.

Today, the traditional family faces radical redefinition. The issues of *Keely and Du* touch us all. No matter what our beliefs, Martin's questions deserve our attention.

Marcia Dixcy

Characters

Du, Walter, Keely, Cole, Prison Guard, Orderlies

Directed by Jon Jory

Cast of Characters (in order of appearance)
Du	Anne Pitoniak
Walter	Bob Burrus
Keely	Julie Boyd
Cole	J. Ed Araiza
Prison Guard	Janice O'Rourke*
Orderlies	Jeremy Brisiel*
	Jeff Sexton

* Members of the ATL Apprentice Company

Scenic Designer	Paul Owen
Costume Designer	Laura Patterson
Lighting Designer	Marcus Dilliard
Sound Designer	Darron L. West
Props Master	Ron Riall
Stage Manager	Paul Mills Holmes
Assistant Stage Manager	Emily Rox
Production Dramaturg	Marcia Dixcy

Casting arranged by Judy Dennis

Setting

The time is now. The Place is Providence, Rhode Island.

KEELY AND DU

SCENE 1

An unfinished basement in a working-class home in Providence, R.I. Details could be kept to a minimum. We are aware of pipes and a water heater. There is a cement floor with a drain. In the middle of the room is an old cast-iron bed, bolted to the floor, neatly made up with an old quilt. Somewhere there is a new, small (knee high) box refrigerator. There is also a rocker and a stool. One door, framed in and made of sheet metal. It has a viewing slot and two inside and two outside locks. Above the door is a speaker/monitor. The play is made up of numerous scenes and, in most cases, the lights come back up instantaneously. In the room, a 65-year-old woman sweeps. She wears a housedress. The time is now.

DU: (*Singing, absently, her mind elsewhere.*) "K-K-K-Katie, beautiful Katie, you're the only da-da-da-da that I adore, and when the m-moonshine falls on the cowshed, I'll be waiting by the . . ." (*She dumps trash into an open leaf bag. She starts the song again.*) "K-K-K-Katie, beautiful lady." (*The buzzer rings through the speaker monitor. DU moves to it and presses the button.*) Yes?

WALTER: (*On the speaker phone.*) She's here. (*DU stands for a moment lost in thought.The message repeats.*) Hello. She's here.

DU: (*Pressing bag.*) Yes. (*She closes trash bag and ties it and puts it by the door. She goes to the bed and pulls the covers down. She puts her broom in a corner. She goes to the door and opens it. She picks up tiny pieces of trash and palms them. WALTER enters. He is a man of 50, neatly dressed in inexpensive slacks, sport shirt and jacket. He wears an animal mask. DU laughs.*)

WALTER: I know. I know. (*He looks over the room.*) You need to put yours on. (*DU crosses to get her mask.*)

DU: I hope she's not allergic. I scrubbed, but. . . (*She gestures helplessly.*) Old basements . . . uh. . .you see.

WALTER: It's fine. (*She puts on her mask. He moves to the door and speaks out it.*) Now, please. (*He re-enters. Moments later two men bring in a hospital gurney. On it is a young woman, early 30's, strapped in. She wears a dress. She is unconscious.*)

DU: (*Involuntarily.*) Oh, my. (*The two men wear jeans and T-shirts or short sleeves. One is young; one isn't. They pull the gurney parallel to the bed and unstrap it. They move the young woman onto the bed.*)

WALTER: Thank you. (*One nods, neither speak.*) Please be at dispersal in 23 minutes, we are running seven minutes late. (*The two men look at their watches.*) Seven twenty-two. (*One adjusts his watch. They take the gurney out and close the door. WALTER speaks to DU.*) Is there anything needed?

DU: (*Stands over the young woman, looking down.*) I don't think so.

WALTER: The anesthesiologist says she might sleep through or she might not. (*DU stands looking at her.*) I'll be back in four days. Someone will be upstairs. It went very smoothly and cleanly; we have no reason to be apprehensive. (*He puts down the small suitcase he carries.*) Everything is here. Your husband wishes you well. Please memorize this number. (*He hands her a slip of paper.*) Only in an emergency. (*He takes it back. He takes both her hands in his.*) God be with you.

DU: (*She smiles.*) Yes. (*He suddenly leans forward and kisses her cheek. DU is surprised.*)

WALTER: We will prevail.

DU: I know. (*He goes out the door and closes it. DU takes two keys on a string from her neck and locks the two locks. A pause.*) We're fine. (*The viewing slot closes. DU turns back to the bed. She moves to the bag left on the floor and unzips it. She takes out a cotton nightgown and hangs it over the back of the rocker. She goes to the bed and removes the woman's shoes, putting them on the floor. She unbuttons the young woman's dress, slips it back under her shoulders, goes to the end of the bed and, by pulling, removes it. The woman is now in a simple unrevealing bra, panties and pantyhose. DU puts the dress, for the moment, over a chair arm. She returns to the bed and removes the young woman's (KEELY's) pantyhose, putting them also over a rocker arm. She takes the nightgown from the rocker to the bed and positions the nightgown over KEELY's head; next she gets KEELY's left arm and then right into the sleeves, moves down and pulls the nightgown until it covers her body. DU moves back to the bag and takes out a pair of handcuffs, goes to the bed, realizes something, goes back to the bag, takes out several pieces of paper and stands reading. After a time, she finds it.*) Right handed. (*She puts the papers in the bag, moves to the bed, handcuffs KEELY's left hand and clicks the other cuff to the iron headboard. She makes sure this arrangement is comfortable for KEELY. Now DU folds the clothes* *she has removed from KEELY and places them back in the bag and re-zips it. DU goes to the bed and takes KEELY's pulse. Finishes, she goes and checks the door and then moves to the rocker, where she sits watching the bed and its occupant. She sings "K-K-K-Katie, K-K-K-Katie." The lights go down.)*

SCENE 2

Lights almost immediately up. KEELY is moving.

DU: *(Experimentally.)* Keely? *(KEELY moves.)* Keely?
KEELY: Ummmmm.
DU: It's alright, honey. Keely? You're alright, you're just waking up. *(Nothing from the bed. DU sits a moment. She takes off her mask, thinks, puts it back on.)* Keely? *(Takes the mask off, moves to the suitcase and puts in it. Crosses to the bed.)* Keely, I'm a friend, I am. You're just waking up. You're not hurt in any way. You're in bed, and I'm here to help you.
KEELY: *(Struggling toward consciousness.)* What?
DU: Nothing's wrong with you, you're just waking up.
KEELY: Who were they?
DU: Who, Keely?
KEELY: On the street?
DU: Good people who wanted to help.
KEELY: I feel nauseous.
DU: That's perfectly normal. Try not to move quickly.
KEELY: Thirsty.
DU: I'll get you some water. *(She goes to the large thermos with spigot.)*
KEELY: Hospital.
DU: *(Returning.)* What, honey?
KEELY: Those people. . .I'm so foggy. . .where is this?
DU: Is it a hospital, well, no, it's not.
KEELY: I don't know you.
DU: Well, I'm easy to know. *(KEELY drinks.)* Not too much now. *(She takes the cup.)*
KEELY: Thank you.
DU: You're welcome.
KEELY: Dried out. *(Now aware her left arm can't move.)* Wait. . .
DU: I'll just come sit down with you.
KEELY: What. . .
DU: Right here.

KEELY: Hey. (*Pulls arm against restraint.*) Hey. . .(*She twists to try to look at the arm.*) What, what is that?

DU: Don't worry, Keely.

KEELY: Hey! What is this? Who are you? Get me out of this, you, whoever you are. . .please. . .where am I?

DU: It's for your own safety. . .I'll tell you, but we should.

KEELY: Now! Take this off me!

DU: I can't. . .

KEELY: Take it off, it's hurting me. . .take it off me!

DU: I'm your friend, Keely.

KEELY: I feel sick, I don't feel right. This is. . .I'll start screaming. . .it's cutting my wrist. . .not right. . .take this off.

DU: You'll hurt yourself. . .

KEELY: Now! (*A bloodcurdling scream.*)

DU: Stop it.

KEELY: Help me! Help! Help me!! (*She glares at DU. She twists and fights until she falls off the bed.*) What the hell did I do to you? Hahh? Please. Let me go!

DU: You need to calm yourself, honey.

KEELY: Help! Laura! Help me! (*To DU.*) Who are you? This hurts, it's hurting me. Ow. Ow, ow. I can't stand this. (*She's on her feet, yanking the cuffs, grabbing with her free hand. She tries to drag the bed. She tries to tip it over. She starts to cry out of frustration. She tries to go after DU, yelling. . .*) Let me go! You better let me go!

DU: Please don't hurt yourself.

KEELY: Get these off. My dad's alone. He has to be fed. Do you understand that? He can't move, do you hear me? Come on, what are you doing? Tell me? What do you want me for? Who do you think I am? I'm not anybody; why would you do this? Let me go! This thing is tearing my wrist. I want this off me. Come on, I'm not kidding. Listen, I got seventy bucks in the bank, I can't get laid off. I got two jobs; what time is it? I have to go home, don't you understand me? (*Her diatribe becomes less and less controlled, builds to a peak and then declines into a beaten, exhausted silence that leaves her staring at DU, who sits in the rocker.*) Get this off me. I can't do this. Help! Let me out! Get me out of this. Do you hear me, are you deaf, or what are you, lady? Help! Help! Help me, help me, help me! (*She screams in rage and frustration.*) Let me go. What are you? Help! Come on. Come on! Tell me what you want. Tell me what you want! Please. Come on. Help! Please, talk to me, talk to me. Please. Please. (*She stands, sweat pouring down her face, her voice hoarse, panting. She yanks against the cuff. She stands staring at DU. The lights fade.*)

SCENE 3

Lights up. KEELY lies sleeping. An outside lock turns. DU enters with a bucket of water, a towel, washcloth and sponge. She puts the towel on the stool and the bucket on the floor. KEELY sits bolt upright, startled.She stares at DU.

DU: Rise and shine, the British are coming. In the army my husband had a sergeant used to say that every six A.M.! Heavens. Well. . .would you like to wash up, Keely? I hoped we'd have a shower, but something about the pipes. (*KEELY doesn't respond.*) Are you a bath person or a shower person? I was bath, but I changed over when I got so that I didn't like looking at myself. You're so aware of yourself in a bath, don't you think? Did you sleep at all? Heavens, I don't see how you could, I really don't. (*DU reaches out to touch KEELY's shoulder, but she turns away.*) Keely?

KEELY: Get away from me!

DU: I can do that, yes. Keely. . .

KEELY: Don't talk to me!

DU: I thought you might want to wash yourself.

KEELY: You heard me!

DU: (*Sits in rocker.*) You can tell me if you change your mind. (*KEELY doesn't move. The lights fade.*)

SCENE 4

In the dark, a tray falls. Lights up. KEELY has knocked a breakfast tray presented by DU to the floor.

DU: (*Looking down.*) Well, honey, what is that? What does that mean? I would like you to keep my arthritis in mind when I'm on my hands and knees cleaning that up.

KEELY: (*Eyes flaming.*) I'll keep it in mind.

DU: You need to eat.

KEELY: I'm not eating.

DU: Then they'll feed you intravenously. Well, I'm upset if that's satisfying, I'm not cleaning this up now. (*She sits in the rocker. She waits. KEELY will not respond.*) No ma'am. No ma'am. Eggs. I'm scrambled, but you might be over easy. My middle son, he was poached, and he's still poached if you ask me. That boy was, is, and will be a trial. It was his born nature and his grown nature, I swear I had no effect, but that child can make you laugh! Lordy. From this high. Three boys, and lived to tell the tale. Every single one of them on the basketball team, and if that's not the dumbest human activity the mind could come up with, I don't know what is. Run one way, put it in a hole, run the other way, put it in a hole. Lord have mercy. (*No response.*) You can talk or not talk. You'll be here almost five months, here in this room with me. How will we pass the time? You have a special burden, I believe that. I would lift it from you if I could. You are not what I would have chosen, but wiser heads. What we think is not everything in this world. You'll be having a baby; perhaps we should start from there. (*Lights down.*)

SCENE 5

In the darkness we hear a buzzer. WALTER, on the speaker: "I will be coming down." Lights up. DU moves to the door, pushes the speaker's button, and says . . .

DU: Yes. Good. (*She turns to KEELY.*) I hope you aren't so angry that you can't listen, because it would be important to listen now. Keely? He is blunt spoken sometimes, and he is a man, don't let that close your heart. Keely? (*DU goes to the suitcase and puts on her mask. There is a light knock on the door. She goes to it and unlocks it. She opens the door. A man wearing a mask, dressed in a suit and tie enters with a briefcase. He speaks to DU.*)

WALTER: Good morning, sister.

DU: Good morning.

WALTER: Good morning, Keely. (*No answer. He goes to the rocker and pulls it closer to KEELY but still beyond her reach.*) Nana is taking fine care of you, I'm sure. (*He looks at the tray on the floor.*) I see you've had your breakfast. You seem alert and well. The anesthetic we used, Lomalathene, is very mild and will not harm the baby, we're very sure of that. I know you have other concerns. Funds have been arranged for your father's care. I wanted to reassure you. (*A pause.*) Will you talk to me at this point, Keely, or shall I just talk to you? I know this must be hard to take in.

KEELY: Who are you?

WALTER: I am a member, Keely, of Operation Retrieval. We are a group of like-minded Christians motivated by a belief in the sanctity of life and the rights of unborn children. (*KEELY puts her head in her* *hand.*) Now, Keely, western man has firmly held to life-supportive principles as promoted by Hippocrates from 450 B.C. until the turn of the century. Since then, certain groups and individuals have been promoting death as a solution to social problems. I do not condone that. You are almost three month's pregnant, Keely.

KEELY: I was raped.

WALTER: You were, Keely, and I find that horrifying. That a man you knew and cared for. . .

KEELY: Wait a minute; wait a minute.

WALTER: You are the injured party. . .

KEELY: Yeah, right. . .

WALTER: In God's eye, and in ours. . .

KEELY: And handcuffed, and kidnapped.

WALTER: . . . but your unborn child is separate from that issue.

KEELY: No, it isn't.

WALTER: It is a separate life which may not be taken to solve your very real problems.

KEELY: Hey, it's cells, little cells.

WALTER: (*Very clearly.*) It is a separate life.

KEELY: And what about my life?

WALTER: I need to clarify the situation for you. . .

KEELY: (*Pulling on her restraint.*) Oh, it's clarified.

WALTER: Keely, there are 1,500,000 abortion deaths on this planet each year, and that is spiritually unbearable.

KEELY: I was raped, do you know that?

WALTER: Yes, I do. We must do all we can for you, Keely, and for the child.

KEELY: It's not *your* child.

WALTER: You know the answer to that, Keely. (*A pause.*) You are one of four young women, geographically distributed, all with child, all seeking abortion, who have been taken into protective custody. Each of you sought out a clinic for different reasons and in different situations. There is, of course, a political dimension here. We chose you as a rape victim, Keely. Rape has always been understood as the extreme edge of abortion policy, and we must make clear that infant rights extend even into this catastrophic area. The rape victim must be given support on every level, but the fact of the child is critical. If medically we must lose or severely harm mother or child, we must choose. If both can survive, both must survive. We intend to document and assist these children's lives, which would otherwise have been lost.

KEELY: Hey, I want an abortion, man. This is my life, right? Who the hell are you? Screw you people. I'm not a goddamn teenager. You're not

God. I want an abortion!

WALTER: Keely.

KEELY: What do you want from me?!

WALTER: We want you to hold your baby. We will care for you here until the seventh month of your pregnancy and then return you home for the birth in the best medical circumstances.

KEELY: Oh, man.

WALTER: We assume the following responsibilities: all expenses relating to the birth of your child will be taken care of, adoptive parents eager to raise the child and capable of so doing will be in touch with you, should you decide to raise your child. . .

KEELY: How the hell do you think I'm going to do that, huh? You knew I was pregnant, you knew I was raped, do you know I take care of my dad? Do you know he's paralyzed? Do you know I hold his bedpan? Is that part of what you know? Do you know I work two jobs? Do you know what they are?

WALTER: A child-care subsidy will be provided for the first two years, and there will be an education fund. . .

KEELY: What is your name? What. . .what. . .who are you?

WALTER: You're going to be famous, Keely. You're going to be a famous American. There will be many opportunities open to you and your child. This is difficult for you to understand, but your life has already changed for the better. . .(*KEELY laughs.*) I know it's ironic. Are the handcuffs hurting you?

KEELY: Yes.

WALTER: I'm sure there is something we can do. Everything I know about you, Keely, and I know considerable, leads me to believe you will fall in love with your baby.

KEELY: My sister-in-law, she threw her baby on the floor, she was so screwed, on the floor one day. . .guy down the street messing with his 3-year old daughter. You think "in love with your baby. . ." is all that's out there? We got 12 year old gangs setting fire to homeless. . .who loved those babies?

WALTER: You are in your third month, Keely. Your baby is sensitive to the touch. If you stroke its palm, it will make a fist. The baby has fingers and toes and fingerprints.

KEELY: You're going to prison, Mister. I'll put you there.

DU: She's exhausted.

WALTER: Of course. One of our doctors will visit you weekly. This lady is a registered nurse.

KEELY: What about my dad, right? He's alone in the house, you understand me? I don't feed him, he doesn't eat.

WALTER: There is money for nursing care, we've arranged a conduit.

KEELY: What kind of care?

WALTER: Sufficient, Keely.

KEELY: I take care of him.

WALTER: It's sometimes hard to recognize a friend at first, Keely. We know your needs and the needs of your family.

KEELY: Screw off.

WALTER: Keely, we need direction sometimes, we need people to tell us what to do when we act out of panic or fear or confusion. I have limited your options and taken control to give you the chance to step outside your runaway emotions. You are frightened and out of control, and I will return your options to you when you are thinking clearly and ready for them. You may send me to prison. . . *(He gestures toward DU.)* we are both prepared for that spiritually and practically. We have committed our lives. What can I say to you? I am a father, and caring for, learning from my children. . .well, you wouldn't understand. They resurrected my life through our Lord Jesus Christ. *(A pause.)* I am a pastor if you wish counseling about your rape or your pregnancy, or we can provide someone else, someone not connected with restraining you. *(A pause.)* You could be my daughter, Keely, and if you were I would do this for you. I'll see about the handcuffs.

KEELY: *(Indicating DU.)* She took off her mask, I'll remember her. *(WALTER looks at DU. A pause, and then he takes off his mask.)*

WALTER: There, now you've seen us both. Hello. *(KEELY doesn't reply. DU takes off her mask. WALTER looks at her again briefly. He rises and moves to the door.)* Keely, the abortion procedure you were seeking Wednesday morning is called Suction Curettage. A powerful suction tube is inserted through the cervix into the womb. The baby's body and the placenta are torn to pieces and sucked into a jar. The baby's head is crushed and then extracted. Goodbye, Keely. *(He exits, closing the door behind him. DU goes to the door and locks it.)*

DU: *(Turning back, she cleans up the breakfast.)* I'm sorry they chose you. *(Lights out.)*

SCENE 6

A tray crashes in the dark. Lights up. DU stands over another fallen breakfast.

DU: *(Looking down.)* My husband can eat the same breakfast one hundred times in a row. Goes the same route in the car to the same places. Buys the same color socks by the gross. He is very set in his ways. (*She kneels down and cleans up.*) Please talk to me. (*A pause.*) Please talk to me. (*A pause.*) My husband isn't much of a talker. Well, I don't know if men ever are. Oh, they talk to each other, but talk to us, well they just turn right to stone, don't they? I could never understand it. (*She pauses. KEELY doesn't reply.*) Now Keely, truly, are we going to sit here like this? You talked to him, am I so much worse? Well, he's a. . .he's a good man if there's times he doesn't sound like one. He's just got a lot of starch in his ideas so he can't see past himself. I tell him you can't have ideas about people and then go keep your own humanity in the closet. Oh, we go to it, we have a rare old time.

KEELY: Why should I talk to you? (*Referring to the cuffs.*) Look at this. Why the hell should I talk to you?

DU: (*She has finished cleaning.*) Now, that's a stupid thing to say, and you know it. Is this as far as we can get? Look at us. Is this where we want to be? You want to get out of those handcuffs and put me in? Is that your idea? We should sit here in silence 'til somebody kicks in that door and blows my head off. Lord, child, let's do some talking; let's see if we can get to a third place somehow or, failing that, let's get some hours off the clock, see if we can understand where we are, now that is why the "hell" you should talk to me.

KEELY: (*Not looking up.*) Bullshit. (*Lights out.*)

SCENE 7

The lights come up on WALTER talking to KEELY at the bed. She has her hands over her ears. DU stands somewhere above the bed.

WALTER: By 25 days, the developing heart starts beating; by 45 days, it has eyes, ears, mouth, kidneys, liver; it has a brain and a heart pumping blood it has made itself. I know you can hear me, Keely.

KEELY: No.

WALTER: Three months, right now, there is sexual differentiation. The baby sleeps and wakes and excretes and has vocal cords he even tries to use.

KEELY: You have no idea. . .no idea. . .

WALTER: At four months. . .it has eyelashes and expressions you could recognize from your grandmother.

KEELY: Please stop talking.

WALTER: Why wouldn't you let the baby live, Keely? You never have to see it again if that's what you want.

KEELY: No.

WALTER: The baby isn't rape, Keely, the baby is a baby. . .

KEELY: Please. (*She starts to cry.*)

WALTER: Last year there were 700,000 people wanting babies who couldn't get them. . .listen to me.

KEELY: Don't touch me.

WALTER: I know carrying this baby is difficult and emotional. . .but, after abortion there are frightening emotional side effects.

KEELY: Please. . .

WALTER: . . .serious depression, terrible guilt, mental illness, self-destructiveness.

DU: That's enough.

WALTER: Spare yourself, Keely. . .finish this in a life-giving way so you can respect yourself.

KEELY: Why don't you give yourself a blow job.

WALTER: (*Forcibly turning her face to his.*) Your mouth should be washed out with soap.

DU: That's enough!

WALTER: (*To DU.*) What are you doing?

DU: I am suggesting that she isn't hearing you. . .

WALTER: Yes?

DU: They are important things, and we would want her to hear them.

WALTER: (*Coming back to himself. Understanding.*) Yes.

DU: That's all I'm saying.

WALTER: Thank you.

DU: That's all I'm saying.

WALTER: Sometimes I don't realize. . .sometimes I am over-emphatic. (*To KEELY.*) Please accept my apologies. (*He lightly touches KEELY's arm.*) That certainly won't happen again. (*She stares at him.*) I, umm. . .I'll be back this evening. Is there anything I can bring you? (*No answer.*) Well, then. . . (*He goes and collects his things. To DU.*) Thank you for pointing out that I had overstepped myself. I'm sorry, Keely. (*No answer. He leaves and closes the door.*)

DU: (*She goes to the door and locks it. She comes back and sits on the edge of the bed.*) I'll just be here. I won't touch you or say anything. I'd just like to sit here. (*Lights down.*)

SCENE 8

Lights up. DU is mopping the floor.

DU: . . . so, the stock market crashed, three days later, there I was. The doctor asked my father what they planned on calling me. . "Calamity Jane," he said. There were ten kids, I was the fourth. Would you like me to stop talking? (*KEELY shakes her head "no".*) My mother, Jesus watch over her, died of leukemia at 37, leaving ten children, God help us, you can imagine. Well, God provides. I took care of the little ones, and my sister, 'til college took care of me. So much to learn, such a stupid little girl. Thousands of meals I put together. Sometimes I would step into a closet for the peace and quiet. Oh, mercy! Oh, my father was quiet, Lord he was silence in shoes, I mean it. . .so tall. . . he wore one suit, and he would move through the mess and noise and contention and tears, and he would pick up the fallen, dry the ones who were wet, find the lost and admonish the fallen away with an old wooden spoon. And then he'd go and sit in the midst of the madhouse and read his bible. When his eyes tired he'd have me read it, on the floor beside him, one hand on my shoulder. You know, I remember a hundred things he did and nothing of what he said. He died of throat cancer, and he died so hard I don't even like to think about it. (*A pause.*) What about your father? (*A pause.*) What about your father? (*Irritation.*) I think you're spoiled rotten, what do you think? You care for your father, and you think that's hard? It's a privilege to do that, young lady. You work two jobs and think you're put upon? There are millions suffering because they can't provide. Your husband forced himself on you? You should have gone to the police. You want to end the life of the baby you are carrying? It's contrary to God's will, it's murder, it's not necessary, it's as selfish an act as you could conceive, and we will not allow you to harm that child or yourself. You are better than that, you know you are, and how you feel or what trouble you might have is not so important as a life. Now grow up and talk to me. (*A pause.*) What about your father?

KEELY: My father? He can move his right arm and the right side of his face.

DU: I'm sorry.

KEELY: He's a cop who got shot being held as a shield during a drug bust. You mess with a cop's daughter, they will skin you alive.

DU: I am truly sorry.

KEELY: You know what you get for kidnapping?

DU: Well, not to the year I don't.

KEELY: All you've got left. All of your life.

DU: I'm a bible Christian, Keely, and you can have my life to stop the slaughter is my perspective, I suppose. Not that I could take the prison, Lord, I don't even like low ceilings. I don't know what I'd do. But. . .Isaiah 44:24, "This is what the Lord says—your Redeemer who formed you in the womb: See, I set before you today life and prosperity, death and destruction, now choose life, so that you and your children may live." (*A pause.*) I don't know if you care anything about the bible.

KEELY: (*Flaring.*) Hey, I didn't choose to have this baby.

DU: And the baby didn't choose, honey, but the baby's there.

KEELY: And I'm here. I don't have, you know, bible reading to hold up. I'm not some lawyer, alright, with this argument, that argument, put in this clause, fix the world. I can't do this, take care of my dad, get myself straight, take on a baby, I got, you know, nightmares, stuff like that, I start crying in supermarkets because they're out of carrots is where I am because, I could get messed up, who knows, killed by who impregnated me, not to mention I might, I don't know, hate this baby, hurt this baby, throw the baby or something like that, I'm not kidding, what's inside me. Now, do you have some bible quotes for that, or am I just beside the point, handcuffed to this bed, carrying the results of being fucked by my ex-husband while he banged my head off a hardwood floor to shut me up?

DU: I'm sorry.

KEELY: You're sorry?

DU: That was the act of an animal at that time.

KEELY: At that time? I could tell you many times. Many times. You don't know who I am, and God knows you don't care, with your scrambled eggs and your grandma act, either let me out of here or leave me alone, do you understand me? I wouldn't eat I don't know what if it came from your hands, I wouldn't touch it, I wouldn't let it inside me. You're filth. I don't care what church you come from or who your God is. You're criminal filth, and I will see to it you get yours. Now, leave me alone. (*She turns away. There is silence.*)

DU: I can't leave you alone, honey. Nobody wants to be left alone. Not really. (*The lights fade.*)

SCENE 9

The light comes up on WALTER sitting by KEELY's bed taking things out of a grocery bag beside him on the floor.

WALTER: Feeling the baby move. I've always thought it must be the most extraordinary sensation. Mouth wash. I believe peppermint was required. Nectarines, I hope they're ripe. I'm told you're over the nausea and that must be very welcome. It wasn't apricots, was it? (*DU nods that it was.*) I'm not an expert shopper, if you hadn't noticed. Emery boards. Kleenex. Peanut butter cups. Certainly makes me understand the mouth wash. Catsup. Oatmeal. And the, uh. . . (*Small hangers with panties.*)

DU: . . .underthings.Size 7 if I'm not mistaken.

WALTER: (*DU nods.*) Now. (*Takes books out.*) "The First Year of Life," very informative. (*Another.*) Doctor Spock, of course. Proof you can't spoil good advice with bad politics, and this, on pregnancy, my wife suggested it. (*KEELY doesn't look up.*) Do you know that I love you, Keely? I love and understand your resistance. I am very proud of you, oddly enough. You believe you are right, and you stick to it. If you were swayed by reason or found new understanding, I believe you would have the guts to admit it. (*No response.*) Listen to me. You have life inside you. It cannot be dismissed by calling it a fetus. It now recognizes your voice. Your voice among all others. You understand? The child is separate from how it was conceived. (*He waits.*) The child is separate from how it was conceived and must also be considered separately from you. Separately, Keely. Your emotions about the conception and the child are valid and honest, but they are not the point. The emotion is not the child. I have no wish to choose between you, but if I must, I choose the child who has no earthly advocate. I can love you, but I must protect the child. This is my responsibility, Keely. Keely? You will have the child, Keely, so the book on pregnancy, at least, will be of practical value to you. (*He puts that book on the bed. KEELY doesn't look up.*) This is a pamphlet on abortion. (*He opens it.*) Please look at the picture, Keely. (*Again.*) Please look at the picture, Keely. (*She doesn't.*) If you cannot look at these photographs, Keely, you have no right to your opinions. You know that's true. (*She looks up.*) This. (*He turns the page.*) This. And this. This. This. This. (*The lights go down.*)

SCENE 10

Lights up immediately. DU is in the chair by the bed. She takes a pair of baby shoes out of her purse. She puts one in the palm of her hand and holds it out to KEELY. KEELY looks. She takes it. She smells it. Lights out.

SCENE 11

Lights up on KEELY and DU. They sit silently. The time stretches out to almost a full minute.

KEELY: (*Finally.*) I'm hungry.
DU: (*Rising.*) I'll get you some breakfast. (*Lights out.*)

SCENE 12

KEELY sleeps. DU dozes in the rocker. WALTER enters. DU wakes as the door clicks behind him.

DU: (*Startled*) What is it?
WALTER: Shhhh.
DU: What? What time?
WALTER: (*They converse quietly, aware of KEELY.*) A little after midnight.
DU: Something's wrong.
WALTER: Not at all. I brought you a milkshake. I just got here from Baton Rouge. A note from your husband. (*He hands her a folded sheet of lined paper.*) Your husband's been injured. It's not serious.
DU: What?
WALTER: Du, nothing, read it. He broke a finger in a fall.
DU: A fall?
WALTER: They rushed a clinic. He was right in the front where they told him not to be. I'm a little tired.
DU: He's too old for the clinics. It could have been his hip.
WALTER: He wants to be with the children who protest. He doesn't want them to be afraid.
DU: He's 70 years old.
WALTER: You try and stop him.
DU: (*Reading.*) He's arrested.
WALTER: Trespassing. Out tomorrow. Write a letter, we'll get it to him.

How is she?

DU: Well, she gets her sleep.

WALTER: And?

DU: She's thinking about it now.

WALTER: (*Nods.*) Split the milkshake with me, I haven't eaten.

DU: Did we close the clinic in Baton Rouge?

WALTER: (*Shakes his head "no."*) They put up a chain link fence. They're still killing 25 a day. (*DU brushes hair out of KEELY's face.*)

DU: Thank God we took her.

WALTER: (*Shakes himself.*) I'm asleep on my feet. (*The lights fade.*)

SCENE 13

Lights up on KEELY sitting up in bed eating breakfast.

DU: (*She watches as KEELY eats around the eggs.*) You ever try catsup?

KEELY: What, on eggs?

DU: Oh, we'd buy this spicy kind by the case, Lone Star Catsup. My brothers would heat up the bottles in boiling water so they could get it out faster. (*A moment. KEELY pokes at her eggs.*)

KEELY: (*Finally.*) For what?

DU: Eggs, rice, they put it on cantaloupe which like to drove my mother from the house. (*An involuntary smile from KEELY, and then, sensing her complicity, silence.*) So, he left high school, Cole?

KEELY: Listen. . .(*Having started to say something about the situation, she thinks better of it, then her need to talk gets the better of her.*) He took a factory job. He was into cars, he wanted this car. His uncle worked a canning line got him on. (*A pause.*)

DU: And?

KEELY: We still went out. . .off and on. We got in an accident, we were both drunk, I got pretty cut up. My dad's cop pals leaned on him. After that. . .I don't know, lost touch. (*A pause.*)

DU: Lost touch.

KEELY: I don't want to get comfortable talking to you.

DU: Keely. .

KEELY: Forget it.

DU: Please. . .

KEELY: I said forget it. (*A long pause.*) I'm going crazy in here. I could chew off my wrist here. That paint smear on the pipe up there, I hate that, you know? This floor. That long crack. Everywhere I look. Wherever I look, it makes me sick. (*She tears up.*) Come on, give me a break, will you. I gotta get out of here, I can't do this. (*Mad at herself.*) Damn it.

DU: (*Gently.*) Help us pass the time, Keely. You're not giving up. I know that. (*KEELY looks down.*) You lost touch.

KEELY: Yeah. (*A pause.*) There were guys at school, you know, different crowds. . .37 days, right? (*DU nods.*) I was. . .man. . .I was, umm, waitressing, actually before he left, down at the Gaslight. . .he didn't like me working. I just blew him off. (*A moment.*) If I talk, it's just talk. . .only talk, that's all. . .because this is shit, what you do to me, worse than that.

DU: Only talk.

KEELY: Because I don't buy this, you tell him I don't buy it. (*DU nods. They sit. Then. . .*) So I was at a Tammy Wynette concert, you know, somebody else's choice, and there he was, definitely his choice as I found out, and my date is. . .well, forget him, so we got together and it got hot really fast and we ended up getting married, which nobody I knew thought was a good idea, which made me really contrary which is a problem I have. . .like up to here. . .so, you know, what I said, we got married, plus. . .(*Finishing the eggs.*) The catsup's all right.

DU: Oh, it's good.

KEELY: I mean I knew who he was, and I did it anyway. I knew about the drinking, I knew about the temper, I don't know where my head was, in my pants, I guess.

DU: Well, I married a man deemed suitable and that can be another problem. There is only one way a man is revealed, and that is day in and day out. You can know a woman through what she says, but don't try it with a man.

KEELY: Yeah, he had a line. I even knew it was a line.

DU: I'll just take the tray.

KEELY: And I knew he drank. Oh, hey, he downpedaled it before we got married. . .way, way downpedaled. He would drink, say two, two drinks, say that was his limit, take me home, go out pour it down 'til ten in the morning, I found that out.

DU: They talk about drugs, but it's still drinking the majority of it, now I have never been drunk in my life, is that something? I'm often tempted so I'll know what I'm missing, yes ma'am, I've tried the marijuana.

KEELY: Bull.

DU: Oh, I have, and it didn't do a thing for me and that's a fact, and I've been in a men's room which I doubt you have, and I've kissed three men in one day, so don't you think you can lord it over me.

KEELY: You smoked?

DU: Oh, yes. Found the marijuana in my son's sock, sat on his bed, waiting' til I heard him come in the front door, lit up and let him come on up and find me there doing it. Shocked him down to his drawers I might say. . . .straightened him up in a hurry. That's the one who's an accountant in Denver. All boys. I would have given my heart for a girl baby. (*An awkward pause.*) It's noisy, too many boys in a house.

KEELY: (*A pause.*) Suitable?

DU: What? Oh, suitable. I was keeping company with a slaughterhouse man who could pop your eyes out with his shirt off, but he was an atheist and a socialist and who knows what else, and that was one too many for my father so he ran him off and put me together with a nice German milkman whose father owned the dairy, if you see my point. August. His name, not the month. I married him at nineteen, in 1947, and two months later the dairy went under, so I got no money and he looked just terrible undressed. The fact is he was an uninteresting man, but he got into the storage business and turned out a good provider. Now, listen close here, we went along 'til he bored me perfectly silent, if you can imagine, and God found us pretty late when the kids were gone or near gone, and when God found that man he turned him into a firebrand and an orator and a beacon to others, and I fell in love with him and that bed turned into a lake of flame and I was, so help me, bored no more, and that's a testimony. There is change possible where you never hope to find it, and that is the moral of my story, you can stop listening.

KEELY: Right.

DU: It is. Still nothing to look at but I just close my eyes. The children kept me in that marriage until it became a marriage and the love I bore them kept me alive until the marriage could catch up.

KEELY: So what am I supposed to be? Glad?

DU: Things do change.

KEELY: Yeah, they get worse. He drank more, he got meaner, he screwed around, got herpes, gave 'em to me. My dad got shot, Cole wanted to move to Arizona because he knew I'd have to take care of him. Pawned a lot of stuff, got himself a recliner. I'm waitressing, minimum wage, cashier at a car wash, 70 hours minimum, he drinks himself out of his job, real thoughtful, right? The recession came on, we just fought minute to minute anytime we laid eyes on each other, I said I wanted a divorce, he hit me, and I left. I was out of there 15 minutes after he hit me. . .I was a crazy, out-of-my-mind lunatic I lived with him all that time. Jesus! What the hell was I thinking of?

DU: It was a marriage, Keely.

KEELY: Yeah. After that, he was all over me. I'd look out the window, he'd be in the back yard. The grocery, the library, when I was hanging up laundry, walk into the same bar when I was on a date. He'd come down to the restaurant, say it was about borrowing money, but he knew I wasn't giving him money, forget that, he just liked me to be scared which is what I figured out. Then it stopped for six months, who knows why, then he came back, sent flowers, left messages, begged me to talk to him for one hour, so I invited him over, you know, I thought we could sit down and let go of it. I thought I could take his hand and say we're clear, we're two different people. You know, some dumb ass idea like that. That we could just let it go, you know, be whole and be gone, you know what I mean? So I fixed him dinner, and he brought me this stuffed animal, and we were doing, well, not perfect but all right, and I just touched his arm so he would know it was alright, and he locked onto my hand, and I said "let go now," and he started in. . .said he needed. . .pulled me in, you know, hard, and I got a hand in his face, and he. . .he bit down. . .bit down hard, and I. . .I don't know, went nuts. . .bunch of stuff. . .got me down on the floor. . .got me down on the floor and raped me. That's how he caught up with our marriage, that's how he changed. (*They sit in silence.*)

DU: Change can start anytime.

KEELY: I don't want to talk about it. (*A pause.*) You believe God sees you?

DU: I do.

KEELY: He sees you now?

DU: I believe he does. (*A pause.*) Keely? (*No answer.*) Doctor says you're in as good a fourth month as you can be.

KEELY: Let's give it a rest, okay?

DU: He says that baby is lively. (*No response.*) Almost time for your birthday. (*A pause.*)

KEELY: How do you know that?

DU: Now, Keely, that's the least of what I know, and you know it.

KEELY: From my driver's license.

DU: The man says you can have a cake.

KEELY: The man?

DU: The man in charge. (*A moment.*)

KEELY: If I do what, I can have a cake?

DU: Oh, a few pamphlets.

KEELY: I'm not reading that crap. I mean it. Don't you bring it anywhere near me.

DU: You're not afraid of information, are you, honey?

KEELY: You call that information?

DU: Well, there's facts to it.

KEELY: I'm not having a baby. I'm not having it and have somebody adopt it. I'm not having it and keeping it. It won't be. It won't. (*A pause.*)

DU: What would you like for your birthday, honey? (*KEELY looks at her.*) Besides that. That's not in my power. (*A pause. Will KEELY speak?*)

KEELY: I would like to get dressed. I never liked being in a nightgown. I don't like my own smell, I know that's crazy. You know how you can smell yourself off your night stuff.

DU: Oh, I can share that. That's something doesn't get a bit better with age, let me tell you.

KEELY: I want to stand up. I want my hands free, I don't care if it's for ten minutes, one minute. I want to walk into a bathroom. I want a chocolate cake. I want to stand up, not bent over on my birthday.

DU: Oh, honey. We only do this because we don't know what else to do. We can't think what else. . .I don't know, I don't. . .birthdays when they're little, the looks on those faces. . .those little hands. . .

KEELY: Little hands, little faces, you make me sick. . .Jesus, can you listen to yourself? All this crap about babies. You don't care about this baby, you just want it to be your little. . .I don't know. . .your little political something, right, God's little visual aid you can hold up at abortion clinics instead of those pickled miscarriages you usually tote around. . .hold up, Baby Tia, wasn't that the one you had downtown trying to pass it off like it was aborted? I can't believe you don't make yourself sick. . .throw up. . .you make me sick, how do you talk this garbage?

DU: (*A moment.*) I have that dress you had on. . .something the worse for wear. . .he might let me get it cleaned. . .cleaned for your birthday. (*A moment*)

KEELY: I don't hate babies, if that's what you think.

DU: I know that.

KEELY: What the hell is your name? You can. . .you can. . .you can give me that for my birthday. I would like to know what the hell to call you when I talk to you!

DU: Du.

KEELY: What?

DU: I get called Du.

KEELY: Du.

DU: Uh-huh.

KEELY: Du what? Du why? Never mind, forget it. . .I would like to be free for ten minutes on my birthday.

DU: You might have to read some pamphlets.

KEELY: What the hell happened to you, Du? Do you see where we are? Look at this where you got to. Look at me. You used to be a person sometime, right? You look like one. You sound like one. You see the movie Alien where they end up with snakes in their chests? What happened to you?

DU: They tear apart the babies, they poison them with chemicals, and burn them to death with salt solution, they take them out by Caesarian alive and let them die of neglect or strangulation, and then later on these poor women, they cut their wrists or swallow lye, and then they bring them to me because I'm the nurse. Over and over. Over and over. Little hands. Little feet. I've held babies. I've lost babies. I took a baby through six months of chemotherapy and lost that baby. I need to sleep. That's what happened to me.

KEELY: (*Almost gently.*) I can't raise this baby, Du. I'm so angry and fucked up, I just can't do it. I dream how it happened over and over all the time. I'd be angry at the baby, I think so. I'd hurt the baby sometime and might not even know it, that could happen. If I had a baby, my first one, and I gave it away, I'd just cry all the time, I would. I'm doing this on empty and, if I did that, I would be past empty and I don't know. I have such black moods, it frightens me. The baby would come out of being chained to a bed, you know what I mean. It's not my baby, it's the people's who made me have it, and I couldn't treat it as my baby, not even if I loved it, I couldn't. He'd come around, see. He wouldn't stay off if I had his baby. He would never, ever in this world leave off me, and I think sometime he'll kill me, that's all I can think. Or hurt the baby, whatever, however in his head he could get me, he would do. . .would do it. Really. And I can't have his baby. . .uh. . .it's just not something I can do. . .because I'm about this far, you know. . .right up to the edge of it. . .right there . . .right there. (*A pause.*) So I guess it's me or the baby, so I guess that's crazy, but you don't. . .I don't show you. . .just how. . .how angry I really am. I don't. I don't. (*A pause.*)

DU: He could have changed, Keely. (*A pause. The lights fade.*)

SCENE 14

DU, wearing a stethoscope, sits on the bed, examining KEELY.

DU: Probably just a urinary tract infection, as far as we can tell, oh, very common, practically nothing. The bladder is right there in front of the uterus, and it compresses when the uterus enlarges, so, it may not empty completely and the urine stagnates, and those bacteria just get after it. You see? So we need to wash more down there, lots of liquids, vitamin C. . .(*She moves the stethoscope.*) Now, there's the fetal heartbeat, would you like to hear. . .(*KEELY does not signify. DU puts the stethoscope on her, she doesn't resist. DU moves it on her chest.*) Anything? Anything? Now? (*KEELY nods. DU lets her listen. She does. Suddenly, KEELY reaches up and takes off the stethoscope. DU takes it.*) We should get a Doppler probe, you could hear it better. (*No response.*) Oh, panty liners, I forgot, the vaginal discharge will be increasing. (*She goes to make a note. Lights down.*)

SCENE 15

The lights come up with WALTER and KEELY in heated argument. DU stands upstage.

KEELY: . . .cannot do this!
WALTER: Living in a nation based on. . .
KEELY: . . .do this to people. . .
WALTER: Christian values.
KEELY: Saving these babies while you rip up the rest of us. . .
WALTER: Because it is a central issue in a Christian society.
KEELY: My dad locked in a bed, man, who takes care of him. . .?
WALTER: We address those responsibilities, Keely.
KEELY: . . .like I was some baby farm, baby sow, like they make veal by nailing those calves' feet to the floor. . .
WALTER: Because you will not confront. . .
KEELY: . . .'til I'm fattened up for Jesus, right?
WALTER: That's enough, Keely.
KEELY: Enough, my ass!
WALTER: Do not shout at me!
KEELY: Christ this, Christ that. . .
WALTER: Because you will not take responsibility.
KEELY: So you and a bunch of old guys. . .
WALTER: When you have alternatives that clearly. . .
KEELY: . . .can do whatever you want and ram your Christ right up my. .
WALTER: Enough! You listen to me, young lady, you are carrying a child and you will carry it to term. As to my Christ, he will speak to you, saying "Be fruitful and increase in number and fill the earth. . .
KEELY: Yeah, that's really worked out. . .

WALTER: "For your lifeblood I will surely demand an accounting. I will demand an accounting from every animal. And from each man, too.

KEELY: Animals and men, right?

WALTER: "I will demand an accounting for the life of his fellow man.

KEELY: So I must be one of the animals. . .

WALTER: ". . .For in the image of God has God made man." (*KEELY spits full in his face. WALTER steps back, takes out a handkerchief and wipes his face.*) Thank you. I have no right to speak to you in that tone. You are a young woman under enormous and unfortunate stress in a situation beyond your understanding where decisions must be made for you in a gentle and reasonable way. I apologize, it will not happen again.

KEELY: Fuck you.

WALTER: Thank you for accepting my apology. (*Suddenly, both KEELY and DU explode in laughter, it continues, they are overwhelmed by it. Slowly, they control themselves. It breaks out again. At last, as WALTER watches them, unsmiling, it stops.*) You find obscenity amusing? (*A beat. The women are again overwhelmed by laughter.*) We are one nation, under God. And the moral law of our God. (*He waits for another outburst of laughter.*) . . .is all that makes us a nation and within the boundaries of those laws we may speak and decide as a people. . .(*One last fit of the giggles.*). . .but when we transgress or ignore Christ's commandments we no longer have democracy, we have anarchy; we no longer have free speech, we have provocation; and this anarchy begins in the family, which is a nation within the nation, which sustains and teaches and holds dear these precepts which makes us one. And when that family sunders, and turns on itself, and its children make their own laws and speak only anger, then will the nation founder and become an obscenity that eats its young. (*He waits a moment and then turns on his heel and leaves, closing the door hard behind him.*)

DU: Oh, my.

KEELY: Oh, my.

(*WALTER re-enters, picks up the briefcase he has left.*)

WALTER: We have further business in the morning. (*He exits again.*)

DU: I shouldn't have laughed, I don't know what I was laughing at.

KEELY: You were laughing because it was funny, Christ doesn't want this.

DU: I don't know.

KEELY: Well, he doesn't. (*She throws the pamphlets that have been on the bed on the floor.*) And this stuff is sewage. And I don't want any more hamburgers or catsup or microwaved peas. And I want a woman doctor instead of that dork with a "Turbo-Christian" T-shirt and his icy hands. And how about some trashy magazines, maybe a TV, books with sex scenes, you know, not the disciples and the Last Supper, plus my back hurts, my legs ache, I'm clammy, I'm cramping, and I would like to see Batman VII, or whatever the hell they've got out there, hell, I don't care, take me to traffic school, I'll think I've gone to goddamn heaven!

DU: (*Holds up a key on a key ring.*) Happy birthday.

KEELY: Oh, my God.

DU: (*Tossing it to her.*) Yes, he is, whether you know it or not. (*She goes to the half refrigerator.*)

KEELY: (*Trying the cuffs.*) My God, does this open this?

DU: And from the fridge.

KEELY: What?

DU: (*Taking out the dress KEELY was delivered in. It is freshly drycleaned, on a hanger, in see-through plastic. She holds it up.*) Nice and chilly.

KEELY: Yes!

DU: And one more thing. . .

KEELY: (*The handcuff opens.*) Oh, man. Forget the sex. This is so cool. I can't believe this.

DU: (*Taking it from behind the heater, a six-pack.*) Warm beer. (*She brings it to KEELY.*)

KEELY: I can stand up. Whoa, a little. . . (*DU moves toward her.*) No, I'm alright. Beer, that's incredible. You don't have any idea. Nobody could have any idea. Standing up straight is this unbelievable pure high.

DU: I couldn't do the cake, I tried, I'm sorry. I could only get out once and I thought the dress was better. . .would you have rather had the cake?

KEELY: No, Du, the dress is fine.

DU: I could have gotten the cake.

KEELY: I'll put it on. Just give me a minute.

DU: Okay.

KEELY: Whoa. Walking. Let me give this a try. Oh, man. It feels like a circus trick, you know? Don't let anybody tell you you don't forget how to do it.

DU: Please, please be careful.

KEELY: This is good, Du, this is really, really good.

DU: The beer is hot because I thought if he looked in the ice box I'd rather he found the dress, well, I don't know what I thought, I was so nervous.

KEELY: Hey, no kidding, the end of the nation as we know it, right? Maybe I'll give that dress a try, what do you think?

DU: CanI help you?

KEELY: No, actually Du I would like to do it by myself, call me crazy, it seems like a real treat. Maybe you could crack the beer or something.

DU: I haven't had a beer in 20 years. On my birthday I would split a Blatts with August.

KEELY: Hard to lift the old arm. . .

DU: They don't make that anymore.

KEELY: Does the mystery man actually talk or does he just make speeches?

DU: Walter?

KEELY: That guy's name is Walter? (*DU nods.*) Like he was really human? Okay, this is sort of on. Boy. I'm pregnant. I know I'm pregnant now. (*A pause.*) This life is strange, huh? (*A pause.*) I don't care, I'm in a dress. (*A look at DU.*) Thank you.

DU: Happy birthday.

KEELY: I never realized it had that word in it. Am I supposed to drink beer?

DU: (*Taken aback.*) Well, I don't know.

KEELY (*A moment.*) Could I have the opener?

DU: They twist off.

KEELY: Right. I spit in his face. I can't believe that.

DU: He provoked you.

KEELY: Yeah. (*A moment.*) Whose side are you on?

DU: He is with God, but he is insufferable about it.

KEELY: Yeah.

DU: (*Nods.*) But he is with God.

KEELY: My idea is that after two beers he doesn't exist.

DU: Oh, I think one would be my limit. (*KEELY hands her one.*) Thank you.

KEELY: How do you know I just won't hit you over the head?

DU: Would you? (*No answer.*) Would you do that, Keely? (*No answer.*) Because there are people upstairs. Because I left my keys with them. Because you can't bar the door and, after hurting me, you would still be here.

KEELY: (*A moment.*) There are guys upstairs?

DU: Yes.

KEELY: Do they like beer?

DU: They call it the "blood of the beast."

KEELY: Right. (*Looks at her beer.*) To what?

DU: Honey, I think you're the birthday girl.

KEELY: (*Toasting.*) To the next half hour. (*DU sips. KEELY literally chugs the bottle.*)

DU: My stars! Oh, I wouldn't do that. Keely, have you lost your senses?

KEELY: I'm trying. (*She opens another one.*)

DU: We have all night.

KEELY: And I would like to spend it fucked up, begging your pardon, blasted, Du, I would really enjoy that. (*She drinks.*) Discount beer, don't knock it.

DU: You might want to sit down for a minute.

KEELY: No way. I forgot I had legs. (*Touching DU's shoulder.*) I don't want to sit down, okay? Boy, I never met anybody who would really take it to the limit like you and that guy. Have an idea or a feeling and just nail that sucker to the wall. Cole, my ex. . .you know. . .if you push, he'll pull, he'll just keep on, but he's crazy. . .I don't think you're crazy, are you? (*She drinks.*) Have this idea about how things should be and take it all the way to here? All the way to the hand-cuffs? Never met anybody like that.

DU: You look nice.

KEELY: Yeah, right. (*DU hands KEELY a pocket mirror.*) Whoa. I don't know about looking in this.

DU: You look nice.

KEELY: Was the kid that died a girl? (*DU nods. KEELY looks in the mirror.*) Well, that was a mistake. (*She looks again.*) Oh, God. I'm so wormy. No color. Look at this hair.

DU: I could put it up for you.

KEELY: Yeah?

DU: Curl you up the old way like I did for my sisters.

KEELY: How's that?

DU: Rags. Rag it. Yes, rag curls, they always come out nice.

KEELY: God, someone putting up my hair, that's been a long time.

DU: Make you feel better. My mother, down at the nursing home, nobody at home, but when I ragged her, she'd smile.

KEELY: Okay, if you drink your beer.

DU: Well, I can do that. (*Pats bed.*) You sit down here.

KEELY: Wow, I am already. . .plastered.

DU: Now I can't do it standing up. (*She goes to her purse.*) I brought a good piece of flannel just in case.

KEELY: I would really like someone to touch me.

DU: (*Holding it up.*) My favorite color. (*KEELY sits.*) I do feel badly about that cake.

KEELY: Forget it. A little dizzy here. Cole wouldn't let me put her out for adoption, not even if I could stand it he wouldn't. (*A pause.*) You actually think you're my friend, don't you? I'm serious. It's a serious question.

DU: Yes.

KEELY: You always chain your friends to a bed?

DU: On her behalf, I would.

KEELY: Funny how there's always been somebody around who knew just what I needed and made me.

DU: Good or bad, depending.

KEELY: Yeah, and they were always men.

DU: Yes, they make a habit of it.

KEELY: I mean all the time. *All* the time.

DU: Sit still.

KEELY: My dad, oh yeah, it was real clear to him, my brother, he picked it right up, boyfriends, my husband, my boss where I work, they got right in there on *my behalf*. . .on my behalf. Hell, I even liked it, I even asked for it. I even missed it when I got over it and right then, right then you bastards were back on my behalf once again.

DU: Now, I don't do hair and listen to swear words.

KEELY: No problem, I'd rather have my hair done. Be-half. No kidding. Maybe less than half. Be less than half. I got the message. You finished that beer yet? (*She looks.*) Two more coming up. (*She gets them, opens them. DU knocks one over.*)

DU: Oh, my.

KEELY: Where's your husband?

DU: Out doing the Lord's work.

KEELY: Like you?

DU: Like me.

KEELY: Nice marriage. (*DU nods.*) Somewhere out there? (*DU nods.*) Know who else is out there? The FBI, fed cops, state cops, town cops, drycleaners, every living eye in Cincinnati.

DU: We're not in Cincinnati, honey. (*A pause.*)

KEELY: Where am I?

DU: Well, you're a long way from Cincinnati. (*Pause.*)

KEELY: I know your face, bunch of stuff about you. When I'm one day out, you'll be one day in.

DU: We've been in our Lord's underground for three years, honey. There's not a soul alive who knows where I am.

KEELY: For what?

DU: For lives. Our Lord. For an end to this holocaust.

KEELY: But you don't care what happens to me.

DU: I would give my life for you to be well with a healthy baby. (*KEELY takes a long pull on her third beer.*)

KEELY: Forget this. (*She exhales, she drinks.*) Know what I like to do? I like to climb. Straight up. Straight, straight up. Colder than hell. The colder the better. I like the frost on the eyebrows, you know? (*DU has been working on her hair for some time.*) That feels good. I used to pull my own hair, it was like a habit. Fear of heights. I don't have it. I always thought I would have it, but I don't have it.

DU: Sit still.

KEELY: Cole screwed around with climbing. . .when he was sober. He like kept at me, you know, so I tried it. The pisser was, I was great. . . what can I say, I was, and did it frost his ass and did I love it? I could do stuff in rock shoes without an ice ax he couldn't even get near. It was so cool. Whip up a crack line, leave him on the wall. This one guy said I could be a pro, no kidding. Went solo, what a feeling, man. Cole yelled at me, Dad yelled at me, I really didn't give a damn, I didn't. Met some people, took a week off, caught a ride with these two women out to Fremont Peak in Wyoming. Man, I never saw anything like that. They got these weird sleeping bags you can hang vertically from a sheer wall and get into? So I'm way, way up, right? And some weather blows through, so I roped myself in and got this hanging bag out and spent the night. I was hanging in this bag, see, 3,000 feet straight down, colder than hell, and I thought, well, you may pee from fear or freeze on the wall, but there is nobody up here to do any Goddamn thing on your behalf. I got down from there and got a divorce. Boy, it was a good night's sleep up there, I'll tell you.

DU: Well, you shouldn't do a thing like that by yourself.

KEELY: It was. . .I don't know what it was.

DU: Turn this way.

KEELY: You ever done anything, like that?

DU: I'm not sure I know what you mean?

KEELY: Done. . .done anything.

DU: Raised sisters and brothers. Raised three good boys. (*A pause.*) I guess I'm doing something now.

KEELY: Yeah. You're way out there now.

DU: Yes, I suppose I am.

KEELY: Yeah you are. Get me out of here.

DU: I've thought about it.

KEELY: But you would?

DU: I would do for you, Keely, anything I didn't have to do against myself.

KEELY: You do this against me.

DU: No ma'am.

KEELY: You choose the baby's life over my life.

DU: No ma'am. Your life is in your hands. You liked that mountain because you were perfectly alone, Keely, but what I hope and pray for is perfect union and powerful life-giving connection. . .I long for it, need it, and I'm thinking that if you get your wish and I mine, my spirits will soar, and yours. . .well, I can't imagine "perfectly alone," I really can't. A mother can be together with a child in a perfect way, in a union that surpasses any wish you ever wished for yourself. If you haven't felt it, you can't imagine it, and it's within your power to feel it. There is union with a higher power. The baby though, that's a sure thing, oh, I can guarantee it.

KEELY: I would give all the babies and Gods just to be alone with myself now, I'm sorry but I would. I don't want to be in another box where something else is more important than I am.

DU: There is always something more.

KEELY: Maybe when I get healthy, but not now. They say an animal will go off by herself to heal.That's what I want.

DU: It's the wrong time, Keely.

KEELY: I haven't ever been alone! Sharing with my brother, moving in with roommates, moving in with Cole, moving back to Dad's, always other people in the room, always hearing other people talk, other people cough, other people sleep. Jesus! I dream about Antarctica, you know, no people, just ice. Nobody on your side of the bed, no do this, don't do that, no guys and what they want, what they have to have, just this flat white, right, as far, you know, as far as you could see, like right out to the edge, no items, no chairs, no cars, no people, and you can listen as hard as you want and you couldn't hear one goddamn thing.

DU: That would be dying, Keely.

KEELY: Yeah? Good. I'll go there then, where you can listen as hard as you want and you can't hear one goddamn thing, so if you wanted to hear something you would have to hear yourself breathe, like you were in a white sack and there wasn't anything out there. (*A still moment.*) He said, "You want it? You want it? You want it?" Perfect rhythm, you know, banging my head off the floor. And I thought, this is like a beat, you know, had a beat, and I was inside this sound and I looked up and his eyes were completely blank, man, like moons. I almost got his eye. I came real close. I wanted that eye. I wanted it. Well, you don't get everything you want.

DU: Oh, baby.

KEELY: I kind of drifted off while he pumped. Yeah, I was out of there for sure.

DU: No more now.

KEELY: The sleeping bag. . .

DU: Shhhh.

KEELY: Up there in the sleeping bag. . .

DU: I know.

KEELY: It was real cold.

DU: I know.

KEELY: Then he went home. Hold me.

DU: Yes.

KEELY: More. Tighter.

DU: I got you. I got you.

KEELY: (*Letting herself be rocked.*) Forget this.

DU: Shhhh.

KEELY: (*Rage, not at DU but at the other.*) Noooooo!! (*DU still rocks her.*)

DU: That's right. That's right. It's alright. It's alright. (*She sings softly.*) K-K-Katie. . .beautiful lady. . .you're the only g-g-girl that I adore. . (*The lights fade out.*)

SCENE 16

The next morning. KEELY is asleep in DU's arms. DU sleeps as well. The squawk box springs to life.

WALTER'S VOICE: Coming down. (*They stir.*) Coming down.

DU: (*Waking.*) Oh, my. (*She tries to disengage herself. KEELY wakes.*)

WALTER'S VOICE: Coming down.

KEELY: What is it?

DU: The room.

WALTER'S VOICE: Please reply.

KEELY: Quick. (*They start to clean the room almost in a panic. DU grabs empty beer bottles and stashes them behind the heater. KEELY shoves the hanger and plastic bag under her mattress.*)

WALTER'S VOICE: What is going on? (*DU moves to the microphone. KEELY strips off her dress and puts it under her covers.*)

DU: (*Into microphone.*) Come ahead. (*KEELY puts on the nightgown. DU unlocks the cuffs. We hear WALTER's key in the lock. KEELY gets into the cuffs and sits on bed. The door opens. DU begins to work on KEELY's hair. WALTER enters.*)

WALTER: Good morning.

DU: Good morning.

WALTER: What is going on, please?

DU: I'm sorry. (*WALTER doesn't answer, he simply looks at her.*) Last night was her birthday, I brought her beer as a gift, I didn't answer you because we were hiding the bottles.

WALTER: May I see them, please? (*DU gets the six-pack and holds it up.*) Where are the bottlecaps? (*She takes them out of her pocket. He looks at them.*) There's one more. (*She finds it and hands it to him.*) You used an opener? (*She shakes her head "no." He looks at bed.*) Is this where the handcuffs were snapped? (*She doesn't respond.*) I find this. . .unacceptable. (*An outburst.*) What the hell could you have been thinking of? (*He takes the time to regain control.*) That was stupid and destructive. You broke the discipline that protects us and the work. Alcohol is harmful to the child, which is our primary concern. Worst of all, you've made it impossible for me to trust you. What else were you doing?

DU: I put up her hair.

WALTER: And what else?

DU: I held her until she fell asleep. (*A pause.*)

WALTER: Good morning, Keely.

KEELY: Hey. (*A pause.*)

WALTER: You may finish her hair. (*He moves around the room examining it. DU moves to KEELY.*) Hell is a place, it is not an obscenity. (*KEELY and DU exchange a glance.*) It would be very difficult for two women in this circumstance not to develop complicity. I should know that. (*DU goes on taking the rags out.*) The easy part of this for you, Keely, is that you have been coerced. We have had to coerce you because the laws which should have guided you are made by venal, self-serving politicians who invariably do the easy thing. You will shortly be returned to your home where you will be confronted by hard choices to be made without guidance. You will choose whether to love and raise your child or give the child up to young parents in a functioning and successful marriage who will become that child's family. You won't be coerced, you will choose. I don't need to tell you how difficult single parenting is. You've been kind enough to read the books I provided you. (*DU finishes.*) People who make jokes at the expense of family and ridicule those of us who understand its central, un-negotiable worth are contemptible, callow, duplicitous fools. Believe me, they are the most dangerous people in this society. If I could teach you one thing, I would teach you that. (*A moment.*) Cole is here to see you, Keely.

KEELY: Noooo!

WALTER: Listen.

KEELY: Absolutely not! You keep him out of here, do you hear me? I don't want to see him. I won't see him.

WALTER: Cole is here to see you, you ought to listen to him.

KEELY: If you bring him in here, I'll kill him, or I'll kill myself, or I'll kill you if I get anywhere near you.

WALTER: He is changed from the inside out, actually transfigured, he wants your forgiveness.

KEELY: I'm warning you.

WALTER: You don't believe in forgiveness?

KEELY: Not for him, and you better not bring him in here.

WALTER: He has accepted Christ into his life. He has denied stimulants. He has cast out evil and accepted responsibility. He asked me, Keely, if he might mortify his flesh, begged me to witness, and in seclusion he lashed himself until he fainted.

KEELY: Yeah! Well, I wish I'd seen it.

WALTER: This man who has been cleansed is not the man who attacked you.

KEELY: Goddamn it! Are you, crazy, you are all crazy, do you know that? You think I care about rapists who find Jesus? The two of you whaling away in some back room. He did it to me, and I loathe him in ways you cannot begin to imagine. Let him hold you down and do it and you might have some idea. Keep him out of here, man!

WALTER: He won't touch you, Keely. I have promised him ten minutes to talk to you.

KEELY: No!

DU: Don't make her.

WALTER: (*Looks at DU and then at KEELY.*) I'll give you a moment to compose yourself. (*He exits.*)

KEELY: Du?

DU: I didn't know.

KEELY: Are you sure?

DU: (*A small pause.*) I knew he was saved.

KEELY: How?

DU: They found him and worked with him.

KEELY: They?

DU: We.

KEELY: So you knew?

DU: (*A pause.*) Yes.

KEELY: He was always going to come here.?

DU: It was always possible. (*A pause.*) Let me brush your hair.

KEELY: No, thank you. (*DU comes and sits on the bed.*) Don't.

DU: Keely.

KEELY: Don't sit on the bed. (*DU gets up.*)

DU: If you forgave him, you'd be free of him, don't you think so?

KEELY: I should have put him in jail.

DU: Why didn't you? (*KEELY shakes her head, she doesn't know.*) You should have, honey. You gave us a harder time because you didn't. Sometimes you have to revenge before you forgive, but then the only way to rid yourself and clean yourself is the forgiveness our Lord makes sacred. It's the only armor.

KEELY: So it's my fault?

DU: I didn't say that, honey.

KEELY: I think you said it's my fault.

DU: I didn't say that. I believe that in extremity you must punish, which is God's wrath, or forgive, which is God's grace.

KEELY: This is from nowhere, this is just talk. You haven't been there, you don't have a clue. There are some things it's your job not to forget. That's God's grace if there is any.

DU: Honey. . .

KEELY: I forgive you, you brought me a beer. (*DU moves toward KEELY.*) No more. (*It's quiet. WALTER moves back into the room. COLE enters. He wears a neat blue suit, white shirt and conservative tie. He has short hair, recently barbered, and carefully shined shoes. He is serious and, if possible, handsome. He is, just below the surface, very nervous. The effect is oddly engaging.*)

COLE: Hello, Keely. (*No answer. She regards him.*) Your dad's well. I see him every day. I brought one flower because I didn't know what else to bring. I got it out of your yard. (*He puts it at the bottom of the bed and backs away again.*) Are you all right? You look all right. (*He turns to WALTER.*) Does she have to be handcuffed? (*WALTER nods yes. He goes out into the hall and brings in a straight-backed chair which he places for COLE a few feet from the bed. COLE sits in it. WALTER and DU stand.*) What I did, it was something an animal would do. I should have been killed for it. I would wake up in the middle of the night and think that. Every night. I couldn't stand to look at myself. I didn't like to look down and see my hands or my feet. I wouldn't use a pen or a pencil because then you have to see your hand. I grew a beard because I couldn't shave. I wore the same clothes all the time, I was up to a quart a day.

KEELY: Save it for Jesus. (*A long pause.*)

COLE: They found me. I was out. I wasn't human anymore. I won't describe it. Remember when we went down to Pensacola? That was some trip. Hey, I got your cat. I'm taking care of your cat. You got it after, right? I've been wondering what its name is? Your cat. What its name is? It's a great cat. I call it Stripes, you know, because I don't know. (*A long pause.*) I would cut off my hand, you know, like they used to do. I would do that if it would make a difference.

KEELY: Do it.

COLE: (*A moment.*) Okay, Keely.

KEELY: And don't ever use my name. I don't let you. I don't want your mouth on my name. (*A moment.*) You won't cut off your hand, you don't have the balls.

COLE: I could do anything.

WALTER: This isn't what we're here for.

COLE: Anything.

KEELY: To somebody else, you son-of-a-bitch.

WALTER: We are a family here. Like it or not like it. The father, the mother, two children.

KEELY: You're the father here?

WALTER: Effectively. Effectively, Keely. We are a family, because no family exists for either of you. We are a family because there is a child to be considered here. I ensure the child will live and hope to see it' thrive. Because I have more experience of life than you, I know that later you will understand the wisdom of this position. Both of you have responsibilities to this child. The acceptance of these responsibilities is not optional in this family. I say that as the head of the family. We are here to discuss how to discharge those responsibilities. I will ensure that we do. (*To COLE.*) Say what you have to say.

COLE: Take me back. Forgive me. I loved you in a bad way, a terrible way, and I sinned against your flesh and spirit. God forgive me. I'm an alcoholic but I don't drink now. I don't know. . .I was. . .lived like. . .didn't know right from wrong, but I'm with Jesus now. I accept him as my Lord and he leads me in his path. I will stay on the path. I will stay on the path. We were married, Keely, you are carrying my baby, let's start from there. I put you on a pedestal, Keely, I do, I wouldn't say it, and I am in the mud, I'm drowning and I ask you to lift me up and then we minister to this child. Jeez, Keely, our child. You know in my house, in my father's house, Jeez, what were those kids, they were nuthin', they were disposable. In your house, right, you know what a time you had. You know. But it can be different for him. I'm different, look in my eyes, you know that. Hey, my temper, you know, I don't do that, it's over. (*Indicating WALTER.*) Ask him is it over. I think about you every minute, every day. I want to dedicate my life to you, because it's owed, it's owed to you. You got my baby. I hurt you so bad you would kill a baby! That's not you, who would describe you, you would do that? Jeez, Keely, don't kill the baby. I brought a book we could look up names, we could do that tonight. You pick the name, I would be proud. I'm going to wait on you. You're the boss. They got me a job. I'm employed. Five o'clock, I'm coming home. Boom. No arguments. I help with the house, we can be partners, I understand that guys, you know, we didn't get it, you know, that was yesterday, that's over. I'm back from the dead. I don't say you should believe. me but because the baby you should test me out. You gotta take my hand here, we could start from there, I'm asking you. (*His hand extended, he waits, a long time.*) Come on, Keely. I love you. I can't make love to another woman, you know what I mean. (*His hand is still out.*) You loved me and I destroyed that out of the bottle. But, Jeez, look at me, took off 30 pounds, I don't care what they tell me at AA, I'm never taking another drink. I'm never. I wanted to suffer what you suffered so I had them whip me, I wanted to take off the flesh, I wanted more pain. I wanted more pain. I wanted more pain. I wanted your pain. I wanted to be even with you so I could put out my hand and we could be one to one. Come on, take my hand. Come on, Keely. Come on, Keely. (*A time.*) I dream of your body, baby. For all those years I knew the small of your back, it's burned into my hand. I worship your body, I adore you. Come on. Come on. (*He moves off the chair.*) You don't have to ask me to be on my knees, I'm on my knees. What am I without you? I'm only what I did to you. I can't demand. What could I demand? Choose to lift me up. Who else can you save, Keely, but me? I'm the only one you can save. (*His hand is inches from hers.*) Take my hand, come on. It's five inches, you know what I mean? It's right here. It's right here for us to do. We held hands before we kissed. Who can say that? Like it doesn't work that way anymore, right? You don't have to make me promises, I'm not saying that. How could I expect that? I'm saying take the hand alone. (*A short wait.*) Let me touch your hand. Don't speak. Don't speak, I'm saying. Let me come this far and touch your hand, okay? Okay? Just the touch. Okay? You know what people are when they touch you. You got a sixth sense for that. I'm going to touch you, you know, no more than that. No talking. (*He touches her hand. She doesn't withdraw it.*) Oh, my God. Oh, my God, there is stuff leaving me. Okay, Keely, I thought about a pledge, what I could make to you, if I could touch you. No harm. No harm is what I thought of. Look, I want to turn your hand over, make it palm up, okay? This is make or break, Keely. Right now. Right now. Close your hand, take my hand. You know what I mean? One gesture, you could save me. We could raise a child. With one gesture we could do that. Come on, Keely. Come on, Keely. (*In an incredibly quick move, KEELY brings his hand to her mouth and sinks her teeth into it.*)

Ahhhhhh . . . (*He can't get the hand back, she goes deeper.*) Ahhhhh-hhhhhhhhhhhhhhhhhhh . . . (*He screams. He puts his other hand on her head and tries to force her off.*) Ahhhhhhh . . . (*WALTER grabs him from behind, but he has pulled free and slaps her hard. WALTER pulls him back.*)

DU: (*DU steps in front of him.*) God love and forgive you!

WALTER: Idiot!

KEELY: Get out, go on, get out!

COLE: I can see the bone what she did.

WALTER: Come with me.

COLE: (*His fist doubled.*) What she did to me.

WALTER: Submit your will, come with me.

COLE: (*Angrily.*) I love you, Keely~

DU: There's first-aid upstairs.

WALTER: Come on, Cole.

COLE: Jesus, in thy name!

WALTER: Come on, Cole.

DU: I'll take care of you.

WALTER: (*Leading him out.*) This way now. Walk with Jesus, Cole. This way now. (*WALTER and DU take him out. Without hesitation, KEELY reaches under the mattress and pulls out the wire hanger her dress had hung on. She brings it up to her cuffed hand and untwists the hanger, straightening it out. She pulls the sheet over herself, puts the wire under the sheet with her free hand and works to abort herself. It goes on. The lights go down.*)

SCENE 17

The lights come up. It is minutes later. The bed sheet covering KEELY is soaked with fresh blood. KEELY lies still; she has passed out. We hear WALTER speak offstage.

WALTER'S VOICE: Did we leave it open? (*We don't hear the answer. Moments later, he steps into the room.*) Oh, dear God. (*Over his shoulder, up the stairs.*) Help me! Come down here. (*He goes to the bed.*) Keely. Keely. (*He lifts the corner of the sheet. He drops it. Momentarily he puts his face in his hands.*) God help us. (*DU enters through the door, sees, comes directly to the bed.*) She's aborted. (*DU looks under the sheet; she removes the hanger.*)

DU: Call the paramedics.

WALTER: I'll try to reach Dr. Bloom.

DU: No. No time. (*COLE, who has entered the doorway, starts for the bed. DU speaks fiercely to him.*) Get away! Get out of the room! Go.

WALTER: (*To COLE.*) Go on. (*COLE exits.*)

DU: You have to call 911.

WALTER: That's not possible. What is the wire?

DU: It doesn't matter. I'll call.

WALTER: Think, this is kidnapping.

DU: She's losing blood.

WALTER: I know. (*She starts past him; he stops her.*) You have to give me 30 seconds. (*He walks to the bed and touches KEELY.*) We'll clear out. It will take five to seven minutes. We'll call the paramedics from a pay phone.

DU: I'm not leaving her. I'll call.

WALTER: Think.

DU: I don't care.

WALTER: Du.

DU: I won't implicate you. Go on.

WALTER: No.

DU: We're Christians. You're needed, I'm not.

WALTER: No.

DU: There is a larger world, a larger issue. (*She goes to KEELY.*) I'm getting help, honey, it's coming. I won't be gone two minutes. (*She kisses her forehead. She moves toward the door, touching WALTER.*) God be with you. (*She exits. He stands. He puts one hand over his eyes for a moment. He looks at KEELY. He exits. The lights go down.*)

SCENE 18

Lights up, the stage is empty except for a straight-backed chair off to one side. A female prison guard enters and presses a button on a speaker phone located on the wall.

GUARD: Code 417-26. Officer Carrington. Requesting pick-up 9923739 Visitors' Area. Time unit ½ hour. Over. Doing it now. (*She exits and returns with DU in a wheelchair, dressed in a bright orange jumpsuit, prison issue. She positions her center. Buzzer sounds. She goes to the speaker.*) We're here. (*She waits a moment. KEELY enters. She wears a light summer dress. She carries a string bag filled with items and a McDonald's breakfast in a bag. The guard moves the other chair opposite DU. KEELY sits. DU has had a minor stroke and* *lost the use of her left hand.*) One-half hour.

KEELY: Hi. Breakfast. (*She opens the bag, takes out an egg & ham biscuit, puts it in DU's good hand.*) Catsup already on it. It's an unbelievable steam bath. Not bad in here. I had a migraine yesterday, but it's on the way out. So. You have more color. Any luck with the left hand? (*In a tiny gesture, DU shakes her head "no."*) Well, they said several months. They were saying you were ahead of schedule. Your hair looks nice.I just can't get mine done, I don't know. In this heat. (*She picks up the string bag.*) Let's see. Cranberry juice, tuna packed in water, pretzels, hot sauce, the hand lotion, eye shadow perfect match. I couldn't find that mascara, but see what you think. Sorry about yesterday, I just. . .new Readers Digest, sequel to *The Clan of the Cave Bear*, peanut butter cremes. Let's see. . .the kind of ball points you like. (*To the guard.*) Is that alright? (*Guard shakes her head "no".*) Well, the stationery anyway. Something else, but I can't think what. (*She holds up the bag and the guard moves forward to take it, and then back to her post.*) Cole gave himself up. You probably heard that. Somewhere in Arizona. Dad had the flu. My God, he's ill-tempered when he's sick. The patient from hell, really. I could throttle him. I may throttle him. (*A pause.*) Everytime I come here I come here to forgive you. Why can't I say it? I guess I come here to tell you I'm trying. "God's wrath and God's grace," wasn't that it? I don't seem to have either. (*A moment.*) Oh, there's a new waitress, she wears heels, and green contacts and calls me "the Queen". . .you want to know the truth I think she's into my tips. She brings this dog to work, leaves it in the car, can you believe it, 90 degrees. Oh, I may go on a climb, I don't know, I don't know, the guy is married. . .yeah, I know. . .Boulder, Colorado the end of the month. Listen, he swears he's separated, plus he's paying. I just should get out, you know? I don't get out. Take my mind off. Anyway. We could talk, you know? I would like that. What do you think? Boiling. So, what are you doing in crafts, that antimacassar stuff? Like you need more, right? (*A pause.*) Any more stealing? (*DU shakes her head "no".*) The ring? (*DU shakes her head "no".*) Boy, it never occurred to me like theft would be a problem in here. Hey, how's the Prozac? They still fooling with the level? (*DU nods "yes".*) Maybe you could slip me some. Joking, you know? So, I went to a Judd concert. You know the one that sings without her mother now. . .(*She stops.*). . .without her mother now. I don't know, I left. People, they're about half screwy, you know. People who go to those concerts? There was this guy next to me, he was smoking grass, had a little girl on his lap, maybe two. (*She tears up.*) Had this little girl on his lap. So. I don't know. I don't know. Anyway.

(The conversation burns out. They sit. DU looks directly at her. They lock eyes. The pause lengthens.)
DU: Why? *(KEELY looks at her. A pause.)*
KEELY: Why? *(They sit. The lights dim.)*

END OF PLAY

POOF!

By Lynn Nottage

Playwright's Biography

Lynn Nottage is a playwright from Brooklyn. Her work has been presented in New York at Baca Downtown, The Knitting Factory, and the New York Shakespeare Festival as part of the New Works Project. She recently had work featured in *A...My Name is Still Alice* at Second Stage. Regionally, her work has appeared at Rites and Reasons, The Black Theatre Festival in New Haven, and the Yale Cabaret. She is a member of the Obie Award-winning New Works Project, Playwrights Horizons Writers Unit, The Next Step, and is currently a resident artist at Mabou Mines. She is in the process of developing a new play, *Las Meninas,* with director Tony Gerber. Ms. Nottage has participated in a number of awareness-raising theatre projects, including *Shelter*, a collection of short works by women drawing attention to the plight of homeless women, and she was a producer of *Naked Rights*, a celebration of the Universal Declaration of Human Rights at the Naked Angels Theatre Company. Last year, she participated in the Voice and Visions Theatre retreat at Smith College, and she is a graduate of the Yale School of Drama. Her ten minute play *Poof!* is the co-winner of the Actors Theatre of Louisville's 1992 Heideman Award.

A Note From The Playwright

Nearly half the women on death row in the United States were convicted of killing abusive husbands. Spontaneous combustion is not recognized as a capital crime.

Characters

LOUREEN
FLORENCE

Directed by Seret Scott

Loureen	Elain Graham
Florence	Yvette Hawkins

Set Designer	Paul Owen
Lighting Designer	Karl E. Haas
Costume Designer	Kevin R. McLeod
Sound Designer	Darron L. West
Properties Master	Mark J. Bissonnette
Stage Manager	Julie A. Richardson
Asst. Stage Manager	Amy Hutchison
Dramaturgs	Michael Dixon and Liz Engelman

Setting

Time: present. Place: Kitchen

POOF!

Darkness.

SAMUEL: WHEN I COUNT TO TEN I DON'T WANT TO SEE YA! I DON'T WANT TO HEAR YA. ONE, TWO, THREE, FOUR. . .
LOUREEN: DAMN YOU TO HELL, SAMUEL! (*A bright flash. Lights rise. A huge pile of smoking ashes rests in the middle of the kitchen. Loureen, a demure housewife in her early thirties stares down incredulously. She bends and lifts a pair of spectacles from the remains. She ever so slowly backs away.*) Samuel? Uh! (*She places the spectacles on the kitchen table.*) Uh! SAMUEL? (*Looks around the stage.*) Don't fool with me now. I'm not in the mood. (*Whispered.*) Samuel? I didn't mean it really. I'll be good if you come back. . . Come on now, dinner's waiting—(*Loureen chuckles, then stops abruptly.*) Now stop your foolishness. . . And let's sit down. (*Loureen examines the spectacles.*) Uh! (*Softly.*) Don't be cross with me. Sure I forgot to pick up your shirt for tomorrow. I can wash another, I'll do it right now. Right now! Sam?. . . (*Cautiously*) you hear me! (*Awaits a response.*) Maybe I didn't ever intend to wash your shirt. (*Pulls back as though about to receive a blow. A moment.*) Uh! (*She sits down and dials the telephone.*) Florence, honey could you come on down for a moment. There's been a little accident. . . .Quickly please. . . Uh! (*Loureen gets a broom and a dust pan. She hesitantly approaches the pile of ashes. She gets down on her hands and knees and takes a closer look. A fatuous grin spreads across her face. She is startled by a sudden knock on the door. Loureen slowly walks across the room like a possessed child and lets in Florence, who wears a floral housecoat and a pair of over-sized slippers. Without acknowledgement, Loureen proceeds to saunter back across the room.*)
FLORENCE: HEY!
LOUREEN: (*Pointing at the ashes.*) Uh! (*Loureen struggles to formulate words, which press at the inside of her mouth, not quite realized.*) Uh!
FLORENCE: You all right? What happened? (*Florence sniffs the air.*) Smells like you burned something? (*Florence stares at the huge pile of ashes.*) What the devil is that?
LOUREEN: (*Hushed.*) Samuel. . . It's Samuel, I think.
FLORENCE: What's he done now?
LOUREEN: It's him. It's him. (*Loureen nods her head repeatedly.*)

FLORENCE: Chile, what's wrong with you? Did he finally drive you out your mind? I knew something was going to happen sooner or later.

LOUREEN: Dial 911, Florence!

FLORENCE: Why? You're scaring me!

LOUREEN: Dial 911! (*Florence picks up the telephone and quickly dials.*) I think I killed him. (*Florence hangs up the telephone.*)

FLORENCE: What?

LOUREEN: (*Whimpers.*) I killed him! I killed Samuel!

FLORENCE: Come again. . . He's dead, dead? (*Loureen rings her hands and nods her head twice mouthing "dead, dead." Florence backs away.*)

FLORENCE: No, stop it, I don't have time for this. I'm going back upstairs - you know how Samuel hates to find me here when he gets home. You're not going to get me this time. (*Louder.*) Y'all can have your little joke, I'm not part of it! (*A moment. Florence takes a hard look into Loureen's eyes. She squints.*) Did you really do it this time?

LOUREEN: (*Hushed.*) I don't know how or why it happened, it just did.

FLORENCE: Why are you whispering?

LOUREEN: I don't want to talk too loud something else is liable to disappear.

FLORENCE: Where's his body? (*Loureen points to the pile of ashes.*)

LOUREEN: There!. . .

FLORENCE: You burned him?

LOUREEN: I DON'T KNOW! (*Loureen covers her mouth as to muffle her words. Hushed.*) I think so.

FLORENCE: Either you did or you didn't, what you mean you don't know? We're talking murder, Loureen, not oven settings.

LOUREEN: You think I'm playing.

FLORENCE: How many times have I heard you talk about being rid of him? How many times have we sat at this very table and laughed about the many ways we could do it, and how many times have you done it? None.

LOUREEN: (*Lifting the spectacles*) A pair of cheap spectacles, that's all that's left. And you know how much I hate these. You ever seen him without them, no! . . . He counted to four and disappeared. I swear to God!

FLORENCE: Don't bring the Lord into this just yet! Sit down now. . . What you got to sip on?

LOUREEN: I don't know whether to have a stiff shot of scotch or a glass of champagne. (*Florence takes a bottle of sherry out of the cupboard and pours them each a glass. Loureen downs the glass of sherry, then holds out her glass for more.*)

LOUREEN: He was. . .

FLORENCE: Take your time.

LOUREEN: Standing there.

FLORENCE: And?

LOUREEN: He exploded.

FLORENCE: Did that muthafucka hit you again?

LOUREEN: No. . . he exploded. Boom! Right in front of me. He was shouting like he does, being all colored, then he raised up that big crusty hand to hit me, and poof, he was gone. . . I barely got words out and I'm looking down at a pile of ash. (*Florence belts back her sherry and pours them both another. Florence wipes her forehead.*)

FLORENCE: Chile, I'll give you this, in terms of color you've matched my husband Edgar, the story king. He came in at six Sunday morning talking about he'd hit someone with his car, and had spent all night trying to out run the police. I felt sorry for him, forgot all about the fact that it was six in the morning. It turns out he was playing poker with his paycheck no less.

LOUREEN: You think I'm lying?

FLORENCE: I certainly hope so, Loureen. For your sake and my heart's.

LOUREEN: Samuel always said if I raised my voice something horrible would happen. And it did. I'm a witch. . . The devil spawn!

FLORENCE: You've been watching too much television.

LOUREEN: Never seen anything like this on television- Wish I had then I'd know what to do. . . There's no question, I'm a witch. (*Loureen looks at her hands with disgust.*)

FLORENCE: Chile, don't tell me you've been messing with them mojo women again. What did I tell ya? (*Loureen stands and sits back down.*)

LOUREEN: He's not coming back. Oh no, how could he? It would be a miracle. Two in one day. . . I could be canonized, worse yet he could be. . . All that needs to happen now is for my palms to bleed and I'll be eternally remembered as St. Loureen, the patron of battered wives. Women from across the country will make pilgrimages to me, laying pies and pot roast at my feet and asking the good saint to make their husbands turn to dust. How often does a man like Samuel get damned to hell and go? (*Loureen breaks down as though crying. As Florence consoles her friend, she realizes that she is actually laughing hysterically.*)

FLORENCE: You smoking crack?

LOUREEN: Do I look like I am?

FLORENCE: Chute, I've seen old biddies creeping out of crack houses, talking about they were doing church work.

LOUREEN: FLORENCE, PLEASE BE HELPFUL, I'M VERY CLOSE TO THE EDGE!. . . I DON'T KNOW WHAT TO DO NEXT! DO I SWEEP HIM UP? DO I CALL THE POLICE? DO I. . . *(The phone rings.)* Oh God.

FLORENCE: You gonna let it ring? *(Loureen reaches for the telephone slowly.)*

LOUREEN: NO! *(Loureen holds the receiver without picking it up, paralyzed.)* What if it's his mother?. . . She knows! *(The phone continues to ring. They sit until it stops. They both breathe a sigh of relief.)* I should be mourning, I should be praying, I should be thinking of the burial, but all that keeps popping into my mind is what will I wear on television when I share my horrible and wonderful story with a studio audience. . . *(Whimpers.)* He's made me a killer, Florence, and you remember what a gentle child I was. *(Whispered.)* I'm a killer, I'm killer, I'm a killer.

FLORENCE: I wouldn't throw that word about too lightly, even in jest. Talk like that gets around.

LOUREEN: A few misplaced words and I'll probably get the death penalty, isn't that what they do with women like me, murderesses?

FLORENCE: Folks have done time for less.

LOUREEN: Thank you, Just what I needed to hear!

FLORENCE: What did you expect, that I was going to throw up my arms and congratulate you? Why'd you have to go and lose your mind at this time of day, while I got a pot of rice on the stove, and Edgar's about to walk in the door and wonder where his Goddamn food is. *(Losing her cool.)* And he's going to start in on me about all the nothing I've been doing during the day and why I can't work, and then he'll mention how clean you keep your home. And I don't know how I'm going to look him in the eye without. . .

LOUREEN: I'm sorry Florence. Really. It's out of my hands now. *(Loureen takes Florence's hand and squeezes it. Florence regains her composure.)*

FLORENCE: You swear on your right tit? *(Loureen clutches both of her breasts.)*

LOUREEN: I swear on both of them!

FLORENCE: Both your breasts, Loureen. You know what will happen if you're lying. *(Loureen nods, hushed.)* Both your breasts, Loureen?

LOUREEN: Yeah! *(Florence examines the pile of ashes, then shakes her head.)*

FLORENCE: Oh sweet, sweet Jesus. He must have done something truly terrible.

LOUREEN: No more than usual. I just couldn't take being hit one more time.

FLORENCE: You've taken a thousand blows from that man, couldn't you've turned the cheek and waited? I'd have helped you pack. Like we talked about. (*A moment.*)

LOUREEN: Uh!. . . I could blow on him and he'd disappear across the linoleum. (*Snaps her fingers.*) Just like that. Should I be feeling remorse or regret or some other "r" word? I'm strangely jubilant, like on prom night when Samuel and I first made love. That's the feeling! (*The women lock eyes.*) Uh!

FLORENCE: Is it. . . .

LOUREEN: Like a ton of bricks been lifted from my shoulders, yeah.

FLORENCE: Really?

LOUREEN: Yeah! (*Florence walks to the other side of the room.*)

FLORENCE: You bitch!

LOUREEN: What?

FLORENCE: We made a pact

LOUREEN: I know.

FLORENCE: You've broken it. . . We agreed that when things got real bad for both of us we'd. . . you know. . . together. . . Do I have to go back upstairs to that. . . What next?

LOUREEN: I thought you'd tell me! I don't know!

FLORENCE: I don't know!

LOUREEN: I don't know! (*Florence begins to walk around the room nervously touching objects. Loureen sits ringing her hands and mumbling softly to herself.*)

FLORENCE: Now you got me, Loureen, I'm truly at a loss for words.

LOUREEN: Everybody always told me, "Keep your place Loureen." My place, the silent spot on the couch with a wine cooler in my hand and a pleasant smile that warmed the heart. All this time I didn't know why he was so afraid for me to say anything, to speak up. Poof!. . . I've never been by myself, except for them two weeks when he won the office pool and went to Reno with his cousin Mitchell. He wouldn't tell me where he was going until I got that postcard with the cowboy smoking a hundred cigarettes. . . Didn't Sonny Larkin look good last week at Catrolines? He looked good, didn't he. . . .(*Florence nods. Florence nervously picks up Samuel's jacket, which is hanging on the back of the chair. She clutches it unconsciously.*)

LOUREEN: NO! No! DON'T WRINKLE THAT! THAT'S HIS FAVORITE JACKET. HE'LL KILL ME. PUT IT BACK! (*Florence returns the jacket to it's perch. Loureen begins to quiver.*) I'm sorry. (*Loureen grabs the jacket and wrinkles it up.*) There! (*She then digs into the coat pockets and pulls out his wallet and a movie stub.*) Look at that, he said he didn't go to the movies last night. Working late. (*Loureen frantically thumbs through his wallet.*) Picture of his motorcycle, social security card, drivers license and look at that from our wedding. (*Smiling.*) I looked good, didn't I? (*She puts the pictures back in the wallet. Loureen holds the jacket up to her face.*) There were some good things. (*Loureen then sweeps her hand over the jacket to remove the wrinkles and folds it ever so carefully, and finally throws it in the garbage.*) And out of my mouth those words made him disappear. All these years and just words, Florence. That's all they were.

FLORENCE: I'm afraid, I won't ever get those words out. I'll start resenting you, honey. I'm afraid won't anything change for me.

LOUREEN: I been to that place.

FLORENCE: Yeah? I wish I could relax these old lines (*touches her forehead*) for a minute maybe. Edgar has never done me the way Samuel did you, but he sure did take the better part of my life.

LOUREEN: Not yet, Florence. (*Florence nods.*)

FLORENCE: I have the children to think of. Right?

LOUREEN: You can think up a hundred things before. . .

FLORENCE: Then come upstairs with me. . . We'll wait together for Edgar and then you can spit out your words and. . .

LOUREEN: I can't do that.

FLORENCE: Yes you can. Come on now. (*Loureen shakes her head.*) Well, I guess my mornings are not going to be any different.

LOUREEN: If you can say for certain, then I guess they won't be. I couldn't say that.

FLORENCE: But you got a broom and a dust pan, you don't need anything more than that. . . He was a bastard and nobody will care that he's gone.

LOUREEN: Phone's gonna start ringing soon, people are gonna start asking soon, and they'll care. Maybe I should mail him to his mother. I owe her that. I feel bad for her, she didn't understand how it was. He was always threatening not to come back.

FLORENCE: I heard him.

LOUREEN: It would've been me eventually.

FLORENCE: Yes.

LOUREEN: I should call the police, or someone.

FLORENCE: What are you gonna tell them? About all those times they refused to help, about all those nights you slept in my bed 'cause you were afraid to stay down here? About the time he nearly took out your eye cause you flipped the television channel?

LOUREEN: No.

FLORENCE: You've got it, girl!

LOUREEN: I can't just throw him away and pretend like it didn't happen. Can I? Goodbye to the fatty meats and the salty food. Goodbye to the bourbon and the bologna sandwiches. Goodbye to the smell of his feet, his breath and his bowel movements. . . *(A moment. Loureen closes her eyes as though reliving a horrible memory, she shutters.)* Goodbye. *(Loureen walks over to the pile of ashes.)* Samuel?. . . just checking.

FLORENCE: Goodbye, Samuel. *(They both smile.)*

LOUREEN: Chickens warming in the oven, you're welcome to stay.

FLORENCE: Chile, I got a pot of rice on the stove. Kids are probably acting out. . . And Edgar, well. . . Listen, I'll stop in tomorrow.

LOUREEN: For dinner?

FLORENCE: Edgar wouldn't stand for that. Cards maybe.

LOUREEN: Cards. *(The women hug for a long moment. Florence exits. Loureen stands over the ashes for a few moments contemplating what to do. She finally decides to sweep them under the carpet, and then proceeds to set the table and sit down to eat her dinner.)*

END OF PLAY

TAPE

By José Rivera

Playwright's Biography

José Rivera was born in San Juan, Puerto Rico in 1955. His plays ANGEL OF MERCY, THE HOUSE OF RAMON IGLESIA, THE PROMISE, SLAUGHTER IN THE LAKE, EACH DAY DIES WITH SLEEP, and MARISOL, have been produced at the Ensemble Studio Theatre, Circle Rep., the Los Angeles Theatre Center, the La Jolla Playhouse, Hartford Stage Company, the Magic Theatre, Berkeley Rep., the Actors Theatre of Louisville, and the Joseph Papp Public Theatre, as well as the national theatres of Sweden and Norway. Honors include two Joseph Kesselring Award Honorable Mentions (for THE PROMISE and MARISOL), as well as grants from the National Endowment for the Arts, the Rockefeller Foundation, and the New York Foundation for the Arts. Rivera has received a Fulbright Arts Fellowship in Playwriting, six Dramalogue awards (for MARISOL), a PEN West Dramatic Writing Award nomination (for MARISOL), and, in 1992, the prestigious Whiting Foundation Writing award. In 1983 THE HOUSE OF RAMON IGLESIA won the FDG/CBS New Play Contest and later appeared on the public television series American Playhouse. In 1989 Rivera studied with Nobel Prize winner Gabriel Garcia Marquez at the Sundance Institute. In 1990 he was a writer-in-residence at the Royal Court Theatre, London. In 1991 he co-created and produced the critically acclaimed TV series "Errie, Indiana." Mr. Rivera is married to writer Heather Dundas; they live in Los Angeles with their two children, Adena Maritza and Teo Douglas.

An Introduction To The Play

Imagine that at some point in your life you had to confront all your lies. Lies told not only to others, but to yourself. To be forced to recall that which you thought was finished but, as is turns out, really wasn't.

Through lies, a person will trace his or her entire life. Lies to himself, to others, from the first lie to the most recent, all must be heard again. There is nothing here to make the experience any easier, either. The Attendant offers only water, a small degree of companionship and, only briefly, empathy. The desk and chair are old, the reel-to-reel well-worn, yet "sturdy, very strong from so much use." The lies may vary, but the instruments used are always the same, and everyone must go through it.

And when one does, as the Person in *Tape* finds out, the feelings are enormous, full of recognition, regret and remorse.

Rivera subtly points out that lies encompass all wrong in the world. Whether it be murder, adultery or theft, a lie is at the core. That belief is central to *Tape*. And someone is always watching, but not in a malicious way. The Attendant's feelings towards the Person are sadness and awkwardness, but always with the good of the Person, and ultimately mankind, in mind. About *Tape*, Rivera states that he "wanted to explore a time in which you were meant to review everything that has happened in your life" and cites Christian teachings about purgatory, "taken one step further," as sources of inspiration. He adds that he had toyed with the idea of using film to replay one's lies, but felt that by listening, the impact would be greater on the individual.

Tape, in Rivera's opinion, is a reflection of the 1980's, in which casual lies were an all-encompassing part of society. There is a case made here, particularly at the end, that culture makes it difficult to be honest, that at a young age we learn to lie. Since society as a whole is now dealing with paying up for lies told in the past, *Tape's* message becomes all the more timely.

The ten-minute form is an ideal vehicle for this play of ideas. The images in *Tape* are vivid and given only in snippets, so that we may extract from them our own ideas. In just ten minutes, we learn about these people and their condition, while at the same time, we learn about ourselves.

Tape serves as a reminder that we must, at some point, own up to our actions. We must take responsibility for what we say. In a short period of time, José Rivera captures all of the ideas, all of the agonies of our very existence, in much the same way Samuel Beckett did. Like Beckett's *Krapp's Last Tape*, Rivera's *Tape* journeys to life's most painful moments. There is hope that one may learn about oneself by taking such a trip, regardless of the wounds reopened. It is the pain of the human condition funneled and focused in concise detail.

Tape plays with a variety of images and ideas, yet when the play ends one idea remains crystal clear. Perhaps it will be expressed by the look of horror on the Person's face as he realizes what lies ahead of him. Perhaps it will be symbolized by the tape spooling through the recorder. Perhaps it will be a vision of an attendant writing down your lies. Perhaps a mental picture of you listening to what was recorded. Through all these images, José Rivera's *Tape* demands that we evaluate our words and own up to our actions, lest we find ourselves in a similar condition.

Michele Volansky
Actors Theatre of Louisville

Characters

PERSON   Fred Major
ATTENDANT   Kalimi Baxter

Directed by Scott Zigler

Scenic Designer	Paul Owen
Costume Designer	Hollis Jenkins-Evans
Lighting Designer	Karl E. Haas
Sound Designer	Casey L. Warren
Props Master	Mark J. Bissonnette
Stage Manager	Craig Weindling
Assistant Stage Manager	Amy Hutchison
Production Dramaturg	Michael Bigelow Dixon

Setting

Time: The present. Place: In a dark room.

TAPE

A small dark room. No windows. One door. A PERSON is being lead in by an ATTENDANT. In the room is a simple wooden table and a chair. On the table is a large reel-to-reel tape recorder, a glass of water, and a pitcher of water.

PERSON: It's dark in here.

ATTENDANT: I'm sorry.

PERSON: No, I know it's not your fault.

ATTENDANT: I'm afraid those lights. . .

PERSON: I guess, what does it matter now?

ATTENDANT: . . . not very bright.

PERSON: Who cares, really?

ATTENDANT: We don't want to cause you an undue suffering. If it's too dark in here for you I'll make sure one of the other attendants replaces the light bulb. (*The PERSON looks at the ATTENDANT.*)

PERSON: Any "undue suffering?"

ATTENDANT: That's right. (*The PERSON looks at the room.*)

PERSON: Is this were I'll be?

ATTENDANT: That's right.

PERSON: Will you be outside?

ATTENDANT: Yes.

PERSON: The entire time?

ATTENDANT: The entire time.

PERSON: Is it boring?

ATTENDANT: (*As if the ATTENDANT hadn't heard.*) I'm sorry?

PERSON: Is it boring? You know. Waiting outside all the time.

ATTENDANT: (*Soft smile.*) It's my job. It's what I do.

PERSON: Of course. (*Beat.*) Will I get anything to eat or drink?

ATTENDANT: Well, we're not really set up for that. We don't have what you'd call a kitchen. But we can send out for things. Little things. Cold food.

PERSON: I understand.

ATTENDANT: Soft drinks.

PERSON: (*Hopefully.*) Beer?

ATTENDANT: I'm afraid not.

PERSON: Not even on special occasions like my birthdays?

ATTENDANT: (*Thinking.*) I guess maybe on your birthday.

PERSON: (*Truly appreciative.*) Great. Thanks. (*Beat.*)

ATTENDANT: Do you have any more questions before we start? Because if you do, that's okay. It's okay to ask as many questions as you want. I'm sure you're very curious. I'm sure you'd like to know as much as possible, so you can figure out how it all fits together and what it all means. So please ask. That's why I'm here. Don't worry about the time. We have a lot of time. (*Beat.*)

PERSON: I don't have any questions.

ATTENDANT: (*Disappointed.*) Are you sure?

PERSON: There's not much I really have to know is there? Really?

ATTENDANT: No, I guess not. I just thought. . .

PERSON: It's okay. I appreciate it. I guess I really want to sit.

ATTENDANT: Sit. (*The PERSON sits on the chair and faces the tape recorder.*)

PERSON: Okay, I'm sitting.

ATTENDANT: Is it. . . comfortable?

PERSON: Does it matter? Does it really fucking matter?

ATTENDANT: No. I suppose not. (*The ATTENDANT looks sad. The PERSON looks at the ATTENDANT and feels bad.*)

PERSON: Hey I'm sorry. I know it's not your fault. I know you didn't mean it. I'm sorry.

ATTENDANT: It's all right.

PERSON: What's your name anyway? Do you have a name?

ATTENDANT: Not really. It's not allowed.

PERSON: Really? Not allowed? Who says?

ATTENDANT: The rules say.

PERSON: Have you actually seen these rules? Are they in writing?

ATTENDANT: Oh yes. There's a long and extensive training course.

PERSON: (*Surprised.*) There is?

ATTENDANT: Oh yes. It's quite rigorous.

PERSON: Imagine that.

ATTENDANT: You have to be a little bit of everything. Confidant, confessor, friend, stern task master. Guide.

PERSON: I guess that would take time.

ATTENDANT: My teachers were all quite strong and capable. They really pushed me. I was grateful. I knew I had been chosen for something unique and exciting. Something significant. Didn't mind the hard work and sleepless nights.

PERSON: (*Surprised.*) Oh? You sleep?

ATTENDANT: (*Smiles.*) When I can. (*Beat.*)

PERSON: Do you dream? (*Beat.*)

ATTENDANT: No. (*Beat.*) That's not allowed. (*Beat.*)

PERSON: I'm sorry.

ATTENDANT: No. It's something you get used to.

PERSON: (*Trying to be chummy.*) I know I went years and years without being able to remember one single dream I had. It really scared the shit out of me when I was ten and. . .

ATTENDANT: I know.

PERSON: I'm sorry.

ATTENDANT: I said I know. I know that story. When you were ten.

PERSON: Oh. Yeah. I guess you would know everything. Every story.

ATTENDANT: (*Apologetic.*) It's part of the training.

PERSON: I figured. (*A long uncomfortable silence.*)

ATTENDANT: (*Softly.*) Have you ever operated a reel-to-reel tape recorder before?

PERSON: (*suddenly terrified*) No I haven't. I mean — no.

ATTENDANT: It's not hard.

PERSON: I, uhm, these things were pretty obsolete by the time I was old enough to afford stereo equipment, you know, I got into cassettes and, later, CDs, but never one of these jobbies.

ATTENDANT: It's not hard. (*Demonstrates.*) On here. Off here. Play. Pause. Rewind.

PERSON: (*Surprised.*) Rewind?

ATTENDANT: In some cases the quality of the recording is so poor. . . you'll want to rewind it until you understand.

PERSON: No fast forward?

ATTENDANT: No.

PERSON: (*Getting progressively more frightened.*) It looks like a pretty good one. Sturdy. Very strong.

ATTENDANT: They get a lot of use.

PERSON: I bet. (*Beat.*) Is this the only tape? (*The ATTENDANT laughs out loud—then quickly stops.*)

ATTENDANT: No.

PERSON: I didn't think so.

ATTENDANT: There are many more.

PERSON: How many? A lot?

ATTENDANT: There are ten thousand boxes.

PERSON: *Ten* thousand?

ATTENDANT: I'm afraid so.

PERSON: Did I really. . . did I really lie that much?

ATTENDANT: I'm afraid you did.

PERSON: So. . . everyone goes into a room like this?

ATTENDANT: Exactly like this. There's no differentiation. Everyone's equal.

PERSON: For once.

ATTENDANT: What isn't equal, of course, is the. . . amount of time you spend here. Listening.

PERSON: (*Horror stricken.*) Oh God.

ATTENDANT: (*Part of the training.*) Listening, just to yourself. To your voice.

PERSON: I know.

ATTENDANT: Listening, word by word, to every lie you ever told while you were alive.

PERSON: Oh God!

ATTENDANT: Every ugly lie to every person, every single time, every betrayal, every lying thought, every time you lied to yourself, deep in your mind, we were listening, we were recording, and it's all in these tapes, ten thousand boxes of them, in your own words, one lie after the next, over and over, until we're finished. So the amount of time varies. The amount of time you spend here all depended on how many lies you told. How many boxes of tapes we have to get through together.

PERSON: (*Almost in tears.*) I'm sorry. . .

ATTENDANT: Too late.

PERSON: I said I'm sorry! I said I'm sorry! I said it a million times! What happened to forgiveness?! I don't want to be here! I don't want this! I don't want to listen! I don't want to hear myself! I didn't mean to say the things that I said! I don't want to listen!

ATTENDANT: Yes, well. Neither did we. Neither did we. (*The ATTENDANT looks sadly at the PERSON. The ATTENDANT turns on the tape recorder. The ATTENDANT hits the "Play" button, the reels spin slowly, and the tape starts snaking its way through the machine. Silence. The ATTENDANT leaves the room, leaving the PERSON all alone. The PERSON nervously pours a glass of water, accidently spilling water on the floor. From the depths of the machine comes a long-forgotten voice:*)

WOMAN'S VOICE: "Where have you been? Do you know I've been looking all over? Jesus Christ! I went to Manny's! I went to the pharmacy! The school! I even called the police! Look at me, Jesus Christ, I'm shaking! Now look at me — look at me and tell me where the hell you were! Tell me right now!" (*Silence. As the PERSON waits, terrified and sad, for the lying response, the lights fade to black.*)

END OF PLAY

WATERMELON RINDS

by Regina Taylor

Playwright's Biography

Regina Taylor makes her ATL playwriting debut with WATERMELON RINDS, which has had staged readings at the McCarter Theatre, the Women's Project in New York and at Atlanta's Carter Presidential Center. She also had a staged reading of her play MUDTRACKS at the Women's Project and at Santa Monica's Beyond Baroque Theatre. She has adapted, with playwright Mario Emes, two one-acts by Franz Xavier Kroetz entitled GHOST TRAIN and STY FARM, which were workshopped at New York's Shakespeare Festival. She is currently writing a one-act play for Seven Stages Theatre for their '93 One-Act Play Festival, and she has been commissioned by Atlanta's Alliance Theatre to write the book to the musical based on the Fisk Jubilee Singers. Ms. Taylor has written for the TV drama I'LL FLY AWAY, in which she appears as "Lilly Harper" and for which she was nominated for an Emmy and recently won a Golden Globe Award for best leading dramatic actress. Ms. Taylor also won the 1993 NAACP Image Award and was the keynote speaker for the Brooklyn Academy of Music's Dr. Martin Luther King, Jr.'s Celebration. Ms. Taylor has appeared on Broadway as "Juliet" in ROMEO AND JULIET, won a Drama--Logue award as "Ariel" in THE TEMPEST and was featured in the film LEAN ON ME and in the TV programs CRISIS AT CENTRAL HIGH and THE HOWARD BEACH STORY.

Introduction to the Play

Family reunions. A great idea maybe, but not when they run amuck. Haven't we all attended gatherings that turned into Family feud? How is it that land mines - in the form of memories, secrets, betrayals, jealousies - detonate so often at social events? Why must the past sabotage the present and ruin so many good meals?

Regina Taylor found herself asking those questions awhile back; the occasion was Thanksgiving. "It was my first year in New York City," Taylor recalls. "I was invited to an Aunt's house for dinner, where her husband's family was gathering. I heard topics from the distant past rehashed by 50 year old adults. All sorts of issues sprang up, and suddenly skeletons came flying out of the closet." Several years later, that close encounter of the family kind inspired *Watermelon Rinds*, Taylor's absurdist comedy about African-American family politics.

Taylor's view of life's absurdities in *Watermelon Rinds* is both tragic and down-to-the-bone funny. "People get sucked into the play through laughter, but then it takes a darker turn toward the end," notes the playwright, who heard readings of the script in Atlanta and Princeton. "The title itself refers to what happens when the sweet meat and juices of the watermelon are gone when the seeds are spit out. We're still hungry but we're gnawing on the rind. What do we do? That's the question we're left to ponder in *Watermelon Rinds*.

Watermelon Rinds premiered in a double-bill of plays by Regina Taylor titled *Various Small Fires*. The other half of the evening, *Jennine's Diary*, is currently being adapted and was not available at press time for publication.

Characters

Jes Semple
Lottie Semple
Willy Semple
Liza Semple
Pinkie Semple
Papa Tommy Semple
Mama Pearl Semple
Marva Semple-Weisse

Directed by Novella Nelson

Cast of Characters (in order of appearance)

Jes Semple	Roger Robinson
Lottie Semple	Kalimi A. Baxter
Willy Semple	Donald Griffin
Liza Semple	Regina Byrd Smith
Pinkie Semple	Elain Graham
Papa Tommy Semple	Ray Johnson
Mama Pearl Semple	Yvette Hawkins
Marva Semple-Weisse	Judy Tate

Scenic Designer	Paul Owen
Costume Designer	Toni-Leslie James

Lighting Designer	Marcus Dilliard
Sound Designer	Casey L. Warren
Props Manager	Mark J. Bissonnette
Stage Manager	Frazier W. Marsh
Assistant Stage Manager	Lori M. Doyle
Second Assistant Stage Manager	Emily Fox
Movement Supervisor	Ervon Neely
Production Dramaturg	Michael Bigelow Dixon
Casting arranged by Judy Dennis	

Setting

The time is the present. The place is a household in an urban neighborhood.

* (H/) indicates UNISON: HUSH

WATERMELON RINDS

SCENE 1

JES stands in a spotlight DSR.

JES: I don't like to go to plays. I'd rather sit on the corner and play poker, a little dominoes, talk loud at passing women, watch cats copulating on the sidewalk, turn up the volume and do the loose goose. . . or do the nasty with a lady whose butt costs less than the price of a g-d theater ticket. I bought a theater ticket once. The paper said it was a black comedy. I went inside. I sat there for two hours. I didn't see one black. And it sure wasn't a comedy. Just a bunch of white people talking about throwing babies out with their bathwater and putting hedgehogs up their you-know-whats. (Excuse me ladies.) But and I said, this ain't no black comedy. This is absurd. Then I got up and walked out. (*Blackout.*)

SCENE 2

Lights come up on a living room stacked high with articles of living...clothes, books, furniture, a candelabra, old toy baby carriage...everything including the kitchen sink. Boxes are scattered. Some empty, half full, and full, taped and labeled. Labels read POTTERY, LOTTIE'S CLOTHES, BAR-B-QUE GRILL, SAM...etc...There is a clearing that leads off right to the kitchen. Another path leads to a door USL to the other parts of the house. Off left is the door to the outside. DSL is a window. LOTTIE, fourteen-years-old, wearing a white slip that shows her newly budding form, is standing on the table doing a barefoot softshoe.)

LOTTIE: (*Singing cheerfully.*) YANG YANG YANG YANG. YANG YANG YANG. (*There is a knocking on the door.*) I'll get it.
WILLY: (*Voice off stage.*) Don't touch that door. Nobody lives here. We're moving.

LIZA: (*Voice off stage.*) Are they here already? Everything isn't prepared yet.

WILLY: (*VOS*) You never know who's on the other side —

LIZA: (*VOS*) Lottie, are you dressed yet?

WILLY: (*VOS*) Damn BEAN EATERS.

LIZA: (*VOS*) If they're here and you're not dressed yet. . . (*More knocking*)

LOTTIE: Who's there?

JES: (*VOS*) Jes.

LOTTIE: Jes who?

JES: (*VOS*) Jes me and my shadow. . . Let me in. (*LOTTIE opens the door.*)

JES: (*His best Groucho imitation*) This country club once refused me entrance. I said—Fine, I don't want to join any club that would have me for a member. They said—their swimming pool was for whites only — I said my great-great-grandmother was raped by her slave master—I'm part white—can I go in up to my knees?

LIZA: (*VOS*) Is anyone here yet?

LOTTIE: No, ma'am.

JES: I'm hungry. When we were growing up we were so po'—our parents had to sleep in the same bed. We were so po'. . . (*WILLY enters from upstage right carrying a bundle and a box. He begins sorting.*)

WILLY: They'll all come, they'll eat, they'll leave, we'll move. Get off the table Lottie.

LOTTIE: Guess who I am. (*Tapping and singing.*) YANG YANG YANG YANG. YANG YANG YANG.

WILLY: You're my daughter is who.

JES: Though a man can never tell for sure—

LOTTIE: No. Not your daughter.

JES: A woman can tell a man anything.

LOTTIE: Shirley Temple. Get it?

JES: Shirley Temple Black.

LOTTIE: Shirley Temple in The Blue Bird of Happiness.

WILLY: Shirley-going-to-get-her-butt-beat-for-dancing-on-the-table-when-I-told-her-to-get-off Temple. (*LOTTIE gets off the table.*)

JES: You may be Shirley but your hips are Monroe. Girl, you are getting as big as your mama.

LIZA: (*VOS*) I know I'm not known for my cooking, but this is a special occasion, I can feel it. (*Then:*) Lottie, are you dressed yet? You're getting too big to run around with nothing on. (*LOTTIE takes two nickels and drops them down the front of her slip and sticks out her chest.*)

LOTTIE: TADA! They didn't fall down. Get it?

JES: Do you know another one?

LIZA: (VOS) They'll be here any minute and if you're not dressed yet. . .
(JES takes a glass, puts it to LOTTIE's elbow, pumps her arm and
the glass fills with milk.)

LOTTIE: How did you do that?

LIZA: (VOS) Heard of a girl abducted, half naked from her own house. . .
(JES drinks the milk.)

LOTTIE: How?

LIZA: (VOS) . . . never seen again.

JES: I'll tell you the secret when you get older.

LIZA: (VOS) Found out later that it was a member of her own family.

LOTTIE: I don't want to ever grow up. Do you remember Shirley Temple
in "The Blue Bird of Happiness"?

JES: "Blue Bird of Happiness"? Isn't that the one with Bill "Bojangles"
Robinson? She used to do a lot of films with old Bojangles. He was
one of the best tap dancers in the world. They attributed it to his big
feet. What else can you do with feet that big? I heard he taught little
Miss Shirley everything she knew about dancing. And how she loved
to dance with her Bojangles. Sweet, black, big-footed Bojangles. Always smiling, both of them together—dancing and smiling—That's
why they took him away.

LOTTIE: Who did?

JES: When they found out why they were always grinning—they dragged
him away, kicking and cut off his—

WILLY: JES!

JES: His feet. Nigger with all that rhythm and no feet—what's he going
to do?

LOTTIE: That's not funny, Uncle Jes.

JES: Bojangles didn't think it was funny either. Can't tap with your
hands—though some have tried—just can't get the same kind of sat-
isfaction. (We hear a round of firecrackers. Lottie runs to the
window.)

WILLY: Damn Bean Eaters!

JES: Blow your hands off—Don't come crying to me.

WILLY: That's why we're moving.

JES: "Don't come crying to me." That's what they used to say.

WILLY: Lottie, get away from that window.

LOTTIE: It was so pretty. It shot straight up—a bright red ball—and exploded in mid-air. It sprinkled down like rain. Red rain. . .

JES: "Blow your hands off. . . "

WILLY: I don't want you going out of this house today, Lottie.

LOTTIE: You never want me to go out.

WILLY: Damn neighborhood. BEAN EATERS— try to find any excuse for disturbing my peace of mind. (*To LOTTIE.*) I don't want you to talk to them, touch them, look at them directly. (*Then:*) That's why we're moving.

LOTTIE: When are we moving?

WILLY: Soon. Very soon. Leave everything behind. It's just going to be good things for my little blue bird. (*Tying up the box he has been filling.*) Boxes. Everything I own, memories, conversations—in these boxes. S-h-i-t. Tombs. I've been sitting in the same spot, the exact same spot for the last twenty years and steadily progressing backwards. How can that be? This used to be my favorite shirt. What's left of it. . . rags. . . pieces of something else. . .

JES: Heard you got King Tut's tiara stashed away up in there.

WILLY: Maybe. . . but damn if I can remember which box.

JES: Ain't that the way it goes?

WILLY: One day real soon we're going to move—move forward—move out and get us a big mansion for my little blue bird. Sacrifices have been made and it's any moment now.

JES: People can't move forward without some sacrifice.

WILLY: Mortgages, loans, scraping, saving, hard work.

JES: Man knew from the beginning. While beating on their drums, and getting high on mooloo juice—they dipped their bodies in monkey fat and danced—danced until the earth gave way to valleys. While praying to their gods they burned sacred offerings. . .

LIZA: (*VOS*) Fried chicken. . . bar-b-que ribs. . . smoked ham. . .

JES: . . . the fatted calf, the lamb, the first born male, the virgin.

LOTTIE: Everybody is coming today. YANG YANG YANG YANG.

LIZA: (*VOS*) . . . pickled pig's feet. . . ox tail stew. . . hog head cheese. . . I know I'm not known for my cooking but I've really outdone myself today.

WILLY: She used to be able to cook.

LIZA: (*VOS*) MMMM. It smells good in here.

WILLY: That's why I married her.

LIZA: (*VOS*) I don't want anyone peeping into my kitchen until I'm ready. You're going to be so proud.

WILLY: Every Friday and Saturday, this was before I proposed, she would lure me into her kitchen with a promise of a taste from her pot.

LIZA: (*VOS*) Remember those things I used to fix for you, Willy? I'm feeling it again.

WILLY: Yes, Liza.

LIZA: (*VOS*) You don't believe me, do you? Man doesn't believe anything until it's rolling around on his tongue. You'll see.

WILLY: (*Hopeful.*) It is beginning to smell. . .

LOTTIE: I smell something.

JES: I'm hungry enough. (*WILLY picks up another bundle and exits.*) When we were growing up, we were so po' - our termites reported us to the better housing bureau. We were so po'- we'd wait until the lights went out and stole the leftovers from our rat's pantry. We were so po' - No, po' ain't funny, there is nothing funny about being po' - We were so po' that fourteen of us had to sleep in one bed while the rest slept on the floor - which was pretty difficult considering that we were so po' we couldn't afford a house with indoor plumbing - so po' we lived in the outhouse. We lived in an outhouse so small that those sleeping on the floor were likely to fall into that hole if they weren't careful. Those sleeping on the floor learned to hold on to each other and the walls. But every once in awhile you would awaken in the middle of the night by a surprised echoing scream and you'd know another brother or sister had let go or was pushed and was lost in that bottomless stinky pit. They said that if you were lucky that you would fall straight to China. If you were lucky. We were so po' - we had a dog once. We named him Lucky. He starved to death. Lucky we ate him. I did keep a pet cockroach. He was as big as a dog. Named him Rex. Walked him on a leash. Ever try to teach d cockroach to roll over and play dead? Ever try to curb a roach? Which leg does he raise? Listen, Lottie - we were so PO' - we had to devour our own in order to survive. Do you know what c-a-n-n-i-b-u-l-l spells? (*We hear firecrackers. JES falls to the floor and convulses as if he were repeatedly shot. WILLY re-enters, carrying another box.*)

WILLY: Damn bean eaters.

LOTTIE: (*Watching JES convulse.*) Are you dead yet? Uncle Jes is such a riot.

JES: (*Finally.*) Hear that? -'NAM.

LOTTIE: Were you in 'Nam, Uncle Jes?

WILLY: That's why we're moving.

JES: The summer of '68. Hot, white beach. Beirut.

WILLY: You were never in Beirut. Shooting, killing, raping.

LOTTIE: That's what it's like in Beirut?

WILLY: This neighborhood. Bean eaters with their ghetto blasters and uzi's.

JES: If I wasn't in El Salvador—then—What happened to my hands?— (*JES loses his hands up his sleeves and chases LOTTIE around the room—screaming.*)

WILLY: The real-estate man said that we were buying into a good solid middle-class neighborhood. We moved in. The first on the block. Fine. A couple of families moved out. Fine. Next thing you know another black family wants to move in. White flight. They flew. Mass Exodus. The next thing you know—any kind of nigger and his pit bull is moving in. Drug dealers, bean eaters and their pet cockroaches big enough to walk on leashes. If I wanted to buy into a ghetto—I would have never moved. This is not what was promised. Sacrifices have been made.

JES: When we were growing up, we were so po'—

WILLY: We were never *poor*. Yes, we had to struggle, but we were never poor. Anything worth anything is worth some sacrifice. Remember that, Lottie.

JES: We weren't poor. We were so po' we couldn't afford the extra o and r. Ever been to a all white beach in Alabama with a sign on it -"No dogs or coloreds allowed."?

WILLY: . . . can he go in up to his knees. . .

LOTTIE: That's how it was in the old days?

WILLY: They don't have beaches in Alabama.

JES: 1968. Hot, white beach. Alabama. He said, "Boy, what you doing on this here beach?" I said, "Boy? Who are you talking to?" And he and his friends took out these knives, long enough for shish-ke-bobin' and he says, "I'm talking to you, nigger." And that is how I lost my hands down a white woman's bikini in Alabamy. (*JES loses his hands up his sleeves and chases LOTTIE screaming—around the room.*)

WILLY: First on the block.

JES: No, I've never been to Iraq.

WILLY: Should have been the last.

JES: But I know how it feels.

LIZA: (*VOS. Singing.*) There is a fountain filled with blood Drawn from Emanuel's veins. . .

WILLY: (*Hopeful.*) It's been a long time since I heard her singing in the kitchen. (*We hear a knocking on the door.*)

LOTTIE: Who's there?

PINKIE: (*VOS*) The big bad wolf. Let me in.

LOTTIE: Not by the hair on my chinny, chin, chin.

PINKIE: (*VOS*) Your chin, my ass. Girl, open this door. (*LOTTIE opens the door and Pinkie enters. She is very pregnant.*)

WILLY: Well look what the cat dragged in.

PINKIE: Boy, don't get started with me. I came here to celebrate, to have a good time. This time I'm going to have a nice time with my family. (*To LOTTIE.*) Look at this girl, getting so healthy and fat. I see the bees done bit.

JES: You can't talk about getting fat. . .

PINKIE: (*Rubbing her belly.*) . . . any minute now.

WILLY: What's the count up to now? Everytime I see you, you're pregnant. What do you do, Pinkie?

PINKIE: Well, if you don't know—I'm not going to tell you.

JES: Where are the rest of them?

PINKIE: Left them at home. You know my kids. . .

WILLY: Wild and untamed.

PINKIE: I see you redecorated the place.

WILLY: We're moving any day.

PINKIE: I heard that before. When are we going to eat?

LOTTIE: You know how slow mama is.

PINKIE: Ain't you fast. Why aren't you in there helping?

LOTTIE: She said that she didn't want any help. (*We hear a crash of pots and dishes.*)

PINKIE: Liza, are you alright in there?

LIZA: (*VOS*) Pinkie!—I'm just fine. Everything is fine in here. Never mind me. Any minute, and we'll be feasting at a banquet.

PINKIE: Alright, then. . . (*Lower.*) I hope you got a McDonalds nearby. I'm hungry. My feet hurt and my back. (*She rubs her stomach.*) I might name this one—Jessee.

WILLY: I don't want to hear it.

PINKIE: I didn't say nothing. Let me hush. But this one is going to turn out.

WILLY: Just like your other ones.

PINKIE: They just weren't inspired. They had it in them but they just weren't inspired.

WILLY: Where is little Lumumba?

PINKIE: Big Lumumba. He hasn't written to me in a long time.

WILLY: And coke-head Marion? Heard Eldridge went crazy—

PINKIE: He was a hyper-active child. . .

WILLY: Carmichael fled the country. . . George was in a shoot-out in prison.

PINKIE: He's dead. They were just born in the wrong time, is all. That's what I figure. The time wasn't right. Not for them. But this one—by the time he gets through puberty. . . (*She notices LOTTIE staring at her belly.*)

PINKIE: You never seen a pregnant woman before? Do you want to rub my belly? (*LOTTIE places her hands on PINKIE'S stomach. Then, startled LOTTIE jerks away.*)

PINKIE: Don't be scared. That's just him saying hello. (*To her belly.*) What's that? You saying, "Who's that rubbing on mama's belly?"

That's your cousin, Lottie... no, you haven't met her before.

LOTTIE: He can hear you?

PINKIE: Of course he can. Talk to you too—if you want to get to know him better. He'll talk your ear off.

LOTTIE: (*Her head on PINKIE's belly*) I can hear him breathing.

WILLY: Unborn babies don't breath, Lottie.

PINKIE: Who are you—Dr. Spock? The girl know what she hears.

LOTTIE: I think I can make out... he's saying something... but it's too low.

PINKIE: He can be a bit soft-spoken.

WILLY: I may not be a pediatrician—but most fetuses don't speak.

PINKIE: That's brilliant, Sherlock. Most don't. I think I'll name him X.

JES: X. I like that.

WILLY: First, Jessee and now—X. As far as I know Malcolm X died a long time ago. Just who are you claiming this child is by?

PINKIE: Do you really want to know?—I didn't think so.

JES: X Semple. I like that.

PINKIE: Thank you.

WILLY: And how do you know it's going to be a boy?

PINKIE: How does every mother know?

WILLY: Oh, he told you.

PINKIE: He didn't have to—He isn't just kicking up in there... I can feel him. Three-inch erections pounding against my womb, four or five times a day. That's how I know.

WILLY: Three inches! ... four or five ... Pinkie!

PINKIE: I suppose you're going to tell me that it's not possible. How would you know? You've never been pregnant.

WILLY: My wife has, and she never told me...

PINKIE: How would she know? The only child she had was a girl. X Semple. Finally, a manchild to do credit to this family.

WILLY: And what does that mean?

PINKIE: I mean, that not since our brother Sam, as stupid as he was, has there been a Semple man in this family worth the salt he pees.

WILLY: Wait a minute...

PINKIE: Let me hush. I came here to celebrate and have a good time with my family.

LOTTIE: I can feel it. It is a boy... daddy... it IS a boy!

WILLY: Lottie, take your hands off this second.

PINKIE: Yeah, that's him. Just humping away.

LOTTIE: I felt him!

WILLY: Didn't your mother tell you to go get dressed? Go get dressed, Lottie.

PINKIE: (*Rocking*) um-um. . . that's my boy. . . mmm-hmm. (*LOTTIE reluctantly exits.*)

PINKIE: Why do you want to send Lottie out, Willy? She's a woman now. There are things she needs to know. You always have been overprotective.

WILLY: She's still a child. (*LOTTIE is in her room, dressing.*)

LOTTIE: When the hens come home. . . Sometimes the voices come from outside. My parents. At night I can hear them through the walls. Sometimes I hear the walls quaking, banging. Their voices rise and fall in arias. On the other side. Of the wall. The sheets flapping. Flapping above them. And the beating of bird wings against its bars. In those mornings I sneak into their room. After they've risen. And search the room. The closets, between the bedcovers . . . searching for signs. . . feathers of the slaughtered birds. Sometimes I find a spot of blood and always the fresh smell of death. Yang, yang, yang, yang, yang, yang, yang. When the roosters come home? When the chickens . . . What Pinkie's baby whispered in my ear. . . Sometimes the voices come from outside. On the other side. Out there. Like low flying helicopters, their voices. One day—looking out. Three boys talking loud and throwing bottles against the wall. One was black as midnight. One with coiled snakes hissing all over his head. And the third tall and sinewy like a swaying palm. The first one saw me spying and smiled at me. His teeth glistened with gold. Repunzel, Repunzel, let down your golden hair. And he climbed up to her ivory tower . . . . Sometimes the voices come from inside me. Clear as a bell. She was a poor peasant girl and barely thirteen when she saw the visions and heard the voices that told her to pick up the shield and sword and march to. . . New Orleans? One day my voices will tell me what and when. My voices will explode. The walls will be knocked down. And you'll see freedom flapping its wings and crowing. When the morning comes.

WILLY: Some things she doesn't need to know. Not now.

PINKIE: Then when?

WILLY: Some things she doesn't ever have to know about. Not like we knew them. No need. Some things she never needs to hear, see or touch.

PINKIE: No pain, no gain.

WILLY: The things we went through—I went through so she would never have to. I cherish her, protect her, fight for my destiny.

PINKIE: One day she'll have to learn to fight for herself. Locking her in her room isn't going to help. It's just going to make the lessons she's going to have to learn just that much harder.

WILLY: Yeah, you know all about it.

PINKIE: That's right. I have the proof of my life experience written all over my body. From stretch marks to razor scars from a drunken lover . . . I still have the welts on my back which were the gifts from our dear parents.

WILLY: Our parents never beat us.

PINKIE: That's how bad they beat you—BRAIN DAMAGE. You can't even remember. I remember—mama tried to break my neck, one time.

WILLY: If only she had broken your tongue.

PINKIE: You know it's true.

WILLY: The only time our parents laid hand on us was in love.

PINKIE: They loved to lay hand on me, fist on me, extension cord . . . frying pan.

WILLY: It wasn't so bad. Though, there was this time when Daddy chased Jes with a baseball bat.

JES: (*To audience.*) Yeah, yeah . . . I gave him a good run. He was fast back then. I ran into the park and lost him around the lake.

WILLY: You had to come back home sometime.

PINKIE: Daddy sat patiently on the porch.

JES: (*To audience.*) For three days.

PINKIE: Three hours. Dinnertime, you came home.

WILLY: Slunk home with your tail tucked between your legs.

JES: (*To audience.*) He said, "Boy, are you ready?" "Yes, sir." "Then, get on in the house and let down the shades and then let down your pants."

PINKIE: (*Sarcastic.*) They only laid hands on us in love.

JES: (*To audience.*) "This is going to hurt me more than you. I'm only starting what the MAN is going to finish."

WILLY: (*To audience.*) He always said that we couldn't afford to be lazy and undisciplined. That's what they expected from us. And he came down harder on us for living up to their expectations. That was the world. That's what I leaned from the whuppings.

PINKIE: (*To audience.*) Your own will treat you as bad or worse than anyone else. That's what I learned.

WILLY: Pinkie. . .

PINKIE: Sam never got any licks.

JES: I sure do miss Sam.

WILLY: He was always the favorite.

PINKIE: He should have been. He was a saint, as stupid as he was.

WILLY: Like the time he fell out of the treehouse.

JES: (*To audience.*) . . . Some got lost down the hole. . .

PINKIE: Jes pushed him.

JES: (*To audience.*) He jumped.

PINKIE: I was in the house cleaning up after you lazy lunkheads, as usual, when I heard his scream. I never will forget it.

WILLY: I had gone to the candy shop and left Jes up in the tree house with little Sammy. I heard him five blocks away...

PINKIE: I ran to the back yard, yelling "What's going on?", and there was little Sam lying flat on the ground.

JES: He just jumped.

PINKIE: And Jes was up in the tree house, looking down, laughing.

JES: I told him not to.

PINKIE: Just laughing your head off.

JES: (*To audience.*) We were playing—TARZAN—and he was Cheetah. I lost my balance and the next thing I knew—he had flung himself off. He said something about wanting to cushion my fall. I told him not to.

PINKIE: Just laughing your head off.

WILLY: That was just like little Sam.

JES: Saigon.

PINKIE: He volunteered.

JES: (*To audience.*) I was a conscientious objector.

PINKIE: How was Canada?

JES: 1968. Hot, white beach. The Bahamas.

WILLY: One of my legs is longer than the other.

PINKIE: He was a real hero. Worth his salt. Stupid as mud, but a hero, just the same. He should have died over in Vietnam for his country. What'd he die for? Should have been blown to bits on some land mine, fighting someone else's battle. Instead of... What did he die for? (*Silence.*) Don't look at me like that. You're the one with all this stuff. (*Indicates box marked "SAM".*) Look at this. What's in here?

WILLY: Don't start stirring things up, Pinkie. Everything's packed down and ordered...

PINKIE: (*In Sam's box.*) His uniform. His football trophy, basketball trophy, baseball... track... honor roll pin, medals of honor, dog tags.. . his varsity jacket... (*Cradling the rag.*) Wasn't enough to piece together for a decent funeral.

WILLY: This isn't the time, Pinkie.

PINKIE: When? When, then? What did our brother die for?

WILLY: Too late now to look back. Time now to look to the future.

PINKIE: Keep your eyes on the prize... And what a sweet cracker jack prize you got. Big old house, two car garage, a fence for them junkies outside to lean up on... and now you're moving to a bigger, brighter, whiter neighborhood. Leave all us po' dunk Negroes behind. You and

Marva. Especially Marva, living fat.

WILLY: Everyone got theirs. You grabbed your share with both hands.

PINKIE: My children were hungry -

WILLY: Weren't we all. Enough said.

PINKIE: Let me hush.

JES: All of that is past and done. Let it go. Spit it out like a old woman's dried up tiddy. No use sucking on that. Set your teeth on the future's firm sweet breast. (*We hear a clear sweet bell. A light comes up on LOTTIE in her room. Then:*) Look at this—Aunt Celine's iron, great grandma Semple's quilt. . .

PINKIE: My first baby carriage. . .

JES: Uncle Matt's lucky horse shoe. . . Margaret Ann's straightening comb. . . Shaka Zulu's spear, I expect. And these. . . (*Holding up shackles*) You're taking these?

WILLY: I'll sort things out once we get there. (*LOTTIE enters in a white dress.*)

LOTTIE: We are gathered here today, though everyone isn't here yet. . .

PINKIE: I hope that Marva, heifer, doesn't show.

LOTTIE: . . . to celebrate the death of. . .

PINKIE: BIRTH.

LOTTIE: . . . to celebrate the birth of the King. "His life was the manna that fed the soul weary masses." I read that in a book.

JES: (*Overlapping.*) K-A-N-I-B-. . . I may not be able to spell it—but I know what it means.

LOTTIE: I don't remember the King, I wasn't born back then, but from the films in schools. I saw the marches and the people in dashikis and 'fros, carrying signs and singing those old negro spirituals. Those were the days of the King, of Camelot, when legendary heroes arose. Women like Angela. . . Angela. . . something. . . Angela and her brothers in prison. . . Soledad. Angela Soledad.

PINKIE: Angela DAVIS.

LOTTIE: Angela Davis? Angela Davis and her sister, Patricia Lumumba.

PINKIE: (*Remembering, longingly.*) PATRICE Lumumba was a man.

LOTTIE: It reminds me of when we studied that French woman who fought alongside her brothers and she heard voices and bells and was burned at the stake for her beliefs.

JES: A steak sounds good. I'm hungry.

LIZA: (*VOS*) Any minute now we'll be sitting at the table. The day of feasting has arrived.

LOTTIE: And the King and his knights sat around the table. . .

PINKIE: What knights?

JES: Ku, klux, and klan.

LOTTIE: Jackson, and Bond, and Young Andrew the lion-hearted. . .

PINKIE: And Toto and Dorothy flew over the cuckoo's nest. . . Willy, I told you to let this girl grow up.

LOTTIE: In the days of Camelot there came forth a king whose holy quest took him to the mountaintop. And he looked over to the other side and heard the voices and visions which he brought back to his people. He brought to them a dream. But before he could lead them to the promised land, he died. But "his life was the manna that fed the soul weary masses." (*Blackout.*)

SCENE 3

We hear voices in the blackout.

VOICES: (*Overlapping and repeating.*) YANG YANG YANG YANG. YANG YANG YANG. It is a far, far better thing I do than I have ever done before. All for one and one for all. . . Ungawa! Kings are not born: they are made of universal hallucination. Fight the power. Free Mandela. Viva Zapata. Remember the Soledad Seven. I have a dream. (*Voices are drowned out by bells. Spotlight comes up on JES.*)

JES: I'm not bitter. I'm not hostile, I'm not angry. I'm not going to sneak into your house at night and slit your throat. I'm Jes Semple. I like white people. There are two kinds of white people. The kindhearted liberals who subscribe to the Village Voice, Jet Magazine, and Town and Country. And then there are those that still believe that Gerry Cooney is the Great White Hope. Not that the white folk can't fight. But you put a black man who's either consciously or unconsciously aware of his over one-hundred years of oppression in the ring with a white man, and he's going to beat the shit out of that white man. And he's getting paid for it, too. Just as if you put a Latino male in the ring, he's going to beat the shit out of that white man and depending on what oppressed dictatorial regime he might have come from— he'll give that black man a good whupping too. You take an American Indian—and this is the fight I personally want to see—he'll beat the shit out of all of them. . . with his hands tied behind his back. . . blind folded. I'm not bitter, I'm not hostile. I'm not angry. Call me Jes Semple. (*LOTTIE enters the spotlight, laughing.*)

LOTTIE: You're so funny, Uncle Jes.

JES: Come here, my sweet naive. Let Uncle Jes whisper in your ear. (*LOTTIE goes over to JES and he begins whispering in her ear. She laughs and laughs and laughs.*)

LOTTIE: Oh, stop Uncle. . . oh, don't, stop. . . oh. . . oh. . . *(LOTTIE laughs until she cries...then laughs some more. Blackout.)*

SCENE 4

Lights up on living room. MAMA PEARL has entered and takes center stage. LOTTIE is at the window watching PAPA TOMMY. Everyone else is in their usual positions.

PEARL: I started out as a singer. Most of my first engagements were in the cotton fields. I was a healthy alto. I could sang. I can't anymore. *(Tries singing.)* Brighten the corner where you are. . . You could hear me a mile away. They used to call me Big Mouth.

LOTTIE: He's wearing a bow-tie! He just got into the gate.

PEARL: Then I started sneaking to Bubba's at night—singing the blues, yeah. I was my mama's only child and this man says to me— "Girl, you sound good, Let me take you to Louisiana with me." I was sixteen at the time or I was fifteen. . . His name was Floyd. A piana player. He said, "Girl, you can be a great singer. Come on with me." And I said that I would first have to ask my mama.

LOTTIE: He's up to the garden.

PEARL: That morning I told mama that I could become a great singer if she would just let me go with Floyd to Louisiana. Don't you know that woman played those evil blues upside my head, that I will never forget. First, for sneaking out at night. Second, for wanting to sing that nasty evil, low-down blues. Thirdly, for hanging around shiftless lazy musicians—My daddy was a musician and had run out on mama and me for some no account, hulleygulley gal. And lastly, for wanting to leave her alone—me, being her only child. She beat me for seven days and seven nights.

LOTTIE: He's past the zinnias.

PEARL: After she finished beating me, she was so tired, she went to sleep. While she slept, I packed my things and took the next bus to Louisiana. I caught up with Floyd and we teamed up. We called ourselves—Big Mouth and Ivory. We toured Mississippi, Virginia, Florida and all the way up to Chicago. That's where I met your Daddy. A tap dancing fool. Talk about some quick pepper feet! As big-footed as that man is, it's amazing how fast he could move them. I met him in this club and I said, "Hey, fool, where you learn to dance like that?" He said that he knew how to tap before he learned to walk. Shoot, people remember Bojangles, The Nicholas Brothers, Sammy Davis. . . Sandman. . . your daddy was the best.

LOTTIE: He stopped.

PEARL: I quit Floyd and teamed up with your daddy. Big Mouth Pearl and Mr. Pepper Feet. We went to New York in '41 or '42.

LOTTIE: He's taking off his hat and pulling out a handkerchief.

PEARL: '41. We were in love. He said that he loved me more than anything in the world and that was good enough for me. So we got married and the same night we debuted at the Apollo.

LOTTIE: He's wiping his head and looking around.

PEARL: Mama wrote to tell me that she was coming up to see the fool I had married.

LOTTIE: He's at the foot of the steps.

WILLY: Maybe I should help him up.

PEARL: Let him be. He said he didn't need any help, the fool. (*Continuing:*) I met her at the train station and she beat me over the head with her suitcase. "When I woke up that morning you were gone." She moved in with us and prayed for our souls every night we went on stage.

LOTTIE: He's on the second step.

PEARL: I got pregnant with Marva, swell up so bad, I was laid up in bed. Tommy was tapping at the Cotton Club and packing them in. Mr. Pepper Feet.

LOTTIE: He's still on the second step.

PEARL: He felt it would help the act if he had a partner. I was laid up in bed. So he hired this stringy-haired skinny gal by the name of Lola.

UNISON: Lola. (*There is knocking on the door. LOTTIE opens the door and an ancient, shuffling, TOMMY enters.*)

WILLY: Come on in. How are you, pop?

TOMMY: Umm-hmmm. Umm-hmm.

JES: Let me rub your head for luck, old man.

TOMMY: Rub my butt.

PINKIE: (*Offering a seat.*) Sit over here.

TOMMY: Naw. (*He continues his slow shuffle, flapping walk past PINKIE and sits on the box labeled—SAM.*)

PEARL: She thought she was cute—that skinny hulley-gulley child. (*TOMMY wheezes and laughs.*) Yeah, you know who I'm talking about. Lola. And she sure was LOW, wasn't she? Mr. Pepper Feet.

TOMMY: (*Enjoying himself.*) Dem was de days.

PEARL: Yes they were. Living in a two room, heatless apartment with a evil mother, laid up in bed swollen to the size of a cow, and you tap dancing at the Cotton Club with LOW-LA.

TOMMY: Yowsah, yowsah, yowsah.

PEARL: I was singing them Saint Louis Blues. . . Blue as I can be. . .

TOMMY: Dat de way. Yo' mom's was a sanging fool. Bi' Mouf. . .

PEARL: Big Mouth and Mr. Pepper Feet.

TOMMY: De Apollo- 19 and 40-somethin'. . .

PEARL: I told them already.

TOMMY: '41. And de Cot-tone Club.

PEARL: And LOW-LA.

TOMMY: Yowsah, yowsah, dem was de days. (*Then:*) I gots to pee.

PEARL: Who's stopping you?

TOMMY: Woman, I's tie-ud.

PEARL: And I's a bony backed mule.

WILLY: I'll take him, ma.

PEARL: When did he become your husband? (*She stands, wide legged in front of him and squats so that he can climb on her back.*)

PINKIE: Mama, you're going to break your back.

PEARL: It'd take more than this fool to break my back.

TOMMY: (*As they exit UR.*) Can't you go no fast-uh?

PEARL: Man, don't you pee on me.

WILLY: Mama, I'll take him.

PEARL: I can take him.

WILLY: I'll take him.

TOMMY: Bony back woman. Let he take me. You too slow.

PEARL: Gone, take him. The fool. (*WILLY and TOMMY exit.*)

PEARL: Calling somebody a bony backed woman. That's the second time. We couldn't find a parking spot in front of the house. Too many people out front running back and forth. I parked a block away. Started walking with him on my back. His feet ain't any good anymore. He know. He called me a bony backed woman. Said I was too slow. You talk about somebody bony. . . Lola was bony. She was the skinniest thing I'd ever seen. The only thing big on her was her knees. She was so skinny you could thread her through the eye of a needle except for them knees. She was as skinny as a tooth pick. Looked like somebody had used her to clean the gunk from between their teeth. She wasn't that clean. Always smelled of that toilet of Paris. She smelled like she poured that stuff all over herself to hide the fact that she didn't bathe regular. It must have gotten pretty funky up there on stage with her. Especially doing them highkicks. They must have smelled her all the way in the back row balcony. She was a skinny, musty-smelling hulley-gulley gal. That was a long time ago. I don't know why I'm thinking about her now for. Haven't thought of her in a long time.

PINKIE: Didn't Marva buy dad a motorized wheelchair, Mama?

PEARL: You know your father. He doesn't go for them new fangled electricized contraptions. He didn't want to sit in it. He didn't want to sit comfortable in somebody's electric chair and then get fried and served up with mashed potatoes and cornbread. He said—What did God make strong backed womens for? I have lost a few extra pounds but my back is still strong. We all have our crosses to bear. And as long as I'm able. . .

PINKIE: All I'm saying is that you shouldn't have to carry a grown man on your back.

PEARL: I didn't have to bear five big-headed children and raise them up. But I did. I didn't have to buy you new clothes and shoes while I wore the same Sears and Roebuck dress that I patched for twelve years and stuff my shoes with newspaper. But I did. I didn't have to take an extra job scrubbing floors at the Sheridan hotel at night scraping knees on the tiles so you could get your teeth fixed and get you that saxophone you begged me for and then played it once, deciding that you'd rather take up bongos.

UNISON: BUT I DID.

PEARL: But I did. Who stayed up with you all night wiping your snotty nose and giving you mustard compresses to ease the fever when you had the flu? Changed your diaper and gave you my tiddy when you were a bawling baby girl. Not that I'm complaining. You do what you are able, to provide the best for your family. Your daddy ain't heavy. Compared to the burdens I've had to shoulder in my lifetime—He's light. When are you getting married?

PINKIE: Who said anything about getting married?

PEARL: That baby sitting in your belly. I swear Pinkie, you should give at least one of your children a name.

PINKIE: All mine have names.

PEARL: Your daddy told me that he loved me more than anything in the world and that was good enough for me. None of my children had to wonder where they came from.

PINKIE: Nobody has to wonder about mine. The truth is. . .

WILLY: Hush now, Pinkie.

PINKIE: Let me hush. I came here to have a nice time. Let me close my mouth. My child will speak for me one day. I'm quiet, now.

PEARL: I've been with one man for over fifty years. Promised to love only me to the day he died. None of mine had to wonder. Let me hush.

PINKIE: (*We hear a clamor of voices outside: "hungry"—"I'm hungry"; "Spare some change..."; "I want a VCR, a Porsche, and chicken in every pot..."; "I feel hungry..."; "My children need food."...Then a rapid knocking at the door.*)

MARVA: (*VOS*) Let me in. . . please, open the door. (*WILLY grabs a base-*

ball bat and opens the door. MARVA rushes in. She looks like a white woman with heavy makeup and disheveled but expensive clothes.)

PEARL: What happened?

MARVA: They tried to kill me. . . they were going to kill me. Three black boys. They surrounded me at my car. Pulling at my purse. . . my hair. . . my hair. . . my suit. Calling me names. They don't know me. They don't know who I am. Calling me out of my name. Who the hell are they? Who do they think they are? No count, worthless. . . my hair. . . my suit. . . my car.

WILLY: (*Re-enters*) Scattered like rats. That's why we're moving. This isn't what was promised.

MARVA: They tried to kill me. They shot at me.

LOTTIE: Fire-crackers.

PINKIE: No one bothered me when I came up.

MARVA: Well, I guess they wouldn't bother you.

PINKIE: And what do you mean by that?

PEARL: Marva didn't mean anything by that. You've always been so high strung, Pinkie.

MARVA: I didn't mean anything by that, surely.

PINKIE: Surely, let me close my mouth.

PEARL: Let me look at you. What'd they do to my baby, my bright morning star. . . oh. . . (*PEARL surveying and smoothing out the damage.*)

MARVA: It was terrible, Mama. And I wanted to look especially nice for this occasion. . . my nails. . .

PEARL: Mama kiss it. All well again—see. (*PEARL kisses her hands and face. MARVA laughs. They hug.*)

MARVA: Jonathan couldn't make it today—he was on call. He sends his regards.

JES: How is Dr. Hatchet?

PEARL: Now, Jes. . . Never mind him. One child crazier than the other. But he's crazy, that's for sure. Always has been, always will be. But the lord never gives you more than you can handle and sometimes he sweetens the pot. (*To MARVA.*)—My chocolate drop, on the cover of Essence Magazine this month, and once again voted Black Woman of the Year. I save the articles, put them in the scrapbook. . .

WILLY: I was voted manager of the month. . . gave me a plaque with my name on it.

PEARL: And your eyes—hazel?

MARVA: Blue.

PEARL: You looked so beautiful on the cover of Jet Magazine.

MARVA: That was the first cover I did.

PEARL: That was back when you looked like Dianne Carol. Then for

Ebony you looked more like Diana Ross.

MARVA: Before Diana Ross looked like Diana Ross.

PEARL: By the time she did Vogue she looked like a young Lena Horne.

MARVA: That was around my sixth operation. And I had just started the chemical peels. They burn away the darker outer layers. . . the nerve endings become so sensitive that you can't touch or be touched. They wrap you in a cocoon until you heal.

PINKIE: When you were little, they used to call you tar-baby. Big lipped, flat nosed, tar-baby, remember?

MARVA: I remember.

PEARL: My daughter was named "The Black Woman of the Year", three years in a row.

MARVA: I take pride in setting a standard.

PEARL: And married herself a doctor.

PINKIE: Who burned, tucked, cut and sucked all the black out of you years ago.

UNISON: HUSH PINKIE.

PINKIE: Let me hush.

TOMMY: (VOS) Gits me off dis shit house.

WILLY: I'll get him. (WILLY exits.)

MARVA: And how is Father?

PEARL: You know your father. . .

TOMMY: (VOS) OOOHHH, Lordy. . . de pain, de pain, de pain o' him-roids.

MARVA: Have you thought of a home?

PEARL: He's got a home.

LOTTIE: (She's been looking out the window.) Sometimes I sneak out and give them things. The homeless. I give them handouts. Left-overs. . . bread, rice, beans. . . fruit to their children. Dried fruit keeps longer. Raisins.

JES: Next thing you know—they'll want a seat at the table.

LOTTIE: It makes me sad to see them. We can spare a little. (WILLY enters carrying TOMMY.)

WILLY: We don't have enough to feed the whole damn neighborhood. . .

MARVA: (Adjusting her face.) Of course we do contribute to various charities. . . SAVE THE POOR. . . UNICEF. . .

WILLY: The whole crippled, mangy-assed breed. They're no kin to me.

MARVA: . . . The Negro College Fund. . . NAACP. . .

WILLY: They're no kin to me.

MARVA: I'm a life member of the NAACP.

LOTTIE: Some live in subway tunnels. . . the children. . . I give them raisins. . . they give me smiles. . .

WILLY: I pay taxes so welfare mothers can sit at home watching the VCR.
. .

MARVA: Just last year we adopted a boy from Ethiopia and a girl from Somalia. They're in the finest boarding schools in Europe. The question is "What is to be done?" and "When have we done enough?"

TOMMY: (*Looking at MARVA.*) Who is you?

MARVA: Who am I? I'm your daughter, father.

TOMMY: Youse ain't mine.

MARVA: I'm not yours? I'm your daughter, Marva, father.

PEARL: Your eldest girl.

TOMMY: Eldest? Cain't be mine. Naw, uh-uh, cain't be mine.

LIZA: (*VOS*) All that's left is the garnish and then I'm done. Set the table everyone. . . the day of feasting has arrived.

UNISON: HALLELUJAH! (*Everyone begins to set the table, finding table cloth, dishes and silver ware among the rubble.*)

LOTTIE: We are gathered here today to celebrate the birthday of Rev. Martin Luther King.

MARVA: I was there. 1963. The march on Washington.

WILLY: I had work to do that day.

MARVA: Thousands of us walking hand in hand to the great lawn. Reverend Martin Luther King uttered his famous speech. He was a beautiful orator. Black as coals. In the heat of the revolution. America had lost its innocence—our sons were in a foreign land fighting strange battles for causes we couldn't understand. This was before the assassinations. Before LBJ threw up his hands and wept. Before the fall of Nixon, the peanut farmer, the movie star, and the lessons of Bush tactics. Back when America lost its first blush, King spoke of a vision, a dream. In the midst of the bombings and fires he spoke of his vision of the future. They killed the man but his memory burns on in an eternal flame. His dream bums on in the minds of the survivors. In those frightful days, America lost its innocence in the jaws of the revolution. (And with that thought some might argue that it was our innocence that fed the revolution.) Point taken. And with the devouring of that innocence came hope. Reverend Martin Luther King Jr. had a dream. And he passed that dream on in a voice that rang out to all on that fateful day. And on that day we were all brothers and sisters. . . in that moment in time we were all family and holding hands. White man, Black man, Gentile, Jew, Arab, Indian. . . I remember sitting on that great lawn and listening to a man, a king as he cast bread upon the waters. And we sang WE SHALL OVERCOME. . .

UNISON: WE SHALL OVERCOME

WE SHALL OVERCOME SOME DAY
DEEP IN MY HEART
I DO BELIEVE
WE SHALL OVERCOME SOME DAY. (*Humming as...*)

PINKIE: Yes. I remember that day. I was there. I can still hear his voice. Our dream was one. It was as if he was speaking only to me, looking only at me. He knew he was going to die. The death threats were common knowledge. Who could carry on his dream? Rev. Abernathy had told me to come to the motel (*Humming stops.*) that night and I could meet him, speak with him. . .

UNISON: Hush, now, Pinkie.

PINKIE: It had always been my dream to conceive a child that would lead his people. . .

UNISON: Lies. . . that's enough. . . hush!

PINKIE: And that night with the revolution burning in my thighs..(H/)..you know it's the truth..(H/)..I laid down..(H/)..the truth will set you free..(H/)..when I laid down. . .

UNISON: (*Overlapping*) HUSH! HUSH! HUSH! (*They sing again "WE SHALL OVERCOME" with fervor as WILLY, MARVA and PEARL tie PINKIE up and tape her mouth. WILLY places her in a box. Song stops at...I DO BELIEVE.*)

PEARL: She always was high-strung.

MARVA: Fantasies. . .

PEARL: I always told her to settle down. No telling who all those children of hers are by. (*WILLY tapes up the box and labels it.*)

PEARL: No telling.

TOMMY: I's just regusted.

PEARL: I cried when Kennedy died. I don't pay any attention to all that sluttish gossip. I don't care what anybody says. . . I cried when King died. (*At TOMMY.*) Lord, seems like he takes the good ones early.

MARVA: (*Pulls up her face.*) How do you put up with it, mother?

PEARL: Put up with what?

MARVA: (*At TOMMY.*) Him.

PEARL: That's your pa, Marva.

WILLY: He's our father.

MARVA: I was the one that was called to pay the bills when he needed the new kidney, the bladder operation. . . the hip joint. . . the gallstone operation. . . the bypass. . . the new teeth. . . You're trying to tell me that what's left of him is my father. . . this babbling, illiterate, incoherent, shuffling, head scratching, dinosaur used to be my father but ceased to exist with Amos and Andy reruns. Yet he attaches himself to our hems as we drag him into the next century and we're supposed to continue to pay tribute by calling him our father. (*Breaking*) You can't be my. . . oh. . . Daddy. . . (*Sits on his lap.*) Dad. . .

TOMMY: (*Low.*) Bastid. (*Pushes her out of his lap.*) And ya'll—BASTIDS. Cain't be mine. (*Getting up.*) No ridim. No ridim. Cain't be mine. uh-uh.

PEARL: Calm yourself.

TOMMY: Damn Bastids. Git outta my way. Yeah, I feel it. Feelin' it. (*Begins to tap.*) Dat de way. uh-huh. Dat de way. Dem was de days. (*His whole body comes to life.*) Yowsah. Dem was de days. All uh God's niggah chirren had ridim. Yeah. dat de way, yowsah. Day knew where it come from. Day could feel it Don't feel nothin' now. But I ain't dead. . . I ain't dead. . . naw suh. . . (*He taps faster and faster then drops.*)

PEARL: Tommy. . . Tommy. . .

TOMMY: (*Whispering.*) Dem. . . was. . . de. . . days. . . Pepper Feet. . . and (*Clutches his heart.*) Lo..la.

PEARL: Lola? Lola? (*Shaking his lifeless body.*) I'll kill him. . . I'll kill him.

MARVA: (*Trying to keep her face from falling apart.*) He's dead. He's dead. . . (*WILLY gently places TOMMY in a box, tapes the box and labels it. LOTTIE covers her eyes.*)

PA: Where's Sambo?

MARVA: Who?

TOMMY: Li'l black Sambo. Now he could dance. Only one of my chirren who could feel it. Feel where he come from.

PEARL: You know he's dead. Tommy. Been dead for a while now.

MARVA: Sam.

TOMMY: That's right. mmm-hmmm—he was good. mmm-hm. Lip-smacking good served up with them pancakes.

MARVA: What?

TOMMY: Pancakes. With pancakes. That's how we ate 'im.

LOTTIE: (*Laughing.*) Pancakes and Aunt Jemimah's syrup.

WILLY: Shut up.

LOTTIE: But, dad, it's just a joke—get it?

WILLY: Go to your room.

LOTTIE: You can't send me to my room for the rest of my life—

WILLY: Shut up. Shut him up.

MARVA: He's just an old man, talking out of his head. Sam had a proper funeral. Just close your ears child.

JES: Though there wasn't enough of him to piece together for a decent funeral.

PEARL: He was the one that wanted to be cremated.

LOTTIE: SAMBO! PANCAKES—FRIED. . .

WILLY: SHUT UP. This is not the time to get into this. This is not the time.

PEARL: It was an accident. He's the one that bought the insurance.

JES: Blow your hands. Don't come crying to me.

MARVA: It was declared by the authorities as an accidental death.

JES: Don't come crying to me.

WILLY: Not murder. Not suicide.

JES: We each got a piece.

TOMMY: Leg, thigh, wings. . .

PEARL: He was a saint.

LOTTIE: You're joking, right? Aren't you?

JES: Some got more than others.

MARVA: We all got the same inheritance. Some used it more wisely than others.

JES: Life insurance.

WILLY: For the lives of our children.

TOMMY: Paid in blood. Still gnawing on his bones.

MARVA: He was cremated.

JES: What was left of him.

TOMMY: Burnt offerings.

LOTTIE: (*Covering her ears and singing loud.*) Yang yang yang yang yang yang yang yang. . . (*Pause.*)

JES: (*To LOTTIE.*) What happens to a dream deferred? Does it dry up like a raisin in the sun? Does it fester like a sore and then run? Does it stink like rotten meat? Or sugar over like a syrupy sweet Does it sag like a heavy load?

LOTTIE: (*Uncovering eyes.*)

JES: Or does it explode? (*We see smoke coming from the kitchen.*)

LIZA: (*VOS. Hysterically repeating*) Everything is fine. I don't need any help. Soups on. (*Smoke billows from the kitchen as everyone runs in*)

EVERYONE: Water, more water. . . Save that turkey. . . etc. . .

PINKIE: (*Voice from box.*) What's going on out there? Somebody let me out. I came to celebrate. (*LOTTIE hearing Joan of Arc bells, she runs out the front door with armfuls of food to the clamoring masses.*)

LOTTIE: (*As she exits, singing - *) YANG YANG YANG YANG. . . (*MARVA enters from the kitchen trying to fix her face, which has melted to one side.*)

MARVA: I don't know what else I can do here.

PINKIE: (*FB*) OH! I feel him. . . OH. . .

MARVA: Lottie! Lottie! (*MARVA exits after LOTTIE. Outside we hear gun-*

shots. *PEARL enters from the kitchen and lays herself across
TOMMY's box. A huge bone is thrown through the window, shatter-
ing the glass, as...)*

BONETHROWER: UNGAWA! BLACK POWER!

PINKIE: (*Voice from box.*) He's coming. . . Jesus. . . Jesus. . . Jesus. . .
HE'S COMING! (*Blackout.*)

SCENE 5

> *Spotlight up on JES.*

JES: (*He's eating a whole pie.*) You can only slice an apple pie so many
ways. Somebody is always going to go home hungry.

SCENE 6

> *The room is cleared except for a few boxes—including those la-
> beled LINEN, STEREO, PINKIE, MA, PA, AND MARVA. LIZA sits
> in the living room wrapped in gauze from head to toe. LOTTIE
> sits, her white dress ragged, soiled and bloodstained.)*

WILLY: Signed the papers. Ha. Ha. Highland Hills. This is the open door
we've been waiting for. That step into the future. My little blue bird's
future. We're moving. (*WILLY picks up a box and exits outside. LOT-
TIE gets up on the table and begins to do a lewd grind-dance.*)

LOTTIE: (*singing, bitterly*) YANG YANG YANG YANG. YANG YANG
YANG. (*WILLY re-enters.*)

LIZA: (*Voice in bandages*) Don't forget my good china.

WILLY: Yes, Liza. (*WILLY picks up a small box next to PINKIE'S box. As
he exits he stops, measures its weight and then curiously shakes it.
Sound of baby crying comes from within. Spotlight up on JES, he
puts on a record—and watches LOTTIE'S dance. We hear a recording of MLK.*)

MLK: Today I want to tell the city of Selma, today I want to say to the
state of Alabama, today I want to say to the people of America and the
nations of the world: We are not about to turn around. We are on the
move now. Yes, we are on the move and no wave of racism can stop
us. The burning of our churches will not deter us. The bombing of
our homes will not dissuade us. The beating of our clergymen and
young people will not divert us. The arrest and the release of known

murderers will not discourage us. We are on the move now. Like an idea whose time has come, not even the marching of mighty armies can halt us. We are moving to the land of freedom. (*LOTTIE's dance becomes a stomp shuffle stomp. She picks up spear and continues her warrior dance which evolves into a summation out of space and time evoking spirits past and present from child to woman.*)

MLK: However difficult the moment, however frustrating the hour, it will not be long because the truth crushed to the earth will rise again.

LOTTIE: HOW LONG?

MLK: Not long because the arc of the moral universe is long but it bends towards justice.

LOTTIE: HOW LONG?

MLK: Not long, because mine eyes have seen the glory of the coming of the lord.

LOTTIE: HOW LONG? (*Blackout.*)

END OF PLAY